Leila's Secret

Kooshyar Karimi was born in Tehran and now lives in Sydney. He is the author of several books on Iranian, Chinese and Assyrian myths and history, one of which was banned from publication by the Iranian government. His memoir *I Confess: Revelations in Exile* was published in Australia in 2012. He is also an award-winning translator of Gore Vidal, Kahlil Gibran and Adrian Berry, among others.

ALSO BY KOOSHYAR KARIMI

I Confess: Revelations in Exile

KOOSHYAR KARIMI

Leila's Secret

VIKING
an imprint of
PENGUIN BOOKS

VIKING

UK | USA | Canada | Ireland | Australia
India | New Zealand | South Africa | China

Penguin Books is part of the Penguin Random House group of companies
whose addresses can be found at global.penguinrandomhouse.com.

Penguin
Random House
Australia

First published by Penguin Group (Australia), 2015

1 3 5 7 9 10 8 6 4 2

Text copyright © Kooshyar Karimi 2015

Cover design by Laura Thomas © Penguin Group (Australia)
Text design by Samantha Jayaweera © Penguin Group (Australia)
Cover photograph by ilse schrama/Alamy
Typeset in Adobe Caslon Pro by Samantha Jayaweera, Penguin Group (Australia)
Colour separation by Splitting Image Colour Studio, Clayton, Victoria
Printed and bound in Australia by Griffin Press, an accredited ISO AS/NZS 14001
Environmental Management Systems printer.

National Library of Australia
Cataloguing-in-Publication data:

Karimi, Kooshyar, author.
Leila's secret / Kooshyar Karimi
9780670078165 (paperback)
Women – Iran – Social conditions.
Pregnant women (Islamic law) – Iran.
Physicians – Iran – Social conditions.
Iran – Social conditions – 1997–

305.420955

penguin.com.au

To my wife, Misha Karimi,
who has the spring of Tasmania in her eyes,
the innocence of Leila in her heart,
and the warmth of home in her voice

AUTHOR'S NOTE

This is the true story of some of the many women, and of one woman in particular, who under the laws of Iran have faced execution for becoming pregnant or losing their virginity outside marriage. While the events described in this book occurred in the late 1990s, nothing has changed in respect of these laws, and Iranian women continue to suffer at the hands of extremists.

According to many historians, Iran is the oldest intact civilisation in the world. The Persian Empire, as Iran was known, endured wars with the Greek and Roman empires, had the world's longest continuous royal dynasty, and in 550 BC became the first realm to issue a declaration of human rights. But in 1979 this ancient cradle of civilisation underwent a fundamentalist Islamic revolution that re-established seventh-century Islamic rules in its constitution, turning the country into a nest of fanaticism and intolerance. Today Iran is one of the largest jailers of journalists of any country, and it still executes minors, stones women to death for adultery, and hangs men for homosexuality.

Sadly, the story of Leila echoes that of millions of women in Asia and Africa. Every year in the Islamic world, more than twenty thousand women are murdered in so-called honour killings. I have written this book in the hope that one day we will start tolerating and stop tormenting; in the belief that if we learn to forgive, freedom will come.

While this is a true story, it has been necessary to change the names of some people and places in order to protect identities. I have also taken the liberty of elaborating on the details of an individual's thoughts, interior life and surroundings, while never altering crucial facts.

Kooshyar Karimi, January 2015

The heavy silence in the room is interrupted now and then by the sounds of a television cartoon trickling in under the locked door. Funny voices, comedic sound effects, light-hearted music – they don't suit the occasion, but there's no other way to ensure my young daughter remains oblivious to what will shortly play itself out at this end of the hallway.

On a July day in 1997, a pregnant Leila sits stiffly on a chair in the spare room, which has been turned into a makeshift operating theatre. Her hands are balled into fists, her body twitches with tension. She is young, beautiful and unmarried, her shame at what has happened to her so deep it is almost a physical presence. She has committed a capital crime in the Islamic Republic of Iran – she has fallen in love.

Love is not allowed in this part of the world, and someone must die for it. Either her or her child.

Leila seems much younger than her twenty-two years, her vulnerability poorly hidden under a thin layer of tenacity. But in a way she is fortunate. When I terminate pregnancies I must do so as an underground doctor; only a few women are lucky enough to meet one of my connections and so come to me. I break the Hippocratic oath every time I end a pregnancy, and I do it because my mother once said to me, 'Kooshyar, sometimes in life, for a greater good, do a little bad.'

But what I can't do for these women is restore their pride.

Leila's expression is one I am familiar with. In fact I've lost count of how many times I have seen that strange combination of fear, desperation and determination on a young woman's face. But this case is different. Leila is not just another desperate girl, still horrified, still withdrawn from the recent discovery of her pregnancy. She is eight months along.

When, on my request to examine her, she hesitantly removed her chador and unbuttoned her trench coat, my eyes had widened in disbelief. She couldn't be serious, could she? Her stomach was rounded completely; how she had been managing to hide it I hadn't a clue. She was pale and weary, sweat clinging to the strands of hair peeping out from her headscarf. She looked ready to collapse, and not surprisingly. No one in her condition should have been trekking across the city in this blazing heat. I had no idea what she was doing here. Surely she didn't think I would even consider ending a pregnancy this far advanced?

'You're too close to delivery,' I say. 'Far too late for a termination. I'm sorry, I can't do this.'

As I'm about to leave the room I find her clinging to my sleeve, tears rolling down her cheeks, begging me for help, and I relent. But the help I'm to give her is not what I had expected.

Later that evening, lying on the table with a drip needle in her vein, Leila told me a story that I will carry in my heart for the rest of my life. She left many questions unanswered during the long hours of her ordeal, but I came to know the full details later. I will be forgiven, I hope, for telling her story in instalments. It is a story so deeply intertwined with my own that I can no longer think of her life and my life as distinct and separate, because I too had been an unwanted child.

In 1945 fanatic Muslims killed a Jewish man who was planning to open a liquor shop in Isfahan. A few months later the man's widow gave birth to her fourth daughter. They called her Turan. Four years later Turan was given into the care of her uncle because her mother had left with her new husband. Turan was forced to work from the age of six, for her food, clothing and education. When she was sixteen she met a handsome Muslim bus driver who promised to save her from her cruel uncle. At seventeen she eloped with him, only to learn two weeks later that he had two other wives. By the time she found herself pregnant for the second time, her first son being just sixteen months old, her husband was barely visiting her in her wretched basement residence. Turan tried multiple times to abort the second child but he came into the world regardless. He was born after midnight in the back seat of a police car, to the unkind and diseased world of Tehran's slums. That son was me.

When I was eighteen months old I almost perished in a house fire lit by my father's second wife, who wanted to get rid of me. At the age of six I nearly died from typhoid. I survived against all odds with only one hope, one reason and one belief: forgiveness.

It seemed to me, after hearing Leila's story, almost as if she and I had transacted a marriage of anguish and sorrow, a ritual bonding that left some of her blood flowing in my veins, and some of mine in hers.

Leila

Holding my chador together with my hands, I push through the crowd on the footpath. The wind blows the black fabric about like a flag. It annoys me, this garment. Whenever I put it on or take it off, I wonder if the world would really end if I left the house without it. But I know the answer to this already, and you know the answer too, Doctor Karimi, with all your understanding of what women endure in our country. The world *would* end, at least for me. If I left the house not wearing my chador my father and brothers would swoop upon me like vultures and tear me limb by limb. On such trivialities people in Iran construct monstrous conceits that can, and do, end in state-sanctioned murder.

I have been folding myself into this dark fabric since the age of seven, yet I still have moments when I long to tear the cloth from my head, from my body, to breathe freely. But I dare not speak such thoughts aloud. My fear of the consequences remains more powerful than my desire to be rid of the chador. I lie awake at night in dread, wondering if a time will come when I can't control this urge any longer. I say to myself, Leila, have some sense.

Aunt Sediqa fans these flames, without realising it. Whenever she visits us I treasure the time she dedicates to being alone with me. The two of us talk fearlessly of things I would never utter aloud to anyone else. And it has saved me, so often, being able to have these moments; however few and far apart they are, at least I know that I am not alone in this desire for freedom, in thinking dangerous thoughts. But while Aunt Sediqa is a beacon in my life, there are times when my thoughts make me feel like a monster, or if not a monster, one of those people in circus shows who attract the horrified attention of an audience because they are so different to everyone else. In such shows (I have never attended one because they only visit Tehran) I have heard that a woman will display a long beard on her face, or a man will cross his legs behind his head; another man will reveal that he has six fingers on each hand. 'Freak' is the word I am looking for. I am a freak. Something in my mind craves to think in a way that makes me stand out, like a freak.

Here is an example: I think women should fly aeroplanes. And another: I think women should be allowed to walk freely on the streets at any hour of the day or night. And visit a library to choose any book she wishes, and read it under a tree in the park. There are many other examples. I should be horrified to find my imagination harbouring such appetites. And I *am* horrified, sometimes. You see, this is the problem. I have too much imagination for my own good, too strong a desire for learning and freedom. I am the bearded lady. There are times when I wish I could change my brain for one that would cause me less anxiety.

And it is Aunt Sediqa who infected me with my love of books. She describes to me the wonderful volumes of literature she has in her home, 'stacked up to the roof', as she says (an exaggeration). When I was younger she would sneak a novel or history book to me and I would greedily eat up every word on every page. Now, as I have grown older, my sister Samira and I are sometimes granted an hour out of the house, away from our chores, to visit the local library. But you see how it is? I did not ask for the mind I have, and Aunt Sediqa did not ask for hers. And both of us must deal with the thoughts that come our way.

I continue to press through the dense throng of people, draping my chador back over my head when it slips. I try to pretend that I am not in the small town of Quchan with its cracked roads, but walking the streets of a modern Iranian city instead, with tall, shiny buildings. I envisage myself dressed as the fashionable women are, in a beautiful long beige coat with golden buttons, my hair pinned behind a colourful scarf that frames my face. I picture the pretty pink leather gloves I have seen in an advertisement, and imagine how they would feel on my hands. I can see myself in white boots, carrying a stylish purse, and proudly wearing a pair of sunglasses that give me an air of mystery. I can almost smell the imaginary perfume, night flower and ocean breeze, floating in the air around me. And just as quickly as the fantasy comes it is gone, with a shove from a passing stranger in the crowded street.

Perhaps if this vision had even the slightest possibility of becoming reality, I would yearn for it with even greater longing. But of what use are such desires? I may never in my life leave this decaying town. I may never in my life know the freedom of coats and coloured scarves. I may never see the sparkling buildings of the city kissing the skies. I cannot yearn for what cannot ever be.

I hear Samira calling my name distantly. I have been so lost in my daydreams that I've drifted away from her to the other side of the road. She quickly crosses over, avoiding the speeding cars and bikes that kick up storms of dust.

'Is your head always in the clouds, or only when you're in my *boring* company?' she teases. 'You nearly got run over; did you not hear the blaring horns?'

I hang my head in apology. Too often I do this to my older sister, so caught up in my fantasy life that I don't hear what she says half the time.

Samira rolls her eyes and sighs in defeat, squeezing my arm in a gesture of forgiveness. 'Let's just go home,' she says, nodding at the darkening sky. 'Mother will be worrying about us.'

We arrive home five minutes later than usual, and predictably my mother sticks her head out from behind the kitchen door, glancing at the clock and muttering words of disapproval. Samira and I both scoff at the not-so-subtle message. Being treated like schoolchildren is something we both despise.

I am already twenty-one years old and Samira is twenty-nine. Most of the girls we went to school with are married by now and have children of their own, but Samira and I still live with our parents and three brothers in an old house at the east end of Quchan. This isn't how we had imagined our lives would unfold, but we don't complain. There is a power structure in our home, as in every home, and we sit in humble resignation at the bottom of it. At the top is my father, Abdollah, fifty-nine years old, who rules the house with unquestioned authority. Our main income is from a small farm he runs a few kilometres out of town, into which he puts long hours. My brothers also contribute some of their trivial income, but they have to save for their future families.

Second comes my mother, who runs the household at a practical level. She makes all the decisions about how the budget is spent, on toothpaste, potatoes, salt, spices, apples – everything, including clothing for each family member. One of my brothers might say, 'Mother, I need a new shirt,' and that will be the beginning of a long campaign waged by my mother for the best bargain to be found in Quchan. Sometimes I watch in awe as she sorts through racks in the bazaar, making a big deal out of the quality of the stitching along the collar, shouting at the shirt-seller, accusing him of being the worst rogue in twenty centuries of Persian history, all but demanding that *he* pay *her* for taking the shirt home to her son. I think to myself, Could I ever do this? And I answer no. I'd accept the price the shirt-seller proposed, which would be considered not only madness but almost a sin.

So Mother is second in charge, but in a particular way. My brothers, as males, still feel that they can bully her, and she will accept the bullying, up to a point. But there are invisible markers in the relationship of a mother to her grown sons, and if my brothers ignore one of those markers, my mother will turn and fight, and win. Like with the shirt.

Third in command is Ali, my 28-year-old brother, who works alongside our father raising sheep and cattle. My two younger brothers place fourth and fifth, Hosein, aged twenty, and Majid, who has just turned eighteen. They have begun work as mechanics in town.

Samira and I help our mother clean and cook and tend to the demands of the male members of the family, as is traditional in Iran. While I am older than two of my brothers, there has never been a question of who holds the authority among us. My whole life I've had to cater to my brothers as though I owe them some debt for being born a woman. I have ambitions like no male in my family, but my dreams do me little good. Both Samira and I wanted to go to university, but Father wouldn't hear of it. My mother did try to convince him.

'Leila's wanted to teach children her whole life,' she said.

And my father replied, 'You need the help here. You're not so young anymore and can't do everything for four men by yourself.'

'Samira knows how passionate Leila is about a university education,' my mother said, 'and she even offered to stay at home in exchange for Leila going.'

But my father still said no, and just like that the prospect of an education for me died. My entire future had been settled in the space of two minutes. Everything my mind craved for itself – dismissed.

I know I am intelligent. Can I say that without sounding conceited? Because I am not conceited. It is simply something I've noticed about myself, as I might about another person. I take pleasure in being intelligent, except when I become the bearded lady. It doesn't make me proud in the wrong way. There have been many intelligent people – men and women – with nothing in their heads or hearts but cleverness. As I've said, in some ways having a few wits makes life more difficult. Often it is hard for me to keep my mouth shut. Sometimes I say to myself, Leila, better if you were an idiot, because that's what you're expected to be. How much easier if it came naturally! My mind wants to be engaged.

Dear Allah – it just struck me that I have something in common with those boys and men who hunger for martyrdom, who sing the praises of Allah and the Prophet as they walk through a minefield. They learnt what they believe from the mullahs, just as I learnt my own dangerous faith from Aunt Sediqa. Their love of their faith is so intense that they will walk straight towards the enemy with arms at their sides – this happened in the war with Iraq. Am I like that? Do I have a hunger for martyrdom simmering within me? I don't want to die for what I believe. But maybe when you have this sort of thing going on inside you, you make a decision at a level too deep for you to be aware of. My mind hungers for nourishment. And I fear that this hunger will kill me one day, that I will find myself walking through a minefield, singing songs in praise of great writers and poets, and then all at once – the explosion.

I am to rot away in this house, unless I find a husband. But until Samira is married I will have to stay single. That is the unspoken rule. It will make Samira look undesirable if her younger sister is married off before her. Yet with every passing day it is less and less likely that we'll find a suitable husband for my older sister. As sweet and good-natured as Samira is, most men do not consider her marriage material. The only suitor she's had was a 42-year-old car dealer with a reputation for being untrustworthy and short-tempered, who had divorced his wife and left her with three young children. It's heartbreaking to know that the reason she is denied the marriage, happiness and fulfilment all young girls dream of is a long, crescent-shaped scar on her left cheek. One scar, a lifelong curse.

It might occur to my mother that Samira is even less likely to find a suitor when she spends her life imprisoned in the house. But Mother is herself almost as hidebound in her devotion to custom as my father. In her opinion girls and young women need to stay home most of the time, otherwise they won't seem virtuous. Shopkeepers and people in the street would gossip about us, accusing us of flirting, and it would be fatal to be labelled a flirt. And a female doesn't have to do anything outrageous in Iran to be branded a trollop. Mother has seen more than one good girl lose her chance of marriage because she smiled too much or exchanged greetings with a man when out shopping or visiting friends. The safest strategy, my mother believes, is to keep us sequestered from the world. She thinks she must guard against not only a possible error of judgement by Samira or me – the gaze drawn involuntarily to the face of a handsome man and allowed to linger for a half-second too long – but also the mendacity of competing parents. That lingering gaze, too brief to be noticed in other societies, becomes intelligence that is stored away. The mother of another girl might mention it, almost as if she'd seen us emerging from a VD clinic. The slightest hint of impropriety can be the molehill on which a mountain of damning gossip is erected.

Still, if we are indoors all the time, we are invisible. We must at least be glimpsed in order to announce our existence. So once a week, as long as we have obediently done our chores and aren't needed at home, Mother lets us go to the library or to shop in nearby stores for a very short time, usually less than an hour.

On this day in June 1996, my sister and I are particularly excited because Samira is taking several of her hand-crafted dolls to Mr Taqavi, a store owner who sells trinkets and knick-knacks. The dolls are cleverly and artistically made from fragments of old clothing. Mr Taqavi sells them for much more than he pays Samira, but she is still happy to earn the extra bit of pocket money.

When we have the opportunity, Samira and I split up to maximise the precious outside time we have. We've agreed that I will go alone to the library and we'll meet back at home. Neither one of us wants to be late, since that will almost certainly mean our mother won't let us go out the following week.

Holding our chadors tight despite the blistering heat, we make our way through the narrow alleyways to the bazaar, the city's largest shopping area. Here people fill the streets, hunting for bargains, haggling over prices. The scent of spices and oils and the aroma of lamb and beef sizzling over open flames fill the air. Cars jostle for space, coming to a standstill when chickens and goats get in their way. Everywhere we look we see little dramas played out between shopper and storekeeper, mothers and children, men conducting business, people galore searching for the right place to eat. I walk with Samira across the road to Mr Taqavi's shop.

'Soon you'll be so busy making your dolls that I'll have to become your business partner, and we'll open up shops all over the world,' I joke with her.

Samira takes up the fantasy. 'Yes, and we'll find an apartment of our own in the city, and you can go to university.'

We lean our heads together, whispering softly so nobody will think we're too happy and wonder what we're up to.

'We'll have a special room for you,' says Samira, 'a library of your own, with a bookshelf that begins on the floor and doesn't stop until it reaches the ceiling. You'll need a ladder to reach all your fine books. We'll entertain great writers and scholars.'

But now Samira resumes her real life, all fantasising set aside. 'Keep your head out of the clouds and don't be late,' she warns me, as she needs to, because I am likely to lose track of time when surrounded by books.

Quchan's one small public library is my favourite place on earth. It's modest, this paradise of mine. The government doesn't spend money on books and the selection is limited. But I'm liberated here from the frowning disdain of my father and brothers for books. At home, reading is accompanied by guilt. I might be discovered in some nook I'd thought private, reading a book I'd bought myself with coins and notes saved from birthday gifts, from odd jobs done for neighbours, sewing, cleaning. And oh, the contempt of my brothers, of my father! But not here. Not here.

Mrs Salimi is the librarian, and one of the people I love best in the world. She waves a quick hello to me as I pass her desk. I notice the clock behind her and realise to my dismay that I've wasted more than half my library time escorting Samira to the bazaar.

The government's rationale for providing any money at all for libraries is that they act as distribution centres for works of propaganda. Some cleric or other writes about the glory and beauty of the revolution, and his book is printed in editions of hundreds of thousands and sent off to libraries from Mashhad to Tabriz to Bandar Abbas. Tyrannies always believe that literature must have a socially edifying purpose, and what purpose could be more edifying than celebrating the wisdom and virtue and kindness of the nation's rulers? But people everywhere, not just in Iran I would guess, know when they are being offered propaganda. In rare cases they might accept parts of it, they might even agree with some of it, but people know an exaggerated claim for the fantastic gains made by government on their behalf – more bread, more motor cars – when they see one.

And now here they are, these works, on display at the front of the library, volume after volume of rave reviews for the government. I never pay them the slightest attention, unless I'm forced to. What I'm looking for is something that will raise my spirits in a very different way, something that will touch my soul.

I choose two books this day, Doctor Karimi, two books that are fated to lift me up to heaven, as exulted as an angel; two books that will be with me when I plummet down to my private hell. One is Kahlil Gibran's *The Prophet*, a book about love, and the lessons of love, the lessons of life. I haven't seen this book in the library before. It is new, just translated into Farsi. The other is also about love, *The Little Prince*, by a Frenchman, Antoine de Saint-Exupéry, recommended to me by Mrs Salimi. Oh Doctor, if I had known, if I had known! But on this visit to the library, to my paradise, I don't know. Nor do I know just how quickly this journey I am about to undertake will begin; how rapidly the days will pass before you, Doctor, will witness my shame. I will see the distress in your eyes; the distress, and may I say, the love.

I know my mother will be wondering where I am by now, but outside I slow down to appreciate the colours in the street. Flowers are on sale everywhere – red roses, yellow sunflowers, daisies, orchids, irises, carnations, zinnias. I pass a weeping boy, his arms reaching out to be carried. His mother, frustrated with his demands and weighed down by the heavy bags she carries, pulls him behind her, ignoring his cries. His tears make little rivers as they run down the dusty skin of his face. He is probably about five years old. His bare feet are dirty, and as he lifts one to rub it over his worn pants, a spot of blood appears on the leg of his trousers. I wonder why his mother doesn't take more care of him. She must be very poor or she would dress him better. Certainly she'd buy him shoes. I watch sadly as the boy drags his tired feet through the dirt after her, and I almost stumble over a sweet-vending cart on the side of the street.

I turn to the old man in charge of the cart. The sun has burnt his scalp through his thin white hair, and his cheeks are bright red from the heat. 'Two lollies, please,' I say hastily. 'Orange ones.'

'Two hundred toman,' he says gruffly, handing the sweets to me.

I quickly turn around to find the little boy, but he has disappeared. I hurry back, glancing down a side street, hoping his mother has gone that way, but he is nowhere to be seen.

Maybe it isn't a good idea anyway. His mother might have been offended. I tuck the lollies into my chador and continue on my way home.

I imagine my own children and how I will shower them with gifts and chocolates and love. Then I feel guilty at the thought, knowing that not all children can have such affection bestowed on them. Poverty is everywhere in this town; starving children draped in dirty rags rip my heart to pieces. I slow to a stop. My mother tells me not to let myself be overwhelmed by the misery I see on the streets. She tells me that it is simply the way things are; what Allah intends. But I don't believe that Allah intends any such thing. I think He intends that those who have will share with those who have not.

'Maman?' I feel someone tug at the back of my chador. I turn to find the little boy. His hand is still raised. 'Sorry! Sorry! I thought you were my maman.' He totters backwards, afraid that he is about to receive a scolding.

I kneel down and whisper, 'Hey, it's all right, it's all right. Are you lost? Have you lost your mother?' He is trembling slightly, looking ready to burst into tears again. I quickly reach into my chador and offer him the treats. His face lights up for a few seconds, then clouds over again, and I realise that he's shocked at being shown kindness. I place the lollies in his tiny hand, closing his fingers around them. 'Take them, they're yours.'

The boy stares up at me with wide eyes. 'Thank you,' he says shyly, and off he runs.

As I turn to walk on I see a man leaning against the doorframe of a nearby clothing store. He is holding a book in his hands: *The Little Prince*.

'Oh,' I say, reaching for my bag and feeling for my book. It isn't there. I must have dropped it while talking to the little boy.

'This is a good book,' says the stranger. 'It's one of my favourites.'

How good-looking he is! Probably in his late twenties, short brown hair, a perfectly groomed beard and warm, dark eyes.

'It's not like a children's book at all.' He hands the book back to me; I accept it quickly and conceal it beneath my chador.

'Um . . . thank you,' I manage to stutter, keeping my eyes on the ground, as far as I can. How well I know that women are not to make eye contact with strangers, yet I find myself fighting a powerful urge to do exactly what I must not.

Someone calls for him from within the store. I glance up to see an annoyed expression passing over his face. He excuses himself with what seems to me reluctance and goes into the boutique. But he turns at the door and says to me, in a way that he should not, 'I hope you come by again.'

My heart is beating as fast as a cat's. His eyes! Oh, I have noticed good-looking men before; I have said to myself, So handsome! But this is different. I am experiencing a new feeling. A strange sense deep in my heart. Is it just that I am older now? Or that secretly I have thought more about romance? I don't know.

Mother is waiting for me when I reach home. 'Where have you been, you foolish girl? Your father will be home any minute. Come and help me clean these vegetables.'

I do as I am told, of course. Yet even as I wash carrots and peel potatoes, even as my mother clashes pots and pans around me in her frenzy to have the evening meal ready for her husband and sons, I hear music in my ears and see those eyes, those eyes.

It has begun.

The Doctor

It is a scorching afternoon in June 1996. I take two steps towards
my front door from my air-conditioned car and am bathed in sweat.
I want to turn back, lock myself in my car again and blast the icy air over
my liquefying body. I have just returned to Quchan from Mashhad,
a trip of 150 kilometres. For the two hours it took I was immersed in
cool air, listening to music, Pink Floyd especially.

My wife hates Pink Floyd, so I can only indulge when I am alone.
Azita insists on Persian music, fearing that listening to a Western band
could land us in trouble. We might be stopped by the police for some
reason, or by the vile Basij militias, and if the Floyd cassettes were
spotted we'd be punished.

I call out, 'Azita, I'm home. Is dinner ready?' I can tell from the sounds of pots being crashed about in the kitchen that in fact dinner isn't yet ready. Azita is from a wealthy family and while she might not relish playing the role of a traditional wife, she takes pride in doing it well. She would be happier with servants to do the cooking and laundry, indeed all of the housework. She has become a housewife by default; she is one thing and another, but one thing she is not is imaginative. Maybe she would enjoy studying further, or taking up some creative pursuit – I don't know what – but if you want to do something that takes you away from the customary role our culture dictates, you have to first be able to imagine it. And Azita cannot. She tries her best to have a hot meal ready when I come home, but today I've arrived at not quite the right hour.

I should have kept quiet about dinner, so as not to add any further grievance to all those that divide us. For the truth is that we are ill-suited, Azita and I. Our politics, our way of looking at life, even the books we read, the music we enjoy are at odds. Growing up in extreme poverty, being deprived of extended family, and feeling lonely and desperate had made me think, and more than anything it had made me read. By the age of seventeen I had read almost every English and Russian classic, and I came to see that my curse was not poverty, or having a polygamist father who did not remember my name, it was my realisation of the futility of ancient rules. While all my friends in the slums were struggling to overcome their adversity by accumulating wealth, I was dreaming of joining an underground freedom movement, of writing a forbidden book on human rights and making peace between science and God.

Azita sees little to criticise in the way the country is run, little to find fault with in Iranian society as a whole. She is an obedient citizen. I am not, and the rigid structures of conservative Iran exasperate me every hour of every day. Azita puts up with our marriage because she thinks that one day I will mellow into a dutiful citizen like herself, that I will steadily build up my medical practice, grow wealthy, and devote my leisure time to writing books that never cause the government censors the slightest discomfort. She likes to boast to her friends that I am a published writer as well as a doctor, but she wants me to be the right sort of writer, the right sort of doctor. If only we could discuss the things that I deal with every day – poor patients unable to pay for treatment, soldiers who come to me badly injured even though Iran isn't at war at this time, women who beg me to perform illegal procedures to save them from execution – perhaps then there could be a bond between us. But it is simply impossible to converse about these issues with my wife. At times I feel sorry for her: she does not have a typical Iranian husband who would be easily satisfied with a beautiful wife, a steady income, and regular picnics on Fridays. While she dreams of a bigger house, I dream of a free Iran with equality for all.

But I am weary of arguing. And really, am I the only husband in the world with complaints to make about his wife? It's so tedious. As I walk down to the kitchen, it occurs to me that Azita is probably as tired of the arguments as I am. She holds on with all her might to a vision of complete normalcy, a dream of becoming undifferentiated in any way from the ordinary, except in the matter of money. I hold on with all my might to the hope of living a life that has some actual meaning. Sighing in resignation, I vow to keep things light for the evening. Peace will be a welcome change.

'It's not ready yet,' she says. 'I'm sorry. But you are earlier than you said you'd be.'

I say, 'No problem, darling,' and inhale the aroma of saffron rice, coriander, cumin, turmeric. 'Beef and eggplant curry,' I murmur with approval. 'My favourite.' My mother was never able to afford such elaborate dishes, but I have quickly grown accustomed to fine dining.

Azita uses many old recipes of her grandmother's, taking pleasure in introducing me to things I haven't tried before.

I pick up a wooden spoon resting on the stove top and scoop out a tender piece of eggplant. I pop it into my mouth before Azita can stop me, and reach for another.

She slaps my hand playfully. 'Don't spoil your appetite. The rice will be ready in just a few minutes.'

'Can't wait,' I say, and dip the spoon in again, this time fishing out a piece of beef. I'm playing the role of affectionate husband to please her.

She shakes her head. 'You forgot to eat. Like every day. And just like every day, you can wait a few more minutes.' Her smile softens the words. The light from a lamp on the table spills across the room at an angle that creates a kind of halo around her head, and highlights her high forehead, her fine, straight nose, her full lips and perfect chin. I watch her for a moment, observing her beauty without emotion.

She cocks her head questioningly, doubtless wondering why I am studying her, and I notice tiny lines forming at the corners of her eyes. She is only twenty-four, but she has been fighting her own battles, which have worn her down. I admonish myself, thinking, She has next to no imagination, next to no curiosity about life, about the world – but she does her best. Grant her that.

'You're making me nervous standing there staring at me,' she says. 'Go watch the news until it's time to eat.'

I stand my ground for a minute, wondering if she sees my flaws too. I don't like to think I have any, but of course I do. I am average-looking but with an easy smile that calms nurses, doctors, and patients alike during stressful situations. I am also average in height and weight. Like most Persian men, I keep my full black beard neatly trimmed, although I wear my wavy hair longer than many, letting it nearly touch my shoulders. My eyes are an unusually light brown and I think this draws people in; most people seem to have a good first impression of me. Even my wife thought me charming when we were introduced. She's told me many times that she found me handsome and clever and cheerful, and that her parents made a good choice of husband for her.

'You won't be a new doctor with military responsibilities forever,' she said. 'You're a brilliant man and one day you'll be richer than my wildest dreams.'

Azita's 'wildest dreams' would have extended to me becoming a multimillionaire, and that's never going to happen. But any marriage is subject to wear and tear, to the slow erosion of the extravagant schemes once entertained. These days she'd probably settle for a good income that fattened our bank account by a little each month without ever amounting to a big enough surplus to cover a Mercedes. This erosion, in our case, has progressed at the same pace as the diminishment of desire. The interest we took in intimacy when we were new to each other was no doubt due to sexual deprivation and curiosity, as well as instinct. Now that interest is not so great.

Azita must sometimes look at me in just the critical and disappointed way I look at her. She must say to herself, Hmm, his hairline is receding, a pity. Or, That way he sits, with his shoulders hunched, it's okay now but when he's older it will make him look like somebody's grandfather. She's probably aware that a pretty face will always catch my attention. Does she wonder, Who does he think he is – Don Juan? Huh!

But she would not think of Don Juan. She would not have heard of him. She would think of Hajji Baba of Isfahan, the Casanova of the Middle East. And maybe she thinks of me as a snob, an intellectual snob. Am I? Yes. Maybe. A little bit. If I were to come upon Azita reading a translation of Tolstoy, my jaw would drop to the ground, certainly. I'd probably say, 'Dear God in heaven, you, Azita, reading

Tolstoy. I don't believe it.' And then I'd add something patronising without realising it, such as, 'Good for you, Wife, I'm so proud of you.' It might be, too, that she resents me hiding myself away to write. She might particularly hate the look of impatience on my face when she interrupts me to ask a question about family matters, advice on a present for her cousin's birthday, whatever. And what about love? Is there enough love in me to satisfy her? Does she think to herself, He never puts his arms around me and says, Azita, dear wife, you mean the world to me?

I wander out of the kitchen, picking up the coat and shirt I draped across a chair and carrying them to the bedroom. I wonder if I could squeeze in a little reading before dinner, then decide against it, knowing that if I get into the history book I've begun, I won't want to put it down. I'll wait until she goes to bed to immerse myself in my research about the clash between the Roman and Persian empires.

I step into the living room and pause. My daughter, Newsha, lies sleeping soundly in front of the television. Treading softly, I cross the floor, squat beside her, and ease the remote out of her hand. Her eyelids flutter and I wonder what visions come to a four-year-old in dreams. Am I in them, watching over her protectively, or does she spend her dream life waiting for me to come home, as she does in her waking hours? I wish it were different, but for now I have to build my practice while also working in the military hospital, which gives me next to no time to spend with my adorable child. Every Iranian man has to do two years' military service when he turns eighteen, although this is deferred until after graduation for those studying at university. Having done three months of tough military training in camps, I am now serving as an army doctor for my remaining twenty-one months. Here in Quchan I work three day shifts and one night shift at the army base hospital, and spend the rest of the week in my private practice.

I settle onto the couch and change the channel to the news. It's full of the usual ridiculous predictions about how much progress the country will achieve in the next five years through economic reforms. I shake my head in disgust. Ever since the revolution of 1979, government stooges on the television network have been deceiving the nation, censoring news, distorting facts. Nobody believes a word they say. Well, no educated person; no one with the capacity for critical thought. It's like when you are forced to listen to someone boasting about his accomplishments – it's usually a male. And you think, If you're really that wonderful, why brag? It will be obvious without drawing our attention to it.

Accidentally I hit the volume control instead of the off button and news about a woman being stoned to death for adultery blasts into the room. Newsha cries out and moves from sleep to being fully awake within seconds, in the way only a child can. She comes and sits on my lap. I turn the volume down, cuddling her while she yawns, at the same time attending with revulsion to the story of the stoning.

Azita comes in and picks Newsha up from my lap, announcing that dinner is ready. She glances quickly at the television. 'That's what happens to people who break laws,' she says. 'They are punished.'

All my good intentions to play the part of loving husband vanish in an instant. I can't believe I've heard correctly. Because that woman was intimate with a man and wasn't married, she should be stoned to death? Azita and I disagree on many things, almost everything in fact, but I thought she, like most Persians, would find stoning barbaric. It's not a subject on which she has offered an opinion in the past, although I've heard her giving pro-government spiels on other issues.

She puts her hands over our daughter's ears, even though Newsha is too young to understand. 'That woman is a lesson to everyone who thinks they don't have to obey laws. She knew the consequences for breaking them. And you can't change the law.' She turns on her heel, taking Newsha with her and calling over her shoulder, 'Hurry or your food will get cold.'

Maybe she's just in a mood to irritate me? Because deep down I do know that Azita is disgusted by this state barbarism. I know exactly what that barbarism has cost her. I also know that, more than anything, she is scared of losing her husband. She wants me to be invincible – the invincibility that comes from blind obedience. She is frightened that one day a black car will snatch me from the street and I will be gone forever, just like all those other men and women who dared to think against the Iranian Big Brother, almost a hundred thousand of them. What Azita doesn't know is that I have never learnt obedience, have never been able to succumb to injustice. She has no idea that the black car is already idling in the yard of the intelligence service.

And that's the end of my appetite. I pick at my dinner, sick at heart at the stoning of that poor wretched woman, and at my wife's absurd endorsement of it. What hope is there for Iran, what hope for the world, if the people who see the monstrous injustice of this punishment choose to sanction it, or stay silent about it? My deepest dread is that one fine day Azita will say, 'Do you know what? Those Jews deserved what they got in the Second World War.' What will I do then? Find a hole in which to hide and weep until I die. While she knows I'm Jewish, Azita openly despises Jews; I have to pretend to be a Muslim around her. She believes the evil myths she's heard, such as Jewish women drinking the blood of Muslim children. The saddest thing is that I'm the only Jew she's ever met in her life.

Azita doesn't know – because I have never told her – that the additional ache I feel when I hear of stoning comes from the fact that my mother was once at risk of this ritual murder. When she married my father she converted to Islam, in the rapid and expedient way that is provided for the infidel by protocols, but she remained a Jew at heart, and prayed as a Jew, and raised my brother and me in the Jewish faith. She made sure we knew who Abraham was and revered him, that we knew the whole story of Moses in great detail, and revered him too. My father was a Muslim only on his papers. He drank alcohol, ate pork and never prayed, not even once. He was a Muslim because it allowed him to have three wives at the same time. In fact the law allowed him to have four, but though he tried to marry a fourth woman, he didn't succeed. He had seven children from his three wives, and as well as never remembering my name, he never knew my age or what grade I was in at school either. His dream was for me to become a bus driver like him and take over his business.

My mother could well have been stoned for raising us in the Jewish faith. She could have been buried in earth up to her shoulders in a portable tub, then displayed in public with her head covered by a cloth while up to fifty Revolutionary Guards and perhaps Basij militias hurled rocks at her (the Guards and the Basij vie for the honour of performing a stoning). These rocks are especially chosen for size, about that of a juvenile fist, and are thrown until a doctor can report, after an examination, that the victim's pulse has ceased. By such time, my mother's brains would be escaping from her skull, her teeth would be smashed, her eyeballs hanging down her cheeks.

She could also have been stoned for adultery, since she slept in a regular way with a certain Haji Heydar, the owner of the bus company my father worked for. She did this against her will, against her pride, and against everything she believed in. She was tormented by it, loathed every single second that Haji Heydar touched her skin. She sold her body to this vicious, arrogant Muslim who was already married so she could provide my brother and me with a little food, and a shirt once a year. And to allow me an education. 'I want you to become a doctor, Kooshyar, so you can treat the poor,' she told me, almost daily. My mother let that evil monster crush her pride so Koorosh and I could have a better life.

When I witness a stoning I don't have to tell myself that the woman being executed could, in a different world, be my sister or wife or daughter, and so bow my head in pity. No, what I think is, That could have been my mother, in this world, and it may yet be my mother. So my hatred for the whole practice, for the men who hurl the rocks, for the vile system that permits it is very, very personal.

'What's wrong now?' Azita's tone verges on anger.

'Nothing,' I say. 'Everything.'

As I leave the table and stride to my study, Newsha calls, 'Please, Daddy. Come back and eat with us.'

But just for a while I need to shut everything out. I open one of my favourite books, Kahlil Gibran's *The Prophet*. I know I'll find solace in his words, in his vision of a world of love and beauty, justice and understanding. I read aloud, pronouncing each word with reverence. *And beauty is not a need but an ecstasy. It is not a mouth thirsting nor an empty hand stretched forth, but rather a heart inflamed and a soul enchanted. It is not the image you would see nor the song you would hear, but rather an image you see though you close your eyes and a song you hear though you shut your ears.*

For a few hours I manage to be at peace.

Walking to my private practice the next day, I glance at the papers on the newsstand. Several men nearby are discussing the headlines and condemning the woman who was stoned.

'She was seeing another man,' a young man said, contempt lacing his words. 'She deserved it.'

'Married for seven years and she does this to her husband?'

'Worse. Her husband was also her cousin. To disgrace her family like that! It's unthinkable.'

Despite my opposition to sensationalising a punishment so out of proportion to what should never have been a crime to begin with, I buy a paper. As I take the stairs to my surgery on the second floor I quickly scan the story, stopping on a landing to turn the page and read through to the end. And what do I read? The woman, Mamoosa, married and with a six-year-old daughter, had met a man a little older than her in a shop. She was drawn to him, despite everything she knew about the danger of surrendering to attraction of this sort. She came back to the shop, again and again. They found somewhere private in the shop and kissed. A suspicious man in a neighbouring shop got word to Mamoosa's husband, who followed her at a distance, then burst in on the lovers in the act of kissing. He stabbed his wife and the shopkeeper, but both survived, the man to endure a hundred lashes, Mamoosa to be stoned to death, after being compelled to divorce her husband and relinquish her daughter.

Arash, my secretary and a male nurse, rises when I enter the waiting room. I wave the newspaper, nearly knocking over a lamp.

'This is savage,' I say, my voice shaking with anger. 'Iran never did this kind of thing before the revolution. Some Middle Eastern countries, yes, but not here.' I try to keep my tone even but I can't. 'Yet to dissent is to risk our lives.'

Before the conversation can continue, the door opens and the first patient of the day arrives. Nodding a greeting, I retreat to my surgery to calm down. I've seen many men die in my country, their jackets pierced with bullets after execution by firing squad. I've seen young men hanged, and the legs of one of them jerking about and sending his slipper flying across the sky to land in front of me. I've treated women who were raped and battered, but none of them were as horrifying to me as stoning.

All day images of Mamoosa flash through my head, making it difficult to concentrate on what my patients say. On my lunch break I hurry to a crowded bookshop in a side street, narrowly avoiding being hit by a runaway goat pulling a lopsided cart, and buy a copy of *Islamic Punishment Laws of Iran*.

That night after dinner, I kiss Newsha good night and wander down the hallway to my study. Taking my new book from my briefcase I slip out into the courtyard for some fresh air. I light a cigarette and sink into a chair near the porch, making sure my wife doesn't see me from the windows. One look at the title of my book and she'd panic, assuming the worst.

Hastily I read the chapters about terminating pregnancies and repairing virginities. I read as if in a trance, my concentration so complete, my horror so intense, that I am totally lost in the words on the page, forgetting about my cigarette until it burns down to my fingertips and scorches my skin.

A doctor who terminates a woman's pregnancy within the first twelve weeks will lose his medical licence, go to jail for two to ten years, and be fined five million toman, which would mean losing his house and all his assets.

If the pregnancy has advanced beyond the first trimester, termination is considered murder and the doctor can be tried and hanged.

The punishment for repairing a girl's virginity allows for no qualifications: death by hanging.

I close the book and hold it tightly against my chest, eyes closed. Since becoming an intern three years ago, I have performed more than two hundred terminations and restored more than fifty hymens. I can't change the law or the culture, but I can help individual women whose indiscretions lead to pregnancies. I say 'indiscretions', but it's more often the case that the woman has been the victim of rape. I've known the penalties from the beginning, but fear grips me now like it never has before. I wonder why this is. Is it the stoning? Yes, that's it, I decide.

It is Iran's religious fascism, its theocratic ideology, that allows the government to get away with any behaviour it wants, from seizing property to kidnapping, torturing and killing its opponents, all of which are done in order to retain power and intimidate dissenters. There is no room for tolerance in a society where a person's worth is judged by their faith and gender. Women are banned from singing, dancing, and uncovering their hair in public. They have no right to divorce or to give testimony in a court of law. Such religious governments are the political manifestation of ignorance.

When I was sixteen I read a book, banned in Iran, about Che Guevara. It was given to me by a young man named Firooz, who was executed three years later for his part in pro-democracy activities. Che, a medical doctor in his native Argentina, one day decided to pick up a gun and fight for freedom. In the book he was quoted as saying, 'In front of me I found a box of medicines and a box of bullets. I chose the box of bullets.'

Thinking of that choice now, I wonder what I should do. Continue with the terminations? Or abandon all that, hoping that the many I have already performed will remain secret, and work at being the best doctor I can be in legal ways? What if one of the women I helped were to say something to a friend, who then went to the authorities? How would Newsha survive without me?

Without any feeling of exultation, without any sense of heroic defiance, I choose the medicine and the bullets.

Leila

Dinner goes by in a blur for me, all my thoughts devoted to the lustre of those eyes. May I ask you, Doctor, do you know *The Little Prince*? And if so, I wonder if it means as much to you as it came to mean to me.

After washing the dishes, I steal away to my room to begin reading. Every word is enchanting; the simplicity and sweetness of the story cast a cloak of wonder around me. And oh, the little prince himself, so full of joy and curiosity – I adore him! I feel we share the same set of eyes as I read his comments on kings and businessmen, accountants and lamplighters.

Curled up on my mattress on the hard floor of the room I share with my sister, I linger over every sentence and turn each page slowly to make the story last longer, to gain a few more minutes with the prince. We are kindred spirits, he and I, both alone in an alien land searching for something, trying to understand things that don't seem to make much sense.

When Samira comes in I tell her what I've been thinking. She tilts her head to one side and studies me thoughtfully before speaking. 'And what are you searching for, darling?' she asks.

I sigh and turn my gaze to the window. 'I'm not sure. Maybe for a life of my own? I'm not *unhappy* here, but it's hard not to feel boxed in.'

Samira nods. 'Yes, our lives aren't really full of excitement.' She pauses for a minute and then lowers her voice teasingly. 'Maybe it's love you're looking for.'

Startled, I deny it. 'Don't be silly!'

'What's silly about wishing to have a wonderful man fall in love with you? Maybe a poet who would write you the most beautiful verses in the world, or a musician who dedicates entire symphonies to you.'

I blush painfully. And Samira notices. She whispers, 'What was that? What were you thinking of?'

I know I've been caught. I know Samira will not rest until I tell her of my encounter, but I'm scared that once I speak the words aloud, once I describe the man in his flesh and blood, the texture of his voice and the colours of his eyes, then he will become real. Not just a passing moment, not just a casual conversation.

Averting my eyes and fiddling with the cover of *The Little Prince* is clearly not the answer Samira wants. She bends over me, giddy and excited. When I finally meet her gaze I sigh and give in.

'I met a man today.'

'What do you mean? Who? What happened?'

'It wasn't even anything important. I dropped my book outside his store, and he picked it up and gave it back to me. That's all.'

'Was he very handsome?' My sister giggles, watching the slow smile spread across my face. 'What did he look like? Did he have a thick curly moustache? Or maybe gorgeous long hair like those actors on television?'

We both break out laughing, burying our faces in pillows to muffle the sounds. As Samira's laughter subsides she looks up at me, her expression of delight fading. 'If it weren't for me, you'd be married by now,' she says, suddenly serious. 'You would have found true love.'

I take her hand in my own and hold it against my cheek. 'Don't say such things. Love isn't what I am looking for. You know what I want most is to go to university so I can become a teacher. I want to teach children about the planets and stars, and have them come into school in the morning telling me that they've been looking at the night sky. I want to read them *The Little Prince* and see them draw pictures of a boa that eats an elephant, like in the prince's picture. But that's impossible, and it's not your fault. So let's just stop thinking about it.'

'Maybe you'll find a husband who wants to see you fulfil your dreams,' Samira says simply. 'I think that could be your fate.'

I change the subject. 'You never said how much you got for your dolls today.'

Samira tells me the price and I frown at the injustice of it. 'Your work is worth ten times that.'

'What does it matter?' she says. 'I have to give it all to Mother for my *jehaz* anyway. I know she's looking out for me, but I don't even get to pick the things that go into it. You and I could buy dishes and silver and a carpet with flowers woven through it. Instead, she chooses everything. She thinks I'm still a child. She thinks I would build a *jehaz* of lollies and pistachios.'

Our mother, like the mother of every young Persian woman, has been saving for her daughters' *jehazes* – what are known as trousseaus in the West – almost from the day we were born.

As if somehow sensing that her daughters are talking about her, at that moment Mother opens the door. She has some sort of extraordinary instinct that tells her such things. 'You need to go to sleep early tonight,' she says, hands on her hips. 'Tomorrow we'll make strawberry and carrot jam. You'll be in the hot sun all day and if you don't get any sleep you'll complain about being tired before noon. No more talking now. Get ready for bed.'

Strawberry and carrot jam. What an adventure!

Samira falls asleep quickly, but not me. I imagine the man from the shop falling deeply in love with me, marrying me, liberating me from my cage. He loves books, as I do. I picture our home full of them, lining the walls from floor to ceiling. And a kiss – what would a kiss feel like? I wonder how those eyes would look in the morning as we wake together in our beautiful home filled with books and art, built far, far away from here. A yearning I can hardly contain tugs at my heart. It seems to get worse, the images more vivid as each hour of the night passes.

The next day we rise early to begin the tasks mother has set for us. We go through the lengthy process of making jam once every summer, when strawberries and carrots are plentiful in the market. We wash the berries and carrots and carry them to the yard, where we peel the carrots and then cut everything into small pieces. It takes all day to make a dozen jars of jam. When evening comes we serve the men, who sit cross-legged on the floor waiting for dinner.

Father complains about the heat and the cost of breeding sheep. 'The government isn't doing anything for farmers,' he says. 'We just get poorer and poorer every year.'

Ali is his usual sombre self. 'I hear you went to the library yesterday,' he says to me, his words more an accusation than a statement. 'And then into one of the shops.'

Mother says, 'The girls had errands to run. Samira sold a doll for fifty toman. I'll use it to add to her *jehaz*.'

And Ali: 'What more could she need for her *jehaz*? She's been adding to it forever.' His tone is cruel and mocking. Samira's feelings mean less than nothing to him. I want to chastise him, but the truth is that I'm afraid of Ali, afraid of all my brothers, and of my father. It's pitiable. Samira and I are like hostages, hoping and praying we won't be tormented, tortured, before being released one day. It's at such times as this I have to remind myself that my father, and even my brothers in their crude way, have what they believe are my best interests at heart. Oh, even as I say that, Doctor Karimi, knowing what was to come, so many phantoms rouse themselves from the shadows. Would I not have been better off if my father and brothers had kept me locked away still more securely from the world? Is that not true?

On this day, though, I strive to recall that their love for me has in the past proved itself genuine. When I was seven years old and ill with meningitis, a common disease in this area, I was expected to die.

My father in his grief went to the doctor and said, 'Save her, I beg of you. I have my own house. I will sell it to pay for treatment. For Allah's sake, please Doctor, please save my little daughter.'

My mother told me this. And she told me more. My father said to the doctor, 'She is the dearest person in this world to me.'

I have never seen or heard of my father begging anyone apart from then. He is such a proud man that I doubt he would beg for his own life.

My brothers, for their part, waited outside the hospital for days, praying without pause for my life to continue. They wept when the news was not good – they wept and my father struck himself on the head in his torment. The morning came when my condition showed signs of improvement, and my brothers and my father shouted aloud their thanks to Allah. That was love. That is what I should remember. If I can.

The men settle in to watch television after dinner – the news, the endless, endless news, and then one of those cheaply made local films about a man who has such faith in Allah and in the mullahs who direct his life that his crop of corn doubles its yield. I sit in a corner to read, enjoying the light breeze that blows through the open window beside me. I've barely read more than a page before Majid takes it into his head to belittle me.

He snatches the book from my hands and sneers at the cover. 'What's this garbage?'

'Give it back! I have to return it to the library. It doesn't belong to me.'

'Oh, look. It even has pictures. When are you going to grow up, little girl?'

Men feel so comfortable in the role of tyrant. Should I say that? Remember, Leila. If you can.

Samira comforts me later, in our room. 'My love, things will change when you get married and have more freedom.'

'Really?' I say. 'They could get worse.' But then I think of the man in the shop and want to bite my tongue off. He would not be a tyrant. He would not bully me. You see what my heart was like, Doctor Karimi. How fragile! It was as if I were carrying into the hurly-burly of life a delicate crystal vase capable of being shattered with one little tap in the wrong place. Completely unaware that not all tyrants were as crude as my brother Majid. That some smiled and gave every appearance of having a tender heart of their own.

Samira changes the subject. 'Do you want to see something exciting?'

'Of course.'

Opening our shared wardrobe, she takes out a bag and tells me to close my eyes. I do as I am told, and when I'm allowed to look, Samira is holding up the most beautiful doll I've ever seen. I pick it up and turn it around and around, taking in every detail of this exquisite work of art. 'Oh Samira, this is better than the dolls in the museums.'

'I worked on it every day for a month,' she says. 'I used the best quality fabric.'

I study the tiny, perfect stitches, the intricate folds and design. 'Don't sell this one to that thief Mr Taqavi. I saw one of your dolls in his store window with a price tag of five hundred toman. He only pays you fifty.'

Samira reaches for her doll and when I hand it back she holds it close to her chest. 'Don't worry, I have big plans for this one. You know the children's ward in the hospital? For children who are terminally ill, and those who've been abandoned? I know it sounds crazy, but I want to go there and give my doll to one of the children.'

'A wonderful idea!'

My sister adores children. She is forever stopping in the street to gaze misty-eyed at some lovely infant trotting beside her mother, his mother. She has an equally strong sympathy for the abandoned and unwanted, whoever they are, children or adults. It is inborn, this great sympathy of hers, and it is part of me too. Maybe it has come down to us from our mother. Who, when she isn't in a towering temper about one thing or another, will stop in the street like Samira and whisper to us, 'Oh, such a sight, such a sight,' when she sees a child in distress, or begging for coins on the kerb.

'This is my plan. I want to ask Mother for one hour out next week. We can go to the ward together. We'll buy some lollies and stay as long as we can. We'll show that people care about them even if they don't have mothers and fathers, or even if they're terribly sick. We'll find a girl who loves the doll and make a gift of it to her.'

I can see so clearly how happy this will make the girl who is given the doll. But what about the many other children? 'I'll save all my pocket money for them,' I tell Samira. 'I'll buy a toy, maybe a small car for a boy. And lollies, many, many lollies for all the kids.'

Samira puts her finger to her lips. 'Mother's coming,' she whispers. 'Don't say anything until I talk to her.' She tucks the doll behind her as our mother enters the room.

'Have you set up the mosquito nets for your brothers yet?' she asks.

'Straight away, Mother,' we both say at once, and leap to our feet.

My heart is all of a sudden so much lighter. I adore the hospital plan. I adore my sister for thinking of it. And just for now, at least, I adore the world.

The Doctor

I want to speak of a time before I'd carried out any surgical interventions of the sort that can put a noose around a doctor's neck in Iran. I want to speak of what happened to the woman who became my wife, of how I know what lies beneath those crazy views she expressed on stoning.

Azita's parents and my mother arranged our marriage. Forty-eight hours after they met we were engaged. In point of fact, as far as the law of the land and our families were concerned, we were married as of the moment our parents agreed. There could be no backing out. Until our wedding ceremony was concluded – a big ceremony that would include all the traditional trappings – sex was out of the question. Even kissing was unacceptable. But we were young, attracted to each other. We made love when we found a way to spend time together without supervision.

Several weeks later, Azita is sitting before me with her head bowed and her hands twisting on her lap in distress. She is pregnant. She's eighteen and I'm twenty-two. It's a catastrophe.

'What are we going to do?' she whispers in anguish. 'My father will abandon me. I'll be an outcast. We'll have nothing. They'll never welcome you into our family. You have no money to support me and a baby. What if you have to leave university to get a job? I can't live like that. If my father lets me live at all. He has a horrible temper and he believes strongly that sex should be forbidden until the ceremony. He won't accept what I've done. We have to find someone who can fix this.'

I tell her, trying to calm her down, 'The wedding isn't that far away. You won't be showing yet. We can say the baby came early.'

My words of comfort only make her sob harder. Her body shakes, almost on the point of convulsions. 'They'll know,' she says. 'Believe me, they'll know. Kooshyar, we *must* prevent this.'

At this stage of my medical career, I haven't even learnt about terminations, let alone considered performing one. I find the name of a traditional herbal-medicine seller and take Azita to see him. He's an old man with wrinkled skin, and thin white hair the exact shade of the cataract covering the pupil of his left eye. He sells us raspberry root.

'Make this into a strong tea, boiling it until it is almost soft, and then drink one cup after another until you vomit.'

Azita goes straight home and as soon as she has the kitchen to herself, she boils the root. She decants the mixture into a big earthen jug and carries it to her bedroom. She pours herself a large cup and hides the jug in the closet, taking it out every few minutes to pour another cup. The taste is strong and unpleasant, and while it makes her gag, she doesn't vomit.

Waiting until no one can overhear, she phones me in tears to tell me it didn't work. I knew from the beginning that we were clutching at straws, that this kind of folk remedy is seldom successful. 'We'll try something else,' I tell her.

And we do. We try the oldest remedy of all. We pray, both together and apart. Do I need to say that prayer didn't work?

Finally, after a month of anxious searching, we find a midwife who will undertake a termination. She plies her trade in Isfahan, hundreds of kilometres from Mashhad, where we live at that time. We go to see Azita's father, asking permission to visit my relatives in the distant city. Reluctantly he agrees. We can go for three days. To pay for the midwife, Azita secretly sells the jewellery her family gave her on her engagement.

As soon as we step off the bus, frightened, lost and exhausted, we set out to find the woman with the shady set-up. The deeper into the city we go, the greater my fears become. There is a panicked tightness in my chest that I have to struggle to control. When we reach her dingy hovel whatever hopes I have are dashed. There is no way this can be safe. There is no way Azita can come out of this alive. I glance at her and see that she is thinking the same thing. The horrified expression on her face makes me sick at heart.

'We can't do this,' I say, taking her arm. 'Anyone who lives in such filth won't use clean instruments. It's too risky.'

Azita says, 'We're here already, there's no other way.'

Before I can say more, the midwife opens the battered door and slides out her arm, keeping the rest of her body in the shadows. She beckons to us with stubby fingers. 'Hurry, before someone sees you.'

We step inside. The midwife wiggles her fingers. 'Payment,' is the only word she utters. With shaking hands, Azita opens her purse and hands over the money. The woman counts the notes speedily, stuffs the money into her pocket and motions to a dirty mattress. 'Lie down and pull your chador up to your waist.'

Without daring to meet my eyes, Azita follows the orders. The midwife sees that Azita is wearing pants under her black chador.

'And them,' she says. 'What a stupid girl not to wear something simple. Take them off. Underwear too.'

Azita lifts her hips and does as she is told. Before I can open my mouth to utter words of encouragement, I'm pushed out of the way. With speed I wouldn't expect of the old midwife, she kneels before Azita, grabs a long metal rod from under the mattress, spreads Azita's legs, finds the opening and jabs the rod inside. She stabs at the uterus until she draws blood – dark-red blood that paints the mattress, then the floor. It resurrects my own dark memories. Forty-five years ago my grandfather was murdered in this very town.

Screaming in pain, Azita tries to move away and I lunge forward to pull the midwife off her. Blood is pouring down Azita's thighs in thick dark streams. She's shaking and her mouth is hanging open in shock. The midwife extracts the rod, dips it into a bowl of water beside her and lays it back under the mattress.

'You can clean yourself there,' she says, pointing to a rusty sink against the wall. 'Then leave. Quickly, before the next woman comes.'

The next woman? How many does she see in one day? I'm in a stupor of disgust and despair.

'Help me,' Azita pleads, choking back sobs. 'Get me out of here.'

I don't dare touch the feculent towels that hang by the sink, opting for a fistful of tissues instead. I stuff my pockets with others for later and carry my weeping fiancée out the door.

'I'm sorry,' I murmur.

Somehow we make it to a hotel, but we don't rest. Azita is in dreadful pain and is still bleeding badly. After an hour of ordeal, she eventually passes out, soaked in sweat and moaning in her sleep. In the morning we catch a bus back to Mashhad, but Azita faints in my arms and I have to carry her off at a stop in Tehran. Her skin is on fire. Frantically I ask someone at the ticket counter for directions to the nearest hospital. 'And a cab,' I plead. 'Right away.'

I know all the signs of septic shock. I watch helplessly while nurses rush Azita into the operating room. I pace back and forth on the spotless white floor, fluorescent lights hissing overhead. A doctor I haven't even had time to talk to will perform emergency surgery to save Azita's life.

What if she dies? She's only a child. This is my fault. Her father will have me murdered. I should never have agreed to a termination, should never have let her set foot inside that squalid house.

Finally the doctor comes to find me. He tells me, with a disgust he doesn't try to hide, that Azita will be all right. 'We need to keep her here for a few days. She'll need intravenous antibiotics.'

'I'm a doctor too,' I tell him, exaggerating the truth. I am still in medical school, but I have enough training to take care of Azita now that she has been treated. 'We have to leave tomorrow. There's no choice.'

The doctor turns on his heel and leaves. I spend the night in the waiting room, and the next morning Azita, still very weak, signs herself out. We are devastated, traumatised. We barely speak to each other, not out of aversion, but because there is next to nothing to say.

I find time over the next several months to learn everything I can about unwanted pregnancies in Iran. It isn't a topic many people talk about, even in medical school. I am shocked to discover how common the problem is, and how many women die at the hands of people promising to help them.

But I understand why women take such risks. If an unmarried couple are discovered in a situation that even suggests intimacy, they will be compelled to marry, without any prospect of divorce, ever.

If the man involved in one of these shotgun weddings attempts to obtain a divorce, he is liable to the punishment of amputation of his right hand and right leg. Such penalties are prescribed by sharia law, the ancient code of punishment and reward comparable to those Old Testament sanctions of punitive torture and execution that are never invoked in the secular West these days. In Iran, if a husband discovers on his wedding night that his wife is not a virgin, the marriage is over. In some fanatically observant families, the father and brothers of the woman accused of having surrendered her virginity before marriage to someone other than her husband will take her life, usually with a knife. Even in families less fanatical, the young woman's family often abandons her because of the disgrace they feel she's brought upon them.

The proof of virginity is the bleeding that occurs following sex on the wedding night. But this so-called proof is highly problematical, in Iran or anywhere in the world. The rupture of the hymen, the thin membrane partially covering the lower vagina, can and often does occur without intercourse. A significant number of females are born without a hymen. Bleeding following the first penetration of the vagina will only be evident in perhaps half of all females seventeen years and older. It's all haphazard, and in fact even in cultures such as Iran's, where virginity at marriage is such a big deal, it has been discreetly recognised as a difficult issue. When wedding-night sheets are ritually put on display to show bloodstains, the blood may well be a pigeon's or a chicken's – or the bride's, but from a small cut made at some inconspicuous site on the body. Why this obsession with blood?

Not all Iranians are insanely sensitive about bridal bleeding. But many more are these days, since the return to Iran of the fundamentalist Ruhollah Khomeini in 1979. That's the feature you notice about fundamentalists, whether Muslim or Christian or Jewish or Hindu or even Buddhist: they create a greater and greater margin between the natural appetites of human beings and what is permissible in their faith. Humans are born with a sexual appetite that is hard-wired to express itself at puberty, but the fundamentalists seek to stifle that expression – in fact to stifle almost every natural impulse, and in doing so crush the joy and vigour out of human life. You can't help but think of Blake's short poem 'The Clod and the Pebble', those lines in which the poet speaks of our perverted compulsion to build 'a Hell in Heaven's despite'.

Let me say here that my disdain for the fundamentalists and their dogma is not something I have come to feel after a dispassionate survey of their program. I have seen up close what institutionalised intolerance brings about. One hanging I witnessed was of a man whose crime was to express criticisms of the regime. All he had done was join a peaceful opposition group. At a less violent level, I was initially denied enrolment at university by the fundamentalist constitution because of my Jewish background. And although I was finally allowed to enrol, I came very close to being expelled in my third year when I unwisely expressed my thoughts about the rights of minorities.

Knowing what their fate will be, every year hundreds of young women in Iran kill themselves when they find out they are pregnant, or fear that their lost virginity will be discovered, even if they have been the victims of rape. How they lost their virginity doesn't matter; the important thing is that they be a virgin on the wedding night. Instead of being a delightful experience, sex is taboo, casting the shadow of death over the young.

I knew of the consequences of having sex outside marriage, but until I experienced them firsthand, I didn't really understand them. I could never have imagined the nightmare awaiting Azita and me. The hunger of sex is so immediate, and can be satisfied in the here-and-now; two bodies unclothed, the avidity of the mouth seeking the flesh of the other. What is pregnancy in that moment? A possibility, something to be cautious about, which will most likely not happen, not until one wants it to. Not the first time, at any rate. And what is caution to a man and a woman on fire with desire? The winking of a tiny candle compared to the burning light of the noonday sun. No one will know what we are doing. No one will ever know.

But sperm, each wriggling little tadpole, is a fanatic, a fundamentalist. Sperm has its own desire, its own hunger for consummation. It yearns to find the ovum and overwhelm it. It shares its faith with the it, lays down its laws, the greatest of which is: grow. Azita grew, and what was remote when we strove together in bed became the single stark fact of our striving.

After her ordeal I vow I will do what I can to make sure no one ever has to go through what Azita has suffered. While I fantasise about marching into parliament and demanding these backward laws be abolished, I know the best I can do is offer my help to one woman at a time. I will not seek pregnant women out, but if they come to me, I won't advise boiling raspberry root and prayer. Nor am I going to scribble a name on a piece of paper and leave a termination in the hands of someone unskilled. I will not let these women commit suicide or be murdered by their fathers. I will perform the terminations, and if someone fears for her life because she's no longer a virgin, I will restore her hymen. I will not hesitate.

Or so I believe. It is in the nature of vows to be written up in categorical terms but my vow is really only a hope, expressed in uncompromising language, that when the time comes, as it surely will, I can find the courage to act.

Leila

This is a day, Doctor, that stands signposted in my memory with the word *destiny*. We surely come to such signposts all through our lives, without knowing. Indeed it is only later, when we look back, that we see them for what they are.

'There,' Samira says, pointing to a dilapidated white building at the far end of the street. 'Can you see the big green door? That's it.'

The street has a row of tall, shady cedars on each side, running down almost to the green door of the orphanage. All the buildings in this neglected part of town are in an advanced stage of disrepair, some on the verge of crumbling. My sister and I hurry along with our chadors drawn tightly around us, sweets clasped in our hands.

An old weathered sign above the orphanage reads: QUCHAN

CHILDREN'S WARD. The building is two storeys high, with windows so small they could belong to a prison. Samira pushes the heavy door open and we enter feeling the anticipation that all bearers of gifts experience, mixed with pity.

A smaller sign just inside the entrance reads: PLEASE DONATE. ANY SUM WELCOME. A long grey desk complements in its drabness the decaying interior, the flickering light bulbs. Scribbling away on one of the hundreds of files and papers that litter the desk, a middle-aged woman wrapped tightly in a headscarf and hospital scrubs sits with a telephone wedged between shoulder and ear. She replaces the receiver when she notices us and looks at us sternly, uncompromisingly. Her name tag reads: MRS GOWHAR. Wisps of dry grey hair escape from her headscarf. She looks like some ancient bird of prey, and yet something in her gaze, some light not yet dimmed, makes me think she can still show kindness.

Samira introduces us and explains, almost apologetically, that we are hoping to visit the children.

'Why?' asks Mrs Gowhar, with what seems genuine curiosity.

'We've brought some gifts,' says Samira. 'We thought the children might enjoy them.'

'Really?' The woman studies us without suspicion, but with a certain amount of puzzlement. 'Come in then,' she says, 'but you can't stay long. The children are just about to have lunch.'

The reek of industrial cleaner becomes stronger as we follow her down the corridor and through a series of doors. I hear the sounds of children chattering and laughing some way ahead. A little boy in grey baggy pyjamas dashes out of one of the rooms opening off the corridor and stops just out of our reach. He is a frail boy, about five years old, with a shaved head and big eyes. A small scar runs across his forehead, and he is so thin his cheekbones show through his skin. Mrs Gowhar doesn't say anything to the boy, who follows us at a distance.

We pass ten more rooms, five on each side of the hallway, and stop when we reach an open area. I see beds in the corner and old metal chairs grouped haphazardly in the centre. The children, all different ages and wearing identical pyjamas to the boy in the corridor, rustle awake in their beds and gaze at Samira and me with curiosity. A few sit up, waiting for an introduction of some sort.

'Children, we have visitors for you today,' says Mrs Gowhar. 'These two young ladies have brought you all some treats.' A murmur goes through the room as the children whisper to each other. There must be at least thirty kids crammed tightly in here, side by side.

Samira asks our guide, 'How many does this place take care of?'

'Fifty-two. Twenty of them are orphaned, including one newborn.' She points to a cot in the corner where a small baby is just waking up. I wonder how they could possibly accommodate so many in such a small place.

I am aware that the little boy in the hallway has joined us, and has worked his way so close he is almost by my side. I want to speak to him but I'm afraid I might scare him away. Better to wait and let him make the first move.

The children have begun gingerly climbing out of their beds, gathering around us with hopeful faces.

'Where's the bag of lollies?' Samira asks me, just loud enough for the children to hear. Excited whispers break out once more.

As I reach under my chador for the bag I feel a light tugging, and turn to find a little girl reaching up, her arm strapped into a cast.

'Hello,' she says softly, and all at once everyone is talking; every child wants to say hello, offer his name, her name.

'All right, children, the young ladies have treats for you but you will only get them if you are quiet,' says Mrs Gowhar, and the second half of her sentence is drowned out by excited squeals.

'Lollies! Lollies! Lollies!' they chant. Just for a moment, the misery of their situation is forgotten. They reach up avidly, their little hands opening and closing like the mouths of baby birds in a nest. We provide a generous number of lollies for each child. Such a joy to me, Doctor Karimi, to see the kids running off to eat their treasure in some special nook.

Suddenly a voice of authority rings out from behind us. 'Be quiet! Sit down! I can hardly believe my eyes! How dare you treat your guests this way?' A tall, thin woman with a bony face, long chin and narrow eyes walks into the room. Probably in her late fifties, this stern woman is clearly in charge, and I can instantly tell she frightens the daylights out of the children.

'Everyone sit down!' she orders. The children become completely silent and drop, sitting cross-legged on the dirty bare floor. Some suck on their lollies fearfully, trying to make no noise. The woman's eyes sweep across the room, daring anyone to defy her.

'It's been a while since we've had such generous visitors. My name is Mrs Zeynab.' She is talking to us but her eyes never leave the children. Her hands are folded behind her back.

'Nice to meet you,' says Samira timidly. I just nod politely.

'Mrs Zeynab, can I —?' one of the children begins.

'Be quiet! You will only speak when spoken to.'

I look at the girl who has spoken. She is around nine years old with a big round face and hair that sticks out of her scarf.

'That is Parisa; she has Down's syndrome,' Mrs Zeynab tells me in an abrupt way, consistent with her severe expression. I feel horrible for the girl. The woman hasn't bothered to lower her voice when she speaks of Parisa's condition. I take an instant dislike to Mrs Zeynab.

Addressing the children, Mrs Zeynab says, 'If you're quiet for five minutes, I'll let you ask questions and talk to the visitors, but only one at a time. If you don't do as I say, I'll have to let the visitors go.' They nod silently, some shivering from sitting on the cold floor in their loose pyjamas.

'Would you like to sit?' Mrs Zeynab asks us, indicating two battered metal chairs. It's not a suggestion, it's an order, and Samira and I obey.

'You can introduce yourselves and tell them why you came here today,' says Mrs Zeynab.

The hall is silent as the children wait for us to speak. My attention is divided between the boy I first saw in the hallway and Parisa, the Down's syndrome girl. I ask myself how their parents could have been so heartless as to abandon them to Mrs Zeynab.

Heartless, Doctor Karimi – the word came to me so easily, to my shame.

Samira says nervously, under Mrs Zeynab's stern gaze, 'My name is Samira. I live in Quchan with my mother, father, brothers and my sister Leila. We came here today with some presents and treats.'

Once I too have introduced myself, several children raise their hands to get permission to talk, Parisa among them.

'You, Naser, you can talk,' says Mrs Zeynab, pointing at a boy of about seven with black eyes and long eyelashes. He sniffs and wipes his runny nose with his sleeve.

'Mrs Leila, thank you for lollies,' he says.

'You're welcome, darling. I'm glad you liked them.' I wish I could scoop him up in my arms.

Mrs Zeynab takes her time choosing the next child. It's obvious she gains some satisfaction in demonstrating her authority. 'You, Laleh,' she says, indicating a girl of perhaps twelve. Parisa continues to wave her arm in the air.

'Mrs Leila, you have beautiful eyes,' says Laleh boldly.

Instantly my 'beautiful eyes' are moist with tears. Even in this dark prison these children want to show kindness.

'Thank you, sweetheart. But you're the beautiful one.'

'Okay, who's next?' barks Mrs Zeynab. Parisa is now holding her arm up with the help of her other hand.

'Ahmad!'

A lanky boy of ten or so stands up to speak.

'Did I tell you to stand, Ahmad? Sit back down!'

He sits, swallows, then says, 'Are you going to come back? Because many people say they will come back but they don't.'

'Enough, Ahmad,' Mrs Zeynab interrupts. 'Be quiet now.'

Samira takes the initiative. 'Yes, of course we'll come back. You'll see us again next week with more treats for everybody.'

'One last question,' says Mrs Zeynab. By now most of the kids are straining their arms and hands as high as they can, hoping to be chosen, Parisa still among them. I'm pleading inwardly with Mrs Zeynab to pick her. Instead she points to one of the older children, a girl with large luminous eyes and rosy cheeks. 'Salmeh, your turn.'

'Can you stay with us until night and tell us a story?' the girl pleads.

'Why do you always ask for a story, Salmeh? You must understand people can't stay here that long.'

Samira says, 'I'm sorry, darling, we have to go home soon. Our mother's waiting for us.'

'Okay, hands down,' says Mrs Zeynab. All the children but Parisa do as they are told. 'Parisa, I said hands down,' Mrs Zeynab snaps.

The child brings her hand down but I cannot restrain myself. 'Mrs Zeynab, can I ask Parisa what she wants to say?'

Mrs Zeynab shakes her head. 'If you let them talk, they'll never stop.'

Mrs Gowhar, who has waited silently by the door, cuts in. 'I think we can spend a few more minutes talking to them. Lunch isn't ready yet.'

Mrs Zeynab glares at her colleague, then grudgingly nods her head. 'One more question.'

Parisa puts her arm up again, and again is ignored. 'You, Ava.'

Before Ava can ask her question, a girl who gives her name as Akram speaks up. 'What does your mother look like?'

I am surprised, but then realise that of course these children will want to know about mothers. 'She looks nice,' I reply. 'She has long black hair and big brown eyes. She's tall. Her name is Fatima.' Akram holds onto every word.

'Our visitors have to leave now,' Mrs Zeynab says. 'Go out and play until lunch.'

Reluctantly the children rise and head to the door, most of them trying to find some excuse to linger. When they are gone, Samira hesitantly asks Mrs Zeynab about the baby in the crib.

'She's our newborn. Two weeks old today.'

'Can we see her?' I ask.

'If you wish.'

Samira and I approach the white cot in the corner. The baby is swaddled in a stained sheet, a rather careworn teddy bear beside her. On her forehead, in blue ink, the word 'Sara' is written.

'Is that her name?'

'Yes. The nurses write the babies' names on their foreheads in the neonatal ward so they don't get mixed up with other kids. It'll wash off soon.' Mrs Zeynab picks the baby up and checks her nappy.

I touch Sara's face. 'Look at those beautiful lips.'

'Mrs Gowhar, bring a nappy,' Mrs Zeynab calls.

'What happened to her parents?' I ask.

'They didn't want her,' says Mrs Zeynab.

With a fresh nappy in her hand, Mrs Gowhar reaches for the infant. 'We don't have enough nappies for tomorrow,' she tells Mrs Zeynab.

'Don't worry about tomorrow, just change her now. We'll do something for tomorrow later,' Mrs Zeynab says with weary resignation.

I realise, as I should have earlier, how hard it must be to manage so many children with a limited budget and next to no staff. 'You must be under so much pressure,' I say.

'You have no idea,' says Mrs Zeynab, shaking her head.

Samira asks, 'What made you want to be a nurse in a children's ward, if you don't mind me asking?'

Mrs Zeynab tries to keep her tone stern, but a softer note creeps into her response. 'I was an orphan too. These children need someone to look after them.'

'Have you ever met your parents?' I ask.

'No.' She sighs and adds, 'Still, to this day my only dream is to see them, even for a moment.' She adjusts her headscarf, taking the moment to gather herself again. 'Now, if you'll excuse me, I have to get back to work.' Without another word she is gone, leaving me to repent of my earlier judgement of her.

Samira asks Mrs Gowhar what the children do for fun. 'They play,' she says. Then she points to an ancient television in one corner of the room. 'And we have a TV. We can't buy them toys, of course. Our budget is so small we can hardly feed them.'

'Can we go into the yard for a minute?' I ask.

'If you'd like.' She ushers us to the back door and we step outside. An old tyre hanging from a tree makes do as a swing, and there's also a rusted slide, crooked and rickety from overuse. The boys and girls play separately. A group of boys are intent on some game in the dust; the older girls scurry back and forth between groups to make sure there are no problems. Salmeh, in particular, rushes from one child to the next and is always the first to reach someone who has fallen or has no one to play with. Despite the meagre provisions for play, the children seem content.

I notice Parisa standing in a corner by herself, facing the garden wall. I make my way to her, put a hand on her shoulder and squat down beside her. 'Are you all right, little one?'

She turns her face to me and nods sorrowfully.

'Did you get any lollies?'

Parisa looks away and shakes her head.

'I promise to bring you some next time,' I say.

'I want something else,' Parisa says without guile.

'What would you like, Parisa? Tell me and I'll see if I can bring it.'

'A piano.'

'Oh, pianos cost so much money, sweetheart. And even if I had enough money, I don't think I could find one in Quchan.'

'That's all right,' Parisa says, her voice catching.

'Why do you want a piano?'

'I saw one on TV, and I want to play one.'

I think fast. I want to give her something to look forward to. 'I can get you a picture of a piano. How about that?'

'Really?'

'Really.'

'Thank you, Mrs Leila.'

I hug the little girl hard against my chest. 'You're welcome, little one. I'll bring you a picture of a piano when I can find one.'

Samira appears and taps my shoulder. 'It's time to go,' she says.

I don't want to leave the children, but if we are even a few minutes late Mother won't let us come again. I squeeze Parisa's hand and follow my sister back into the hall. 'What are you going to do with the doll?' I whisper.

'I don't know. I can't show it to the kids. They'll get too excited.'

'What if you just sell it to the shop and buy more food or lollies for them?'

She shakes her head firmly. 'No. I really want to give her to one of them. It's just so hard to choose.'

'I'd give it to Salmeh, the little girl who asked for a story,' I say.

'Why her?'

'I don't know. I guess because she likes stories. Maybe she can tell the doll stories at night. And I saw her taking care of everybody without worrying about herself.'

'Where is she?'

'Mrs Gowhar will know.'

We knock on the kitchen door and wait for Mrs Gowhar. 'That's so kind,' she says when we've explained the situation. 'Let me find Salmeh and bring her inside so you can give her the doll without all the other children around.'

She heads outside and returns a few minutes later with Salmeh behind her. Samira offers her the doll, but the poor child is so unaccustomed to gifts that she hesitates before accepting it. 'Is this for me?' she asks.

Samira says, 'Yes, this is for you. The way you help the other children is so inspiring. You deserve it.'

Still Salmeh holds back. Whereas more privileged children assume that gifts will come their way regularly, Salmeh does not know what to do; it is almost as if she thinks there is a catch involved. Finally, with Samira's urging and the encouragement of Mrs Gowhar, she takes the doll into her hands and gazes at its beauty in awe.

'It is too beautiful,' she says. She thanks us, and is given permission to return to the other children. She wanders off still dazed, but happy.

As Samira and I are leaving, the little boy who took such an interest in us when we arrived comes out of his room to watch us, surrendering to his fascination. I kneel down in front of him and look into his brown eyes.

'What's your name?' I ask in my most comforting voice.

'Ali.' He speaks so softly I have to strain to hear him.

'Really? I have a brother with the same name.'

This boy is different from the others. He's too quiet. I wonder why he isn't outside playing, why he is always waiting at the door.

'Will you come back?' he asks.

'Yes, darling, I promise.'

Ali stands motionless, staring at the floor. I can't stand his pain any longer. I wrap my arms around him and press him against me. He remains perfectly still, not returning my embrace, but I can feel the warmth of his being.

Mrs Gowhar opens the door and I blink as my eyes adjust to the bright light. I turn back when we reach the pathway, and see Ali's face one final time as the door shuts behind us.

The Doctor

My vow is tested far earlier than I expected. When I made it I was thinking of a time a little further into the future, when I was an independent professional. But the test comes when Azita and I have not been long married and settled into our first apartment, and before I am a fully qualified doctor. I am a few months into my internship.

On one of the rare nights when I am home from the hospital early enough to have dinner with my wife, she tells me her uncle has suggested that a distant relative of his come for a visit.

'Who is she?' I ask absently. 'A friend of yours?'

Azita shakes her head. 'I've never heard of her before, but my uncle says it's important she talks to you.'

I sigh. I'm getting used to this. Even though I'm still only an intern, when my relatives want free medical advice, they think of me.

'What's wrong with her?'

'He didn't say. All I know is that she works in a pasta factory and lives with her mother.'

'Very well. Tell your uncle I'll see her.'

The woman, Marmar, comes to my office the next day, without providing any clue to her condition in advance of the consultation. She sits before me with her eyes downcast. I am used to embarrassment in my patients – a visit to the doctor can be a trial when it concerns something deeply personal – but there is a distress in Marmar that goes beyond mere blushing and stuttering.

'I'm not beautiful,' she says, her voice low. 'I've never been desired, no man has ever wanted to marry me. I've watched all my friends get married, have children, have families. I hear stories all day at work about married life and love and family.'

I try to understand where this is going. I'm expecting questions about a condition, symptoms, anxieties. Why this preamble?

'One day,' she says, 'there was a man. Allah forgive me, because I know it was wrong, but I let him touch me. Just for one time I wanted to know what it was like to be held and kissed and wanted. I knew he wouldn't marry me, but I didn't want to die without ever experiencing the touch of a man. And now . . .'

Marmar's determination to tell me her story quickly and candidly breaks down. Her hands go to her face, and her shoulders jerk as she surrenders to tears. But at least the reason for her visit is revealed.

'And now you are pregnant,' I say, speaking the words that Marmar cannot.

She nods miserably. I hand her a tissue and she dabs her eyes, but tears still trickle over her blotchy cheeks and down her jaw. 'Please help me. My father is dead and this would kill my mother. Our landlord is a very religious man and he'd throw us out on the streets. I'd lose my job, and my mother is too old to work. I've tried to think of a way out of this but it's impossible, no matter how I look at it. Do you know anyone who can help me? I'll try anything. Please!'

A doctor hears these cries from the heart any number of times in the course of a year, not necessarily in regard to pregnancy. This patient or that has come to fear for his life, her life, due to a tumour, blood in the urine, a heart that seems likely to give out any second. The plea is always the same: *Doctor, save me. Doctor, I need a miracle. Doctor, you are my only hope.* You say something soothing, consider the situation, do what you can. The law of the land doesn't come into it. Maybe you will work the miracle the patient begs for, maybe not. The miracle Marmar craves is in my power to grant. I won't have to send her off for a consultation with a specialist; I won't have to call her back for further treatment once I see the results of tests, of X-rays. It is just me, Marmar, and the laws of the Islamic Republic of Iran standing before a dark arena, waiting to see who will live and who will die.

If I don't help Marmar she'll go somewhere else. What if she ends up with a midwife like Azita's? Or rather, what if Azita and I had received proper help? The help we deserved? The help this woman is begging for? I hesitate for about thirty seconds, then step into the arena. 'Call me in two days,' I say.

Marmar lifts her head and stares at me, the tears in her eyes glistening. It's the miracle she'd hoped for but didn't dare believe in.

I can't sleep all night. Azita hasn't questioned me, but she knows why Marmar came to see me. Why else would a woman be in such torment?

'Don't do anything stupid,' she says when I lean over to kiss her goodnight.

The next day I ask another intern, a trusted friend, if he knows anyone who smuggles in medications and sells them.

'Can I inquire what you need?' my friend asks. Many medications, including life-saving chemotherapy drugs, are almost impossible to come by under the regime except through smugglers, but not all smugglers offer the same medications.

'It's . . . for a woman.'

My friend nods, understanding immediately. Taking a pen and a scrap of paper out of his pocket, he scribbles down a phone number.

The guy I purchase the Prostodin ampoules from appears to have learnt everything he knows about being a crook from gangster movies: slicked-back hair, neatly trimmed beard, expensive shoes, laconic manner. Even as I hand over the money, I'm considering what will happen to me if he turns out to be a police stooge, if the whole thing is an entrapment. What will happen is that I will be hanged. And hanging in Iran is not what it is under other jurisdictions. There's no trapdoor, just a noose, suspension, and slow strangulation – about twenty minutes – until the verifiable cessation of a heartbeat, respiration and brain activity. I have seen men hanging from the hook of a crane on the back of a truck, bouncing about as it drives down potholed streets, their head likely at any moment to separate from the body. This might be me one fine day.

The ampoules come in a dark orange plastic bottle with a torn label. I slip bills into the smuggler's outstretched hands, noting that he keeps his fingernails much longer than most men. I hear his slight wheeze as he breathes. His eyes are bright with suspicions of his own, perhaps wondering if *I* am an informer, waiting to slip a noose over *his* head.

Marmar arrives at my house at the appointed time, both dread and determination written on her face. I explain to her what will happen after the Prostodin injection, how many injections will be required, and then I do for her what I've promised. Over the next hour she vomits, she bleeds, she cries out in terrible pain, she gasps as the foetus is expelled, and she thanks me, again and again and again. All that I'm thinking is this: Sperm had encountered an egg inside her, conception occurred – the most natural thing on earth. But here in Iran this natural process might well lead to Marmar being stoned to death. And this not-so-natural process of ending the pregnancy could lead to three deaths: hers, mine, and that of the foetus.

The morning after, I return to my office in the military hospital in a state of hideous distress. I fear doing any more terminations because even the one I have performed puts me and my family in too much danger. Oh, but the knowledge of what Marmar would have faced – one hundred, two hundred, five hundred stones raining down on her skull, her eyes knocked from their sockets, every tooth in her head smashed – I don't know how I can resolve this internal conflict, and decide to put it out of my mind until I have time to think things through more clearly. I also want to talk to Arash about it, but I can't. He is a dear and well-trusted friend, but sharing this lethal secret with him would put him at risk too. He could be punished for being my collaborator. In addition to being my secretary and nurse, Arash is my trusted friend. When I moved my family to Quchan from Mashhad so I could be near the military hospital I had to report to, it was Arash who befriended me and taught me about the culture and people of the area.

'Many, many families in Quchan stick very close to the traditional ways,' he told me. 'Men rule the homes and the women. Children and women are rarely seen without the company of their fathers or brothers or husbands. Women aren't allowed outside their houses without their chadors, and unlike in Tehran and other big cities, they can't let even a lock of hair show. Long coats and headscarves aren't enough to cover women in Quchan. To dress like that in public here would mean severe punishment. Marriages are still arranged by the parents.'

I'd been embarrassed to admit that my marriage, too, had been arranged, so I asked instead if women in Quchan sometimes found employment in the bigger Iranian cities.

'Some, but mostly in low-paying cleaning jobs, or as teachers in schools only girls attend. Women vote here, too, as long as their fathers and brothers don't object. If the man who is head of the household says she can't vote, the woman honours his wishes. Other things you'll see here in Quchan are the same sad story as everywhere. We have orphans and homeless children thanks to so many parents being killed during the war, and to illegal pregnancies. In secret places there is prostitution, and Quchan is also a route for drugs. It's becoming a problem here, but few will talk about it.'

Arash helped me find an office, and I signed a lease for two rooms on the second floor of a three-storey building in a good area of Quchan, which at this time had a population of some ninety thousand. He proved to be a good nurse with excellent social skills, and between his local knowledge and my medical knowledge, I had a thriving practice within six months.

We became close enough for me to tell him I didn't want to charge people who couldn't afford to pay. Self-administered charity of this sort is illegal in Iran, God knows why. As a child I'd seen people too poor to afford medical care suffer and die in our neighbourhood. Many parents, including my own mother, had struggled to feed and clothe their children. In times of illness they resorted to folk medicine and witchcraft.

Arash entered into this charitable conspiracy with a discreet enthusiasm. He told me of a pharmacy where it was safe to set up an account and pay for medications that poorer families couldn't afford without risk of being reported to the authorities. Arash's sister, a school principal, had made him aware of just how few of her pupils could afford to see a doctor, so I began visiting the school every two weeks to check the students for heart conditions, asthma and other ailments. Once, after I'd paid for a particularly costly medication, Arash asked how I could afford to help so many people.

'I'm fortunate that the books I have published are doing well,' I told him, 'and so is my practice, thanks to your help. It's no burden to share my good fortune with others.' At the time, I'd had more than eighteen books published, including translations of Khalil Gibran and Gore Vidal, and I'd won an award for the best translator in the country in 1994. My own books were mainly in the areas of history, mythology and medicine.

'I have to let you know,' he said, 'that some of the other doctors in town are upset with what you're doing. Your reputation is growing, and they're losing patients to you.'

'Who cares?' I said, with a flippancy that, as I was to learn, could not have been more ill-advised.

Leila

Thoughts of the orphans and sick children fill my waking hours. The memory of Salmeh's expression as she slowly realised that the exquisite doll really belonged to her is so vivid I feel as if I could reach out and wipe the smudges of dirt off her apple cheeks. The way Parisa held her fingers over her eyes after she asked for a piano haunts my dreams. The last thing Samira and I whisper about before we fall asleep is how we could reach Ali, a child so hurt and desolate he doesn't even know how to hug.

But it is Sara who has moved into my heart. I can still smell her baby softness, and I long to bathe her in fresh, clear, warm water, gently rubbing the blue writing off her forehead. I'm wondering what could possibly have made a mother leave behind her newborn child. What could make her walk away knowing that someone would scribble her baby's name in blue ink on her forehead, and then send her off to live among strangers who had no time to love and cherish her.

Yes, what mother could do that, Doctor Karimi? What mother could show such heartlessness? And what woman could be so grievously naïve?

I think to myself, Maybe Sara's mother died during childbirth. But then what about Sara's father? Did it not matter to him that he'd played his part in bringing a child into the world? Were his instincts not to protect and love his own infant as he had loved his wife? How could he not want to honour his wife's life by caring for the child she'd died giving birth to?

But maybe that wasn't it at all. Maybe Sara is the daughter of a woman who sold herself to men. Maybe Sara's mother doesn't even know who the father is. Of course I do know the reasons why babies get abandoned in Iran. Many are the left-behinds of relationships outside marriage, often girls who are barely out of childhood themselves, whose families let the pregnancy go through to birth then leave the baby somewhere, expecting it to be taken to the orphanage. The girls may have been raped – that's very likely. I have heard of girls of eleven giving birth, and no girl that age would choose to enter into a sexual relationship with a boy or man. Still others have been abandoned by families who can't afford to keep another child. And then there are those whose mothers were allowed to give birth before they were stoned or hanged. Most of the orphans don't know, I'm sure, who their mothers are or how they have come to be where they are. But some do. Some must surely remember a different time, when a mother's face beamed above them. A mother who subsequently died, leaving a child unwanted by her family.

I urge my sister, 'Make Mother let us go back to the hospital.'

And somehow Samira manages to convince her that we should go to the orphanage in a regular way, for the sake of the children. This is a great tribute to my sister's powers of persuasion. In a household that includes four men, the work for the women is unending. Mother might feel inclined to say she couldn't spare either of us for so much as ten minutes, but she is not a tyrant. She sees the need for her daughters to experience more than household chores. An hour at the orphanage is acceptable to her, or rather, she is willing to concede the hour, but only after adding serious threats if we are late in returning.

I realise, Doctor Karimi, that my sister and I seem to be about ten and fifteen, instead of twenty-one and twenty-nine, slaves as we are to the whims of others, and sharing our little schemes and secrets like children. But this is what growing up as a woman in Iran is like. You work hard, like an adult, but at the same time you are infantilised.

We have promised the children more sweets and we must not disappoint them. Their lives have been catalogues of disappointment, and it would be just too horrible if we were to add to them. So for our next visit I have fifty toman from my meagre savings, enough to treat all the kids. As Samira and I make our way through the crowded bazaar to the lolly shop, I'm already anticipating their smiles. Is it not true, Doctor Karimi, that the smile on the face of a child is one of the most wonderful things in the round world? You have your own beautiful Newsha; you must know what I'm talking about.

We stop at Mama Khadija's sweet shop, where I tell the old lady of our plans, and she adds a handful of sultanas and a handful of pistachios as a gift of her own. Hurrying down Shahid Naseri Street, we make sure our expressions convey a sombreness that suits this location; it would not do to be seen smiling in Shahid Naseri Street. It is named after Mohammad Naseri, a boy of eighteen from Quchan who was killed in 1985 during the Iran–Iraq war and is considered a martyr. In every town in Iran, in every suburb of every city, you will find streets named for martyrs such as Mohammad Naseri. There are more than enough to go around. Young Iranian men and boys died in a slaughter very like that of the First World War in Europe, so my reading of history tells me. They died in their hundreds of thousands, sometimes twenty and thirty thousand in a single day. Our government wants us to remember the dead of the war forever, which is fitting, although I often feel bludgeoned into reverence.

Further along the street, Samira and I are hailed by a woman I don't recognise at first. She says, 'Leila, my dear, how are you?'

I'm at a loss for a few seconds, then I realise it's Mrs Soleimani, who taught me literature in high school. I haven't seen her for some years. We embrace, and I introduce my sister. I'm delighted to come across Mrs Soleimani in this way, a woman who has had such an influence on my emotional and intellectual life, but when she asks me what I'm doing these days, I stutter and baulk and can barely say a word. More than anyone else in my life, Mrs Soleimani encouraged me to dream of university, of a career in teaching – what she would consider a 'proper' life, in which ambition extends beyond running a household. And now, facing her, I have to confess that I am not at university and never will be. A career? Yes, I have a career that exists entirely in my fantasies.

'I . . . I'm not at university, Mrs Soleimani,' I stammer out.

'No? How can that be, Leila? You were the best student of literature I ever taught. Ever. I don't understand.'

Samira can see the state of humiliation I'm in and tries to explain that my mother and father require me at home, but it sounds like an apology.

'Is this so, Leila?'

I shrug foolishly, more embarrassed than I would be if I were caught stealing from a shop. Yes, that's what I feel like – a thief, who has robbed herself.

Poor Mrs Soleimani, realising the situation now, back-pedals, trying to ease my suffering. 'Oh, well . . . university is not all that exciting. Goodness, no. Really, a woman can find just as much satisfaction in her home. Yes, quite as much.'

I know she doesn't believe a word she's saying.

Our second visit to the orphanage is as moving and emotionally gruelling as the first. The children crowd around us like chattering birds, calling our names, reaching out to touch us and to be touched. It seems to me that this is what I was made for, what my heart is best at – responding to the yearning and love of children. Sara with her name in blue on her forehead; Parisa with her ambition to send her fingers flying over the keys of a piano, but willing to settle for a picture of the instrument; Salmeh hugging the doll Samira made her and whispering the name she has given it; Ali, trapped in his prison of dread. Since I can never go to university, I could work so willingly in a place like this. I could make it my life's purpose to be here for these children.

But Doctor, there is another type of love within me, waiting to have its say; another type of longing that will soon course through my veins and shock me with its intensity. Even as tears form in my eyes for poor imprisoned Ali, for baby Sara, that love has filled my heart to the brim and is about to overflow.

A week has passed since the second visit, and for that entire week I have thought of nothing but the orphans. It is too soon to gain

Mother's permission to make a third visit, but perhaps I can persuade her to let me return my library book. While she peels vegetables under the shade of a cypress tree and I hang the laundry out to dry on a rope strung between two walnut trees, I ask if I can go that afternoon.

'Have you finished the rice?' she says.

'It's still cooking, but I can get Samira to turn the oven off in ten minutes.'

'Samira has other chores.'

'Mother, my book's already overdue.'

Heaving an exasperated sigh, she relents. 'Finish cooking the rice, and then you have half an hour. That's it.'

Oh Allah, listen to me, listen to me. Twenty-one years old, Doctor Karimi, and pleading to be allowed to visit a public library. Looking back, I am reminded of reading somewhere that naivety in an adult is simply a polite term for ignorance. I was bred to be ignorant. That's the truth of it.

The weather is gorgeous. The sun shines brightly but a breeze keeps the heat at bay. I dawdle along, despite my eagerness to reach the library, relishing the life of the bustling streets: kids scampering around, the racket of the traffic, merchants calling to each other, old men hawking pistachios and cooked broad beans to passers-by.

I want to throw my arms wide and embrace the day. But I have thirty minutes and no more. And I must remember that I am encircled by spies. Any of my many relatives, my friends, my brothers' and father's friends could be watching me from some doorway, avid to report back to my parents anything mildly out of the ordinary in my behaviour. 'I saw your foolish daughter smiling in the street. I saw her laughing. I saw her stop and stare at the sky.' In other words, 'I saw your daughter behaving like a human being – shocking, shocking!' Nothing can make me believe that a girl or a young woman smiling in the street is doing anything other than what is natural. I wish I didn't think this, but I do. Maybe it's the books I've read, maybe it just occurred to me one fine day and seemed true, took up a place in my mind. So many of the things that I'm supposed to do, so many of the things I'm supposed to avoid, seem unnatural. I confess it.

I wish my Aunt Sediqa lived in Quchan instead of Mashhad. She is my mother's older sister and would never say anything that would get me into trouble. She has two married daughters who live in Tehran, and since her husband divorced her she has lived alone. Aunt Sediqa thinks women deserve freedom and has even asked my parents to allow me to become a teacher, but her pleas have been brushed off. Once a year my family and I visit Mashhad for a pilgrimage to Imam Reza and then my aunt and I are inseparable. If she were my mother, how different my life would be. But since my aunt cannot be my mother, how much more tolerable my life would be if my mother were more like my aunt.

I reach the library within ten minutes and find Mrs Salimi at her desk in front of the high arched windows. She is wearing a dark blue manteau to go with a black scarf. I wish briefly that my father would allow me to wear this instead of a chador. A manteau, being a long coat, is far less bulky and has sleeves, so that I wouldn't have to use my teeth to keep my chador together when I carry things.

I greet Mrs Salimi and quickly apologise for returning my book late.

'Don't worry,' she says. 'I'll fix it. Tell me, though, did you enjoy the book?'

'Too much, I'm afraid. I wanted to keep it forever.'

I walk past the stacks of history and philosophy books, past the children's books and biographies, past popular novels, until I reach the literature section. I've read more than half the books in this small selection already, books by Iranian writers and those from other countries. Tolstoy. Gibran. Carlyle. Dumas.

I pause at *The Prophet*, Gibran's masterpiece. I skim the first two pages and decide this is exactly what I am looking for. As I hand it to Mrs Salimi, she glances at it from above her thick glasses.

'*The Prophet*. You definitely have good taste. This is one of the greatest books in the world.'

I leave the library in an even better mood than when I entered. Not only do I have another good book, but I found it so quickly that I have a few extra minutes to spend at the bazaar. I wonder if I can make it to the orphanage, but I know that even if I risk running there and back, I'll be home late.

I look into shops, not paying much attention to what's on sale until I come to the boutique where I gave the boy the lollies. And I see that the beautiful blue shirt that was in the window that day is still there. If anything, it is even more beautiful than I remember it, as soft as clouds, blue as the sky.

I glance inside. And there he is. The handsome man with the warm eyes, square jaw, perfect nose, trim physique. But it is his knowledge of books that attracts me most. Fixing my chador to make sure all my hair is covered, I enter the boutique, which is empty apart from him.

'Can I help you with anything?' he asks.

'Thank you, just browsing.' I feel so shy I forget why I've come in. Then I go to the window and reach out to feel the fabric of the blue shirt. I am right – it's soft as can be. I imagine myself wearing it without a chador covering me.

'You like that one?' the man asks.

'It's beautiful,' I murmur.

'Would you like to try it on?'

I feel myself redden. 'No, thank you. I just wanted to know how much it costs.'

The man smiles. 'For you, five hundred toman.'

I'd have to save my pocket money for more than a year to afford it. 'Thank you. I'll have to think about it,' I say, glancing at him.

As our eyes meet he puts out his hand as if to touch me, then pulls back. 'Wait a minute. You're the girl with the book. I've been waiting for you to come back.'

I immediately look away, chiding myself for daring to meet his eyes. What if he is a friend of one of my brothers? They'd hear about my boldness and beat me to remind me that I have no right to look into the eyes of a strange man. Worse, my mother wouldn't let me go out by myself again.

As I turn to leave, the man calls after me, 'Wait! I have something for you.'

I hesitate. Had I dropped something else the last time I walked past the store? Surely not.

He walks towards me, his arm extended, holding out a book. I recognise the cover immediately. *The Little Prince.*

'It's yours,' he says. 'I hope you like it.'

A searing blush rushes up my face. 'Thank you, but . . .' I halt, having no idea what to say.

'Take it. I bought it for you. You dropped one last time, remember? A library book. I thought you might like a copy of your own.'

I shake my head. 'Thank you. You're very kind, but I cannot possibly accept it.'

'Why not? It's just a book. I have a copy of my own. It's one of those books one should have forever.'

'You're right, but . . .' Again I forget how to speak. I am so flattered I have no idea how to respond. I've had no experience of talking to men alone, never mind a handsome stranger who wants to give me a gift.

He takes a step closer. 'You bought that little boy you didn't even know some lollies. Now I'm offering you something too. Accept it, please. As a favour.'

He can see my reluctance. Lowering his voice so that it seems we are the only two people in the world, he adds, 'They say one should not refuse a present.'

Boldly I raise my gaze and stare into the depths of his dark eyes. Now that we are standing only half a metre apart, I'm overwhelmed by his looks. His hair is thick and dark, his lashes long and curled, his large eyes as black as the night. His shirt is a beautiful light blue and his pants are neatly pressed.

A slight frown creases his brow and he watches me quizzically, not understanding why I am refusing his gift. 'Please,' he says again, and this time I understand that he will truly be offended if I refuse. Letting go of my chador for a second, I reach out and take the book from him, immediately tucking it away under my chador, which I hold against myself like a shield.

'Thank you for accepting it.' His voice is gentle now, his eyebrows no longer knitted into a frown.

'But . . .' I stammer, then stop.

'But what?' he urges gently.

'But why have you done this?'

He pauses for few seconds and rubs the back of his neck, cocking his head to one side as if perplexed by his own behaviour. 'To be honest, I don't know. Maybe because you were kind to that little boy and I wanted to do something nice for such a thoughtful person. Maybe because it's one of my favourite books and I think everybody deserves their own copy. Maybe only Allah knows.'

I feel my skin redden again, from my neck to my hairline. He is so sincere; there is not the least hint of flirtation in his voice. What could be wrong in accepting his gift? I have no idea how to gracefully end the conversation. As I search for something to say, the door opens and a pudgy, middle-aged man enters.

Quickly I say, 'I should go now. Thank you.' Feeling clumsy and awkward, I force myself to cross the floor.

'See you next time,' the shopkeeper calls after me.

I step into the sun and hurry away from the shop. I'm on fire. With excitement, joy, happiness. I feel so restless, so wild, I am afraid of my own heart for the first time in my life. I collide with a woman holding a child's hand and realise I am walking too fast, oblivious to my surroundings. All I can see is his smile as he put the book in my hands.

The book. Oh, Allah. I look at it. What have I done? There is no way I could explain it to my mother or father.

I am ashamed to imagine what the shopkeeper would think if he saw me in such utter turmoil over his simple gift. For a long moment I stop walking altogether and contemplate going back to return it. Why had I let him convince me to accept it?

But what if he isn't alone? The thought propels me forward again, back to my house.

I open the door softly and slip inside. My best chance of hiding the book is to get to my room before anyone sees me. If I'm asked what I'm holding under my chador I'll have to bring out both books, and one clearly doesn't belong to the library. Either my father or Ali will beat me for accepting a gift from a man. Maybe both of them. Worse than a beating, though, I'd never be allowed outside again. Bruises heal, but the deprivation that comes with isolation would be unbearable.

I hope Mother is in the yard resting under the shade of the trees. She sometimes naps outside during hot afternoons when the men have returned to work. If I'm very quiet I can tiptoe to my room, find a hiding place, join my mother and chat about the roses I saw in town, none of them equal to those you, my mother, grow in your small rose garden. Whenever I find myself thinking that my mother is a cold, unfeeling woman, I remember how tenderly she nurtures her roses, singing to them as she trims them back, scolding any bugs that dare to make a home in their leaves. There is poetry in my mother, but it's fugitive.

I have almost reached my room when I hear her footsteps behind me, heavy and fast. Before I can stop to face her, she reaches out and grabs my arm. *The Prophet* and *The Little Prince* slip from my grasp, but I manage to stop their fall by pressing them hard against my thighs.

'Where have you been? I said thirty minutes.'

'I forgot the time trying to find the right book.' As soon as the words are out I wish I could stuff them back inside my mouth. I've all but invited my mother to ask which one I selected.

But she has no interest in books. 'Borrowing a book shouldn't be such a chore. You walk to a shelf, you see one, you pull it out and take it to the desk. How hard is that?'

I know arguing with my mother is disrespectful, and pointing out to her that all books are far from the same would invite censure. I bow my head as if I'm ashamed. 'I'm sorry that I took so long to find the right book. I shouldn't be so picky.'

Mollified, she nods. 'You've probably read them all already, anyway. Next time don't dawdle, or there'll be no more trips to the library. Now put your things away and go hose down the yard. I don't know what the point of all that reading is to begin with. The rest of us do just fine without filling our heads with the ideas of people who have nothing better to do than make up stories.'

I hesitate long enough for Mother to reach the end of the hallway. When I hear the back door open I gather my books safely into my hands, enter my room and close the door.

I scan the room, searching for a hiding place, but nowhere is safe. My parents and brothers have a right to enter at any time, to go through my belongings if they have any suspicion I'm keeping something to myself. My brothers sometimes take my things if they want them, and sometimes Ali destroys something I like out of sheer meanness, just to let me know he has power over me. Once he took all my pocket money, which I had been saving to buy Samira a birthday present. When I ran to Mother in tears she reminded me that Ali had the right to take whatever he wanted. 'Get used to it,' she said. 'It's good practice. Your husband will do the same.'

My eyes settle on the tall wooden wardrobe. In addition to our clothes, it holds magazines, stationery, papers, and odds and ends Samira and I are saving. Standing on tiptoe, I reach for a big green folder stuffed into the back of the highest shelf and pull it down. I open it and the papers spill out. I gather them up, haphazardly returning various items – my high-school diploma, two papers I'd written that a teacher had read to the class as examples of fine writing, Samira's diploma, and documents my brothers insisted I look after for them. I plant the book in the middle of the loose pages and tuck the folder high up inside the wardrobe.

'Leila, come and give me a hand,' Samira yells from the backyard.

I find her stacking heavy wheat bags on top of each other under a small shelter in a corner of the yard.

'You had a look around the bazaar as well as the library?' she asks me as we lift the next bag. 'Did you see anything for the kids?'

'No,' I reply, too readily.

Samira stops in mid-action, a heavy bag suspended between us. Furtively she checks to see if our mother can overhear us. 'What's wrong?' she asks.

'Nothing.'

'I'm not stupid. I can see it in your eyes. What is it?'

Now it's my turn to make sure we can't be overheard. 'I'll tell you after dinner when everybody's asleep.'

Samira raises her eyebrows. 'Must be exciting.'

'I don't know. I'm confused.'

Mother yells for us to hurry so we can help her carry the rug from her bedroom outside to be cleaned.

I'm anxious all through dinner, feeling as if my secret is written on my forehead as clearly as Sara's name is scrawled on hers. I feel everyone but Samira is a hawk flying overhead, waiting for the right moment to attack. When my younger brothers return from the garage and join us on the rug to eat, I'm afraid to look at them, certain someone has said something to them, that they're only waiting for the right moment to accuse me of flirting. After dinner, we all prepare to pray for the third and final time of the day. As I wash my hands and feet and finally my face before kneeling to pray, I wish the water would wash my guilt, too, down the drain. I pray harder than I have in months, asking Allah's forgiveness for accepting a gift from a man my family doesn't know.

'Tell me what's happening,' Samira says when we're finally alone in our room.

I put my hand over my heart and hold it there for a minute while she watches me curiously. 'Finally my heart's stopped rushing,' I whisper.

'What are you talking about? What have you done?'

'I haven't committed a crime, don't worry, but on my way home from the library, I went to a boutique to find out the price of a shirt I liked. It was the same store I was outside a few weeks ago, when the man picked up my book.'

'What book?'

'*The Little Prince*. The one I borrowed from the library. Today, when I went into the shop, he gave me a copy as a present.'

'Oh, that handsome man you told me about? He gave you a book?'

I nod.

'You're kidding!' Samira moves closer and takes my hand.

'It's true. I hid it in the wardrobe.'

'I want to see it.'

'What if someone wakes up?'

'Everyone's already sleeping. You have to show me.'

I fetch the book from the wardrobe and hand it to my sister. She takes it reverently, handling it as if it were a priceless manuscript that belonged to an ancient king. She holds it up to the moonlight so she can see it better. 'You know what this means, don't you?' she says. 'He likes you. A lot.'

My voice catches in my throat. 'Does he?'

'Of course. He can't get you out of his mind. He remembered your book, then bought it for you and kept it with him, just waiting for a chance to see you again. Do you like him? Is he nice?'

'I don't know if I like him. I mean, he's very nice. And thoughtful. And he reads books. I like that a lot.'

'And he's very good-looking?'

'Shh!' I put my finger to my lips. 'He's the most handsome man I've ever seen.' I cover my face with shame. I've never spoken this way about a man before, even to my sister.

'What's his name?'

'I don't know.'

'A man gave you a present and you don't even know his name?'

'I told you, I've only seen him twice, and both times only for a few minutes. I was so embarrassed I could barely talk. I ran out as soon as I could. He must have thought me a silly little girl.'

We put our hands over our mouths to stifle our giggling. Then, suddenly serious, I take my sister's hand. 'Samira, have I committed a sin?'

'Don't be silly. You haven't touched him. Talking to a man is fine.' But she turns quiet, and now it's I who asks what is wrong.

'I'm so sorry, Leila,' she says sadly.

'Why? You won't have to tell Mother, will you?'

'Of course not. It's not that. But I've held you up. You could have so many suitors, but you can't because I'm not married. You're so beautiful, and now this man is interested in you, but because I have no suitors, you can't do anything about it.'

'This isn't your fault. I'm not desperate to get married. What's the point of marriage, going from a jail cell to solitary confinement?'

Samira shakes her head. 'Maybe one day this man will want to marry you, but you will have to refuse just because I'm not married yet.'

I laugh lightly and lean my forehead against my sister's soft hair. 'Don't worry. He's not coming to ask for my hand yet. Only Allah knows what's going to happen tomorrow.'

Over the next few days, the only time I can stop thinking of the shopkeeper is when I think of the orphans. Finally, after nearly two weeks, Samira receives our mother's permission to go to the orphanage for a third visit.

As Samira and I count out our money I say, 'We have less than last time. What are we going to do? We promised we'd bring all of them treats.'

'We'll have plenty,' says Samira. 'Mother has made a *nazr*. She's asked Allah for something special and so now she has to give money to the poor in the hope He'll grant her wish. And guess what? The orphans are her *nazr*. She's giving us a hundred toman for the hospital. I suggested it to her myself.'

I clutch my sister's hand. 'You're a genius. Did she say what her *nazr* is?'

'Of course not, which means she's asking Allah to find me a husband. She doesn't want to tell me because she thinks it'll hurt my feelings, but I don't care. And if Allah doesn't send me a husband, she'll give even more next time.'

After we don our chadors for our excursion I fumble at the bottom of the wardrobe and pull out a magazine. 'Here. I found this, for Parisa.' The magazine has a picture of a piano on the cover.

'Perfect.' Samira finds a pair of scissors to cut it out. I roll up the picture of the piano and put it carefully in my bag.

'Don't talk to strangers,' Mother warns as we step into the blazing midday sun.

Samira and I have already agreed we won't meander on the way to the orphanage, despite the perfect weather and the temptation to enjoy the sights and sounds, fragrances and flowers of the bazaar. Still, as we near the boutiques, I find my thoughts turning to the shopkeeper. Should I stop and say hello? But no, I decide that's not right. If he wants me he should go to my father and ask to marry me. And if he really wants me, he will wait until my parents arrange a marriage for Samira. But if we stop in the shop on the way back, Samira could meet him and tell me what she thinks of him.

Before I can continue the debate with myself, a window display of small plastic cars catches my eye. 'Wait,' I call to Samira. 'I'll be right back.'

I disappear into the store, returning shortly with my purchase. 'For Ali,' I say triumphantly. 'All boys love cars, and imagine how excited he'll be to have a toy of his own. Maybe he'll even smile.'

Samira's eyes twinkle mischievously. 'Now it's your turn to wait.' And she too disappears into the store. A few minutes later she reappears waving a noisy rattle in the air. 'For Sara,' she says with a grin.

Laughing, we hurry on until Samira asks me, 'Where is it?'

'Where's what?'

'You know, Mr Handsome's store.'

'I'm too nervous. I don't want to act like a fool. Or worse, a flirt. I don't want him to think of me that way.'

Samira nods. 'Okay, we'll just walk past, and I'll look inside and see if I can spot him. We won't say anything at all, and you can act like you aren't even aware you're in front of his store.'

We do as she suggests, and passing the boutique Samira steals a look inside. 'He's not there,' she whispers. 'A woman's stacking something on shelves, but other than her, I see no one.'

'Who could that be?'

'Maybe his sister or an employee.'

'Or maybe he no longer works there. It's the orphans who matter,' I insist. 'Let's not waste time we could be spending with them.'

We reach Mama Khadija's shop in a matter of minutes, buy our lollies, and accept a free bag of pistachios and sultanas for the orphans, just like the last time. 'This is my *nazr*,' she finished with a smile.

'What's your *nazr*, Mama Khadija, if you don't mind me asking?' Samira inquired.

'I'm an old woman and I have only one wish. To see my son. He left Iran ten years ago and now lives in Australia. I've made a *nazr* to see him one more time before I die.'

'We'll give this to the children. May Allah grant your wish to see your son one day soon.'

The hospital door is opened by Mrs Gowhar, a big smile lighting her plain, square face. I hadn't noticed before but there's a small semicircle of moles just under her jaw. I wonder if the children are scared of this oddity. Maybe they think she is a witch. But she's a kind woman under her homely, harried exterior and I hope the children realise that.

Ali runs from his room and stands in the middle of the corridor to greet us. I kneel in front of him, cuddle him, give him his car. His reaction is a shock. His eyes well up with tears and he turns and runs.

I stare after him, distraught. Mrs Gowhar says, 'I'll explain later,' and leads us to the big room. The children race in from the backyard, bringing a dust storm along with them.

'Aunt Leila! Aunt Samira!' they shout. The bolder girls throw their arms around our waists, pressing their faces against our chadors.

The kids have made a playground in the room, using what little is available. Mattresses piled on top of each other act as a mountain to climb and tumble from. Chairs and blankets have been fashioned into a tent. Samira and I make a big deal of the children's ingenuity, inspecting their constructions with words of encouragement. Games follow, and the distribution of toys and lollies. The joy of this, of being made so welcome by these children who have nothing to look forward to in life, hasn't lessened with each visit. For all I know, our visits might be one of the things they will draw strength from in the hard years that await them. Nevertheless I cannot forget that a day like today is just a brief respite from the despair of their present lives.

Ali's response to the toy car still distresses me, and I take Mrs Gowhar aside to ask her what went wrong. She explains that his parents died in a car crash. He half hopes they will somehow, impossibly, turn up at the hospital door one day, but he remains terrified of cars.

'You couldn't have known,' says Mrs Gowhar. 'How could you have possibly guessed that a toy car would plunge him into misery? Poor girl, don't worry. Cuddle him when you get the chance.'

At that moment Samira opens the door carrying baby Sara in her arms. 'There you are, Leila. Look at darling Sara. Hasn't her hair sprouted up like wild grass? And look at her eyes. They're as big as poppies.'

Hoping that the rattle we've brought her will find a happier reception than the toy car, I put it in Sara's hand. She attempts to shake it, with limited success. Cradling her fills me with a strange joy and contentment. Considering what is about to unfold in my life, I should be feeling a type of – what? Warning? But I feel only joy, and love for this tiny human being.

'I hate to cut your time with her short,' says Mrs Gowhar, 'but I need to change her and get her bottle ready. One of the older girls will feed her while I get the rice on for tonight's meal. Being here all alone means I have to rush.'

'We could change Sara for you,' I offer.

'Could you? That'd really help.'

After handing Samira a fresh nappy, Mrs Gowhar goes into the kitchen to heat Sara's bottle.

'I know you don't want to hear this, Leila, but we have to hurry. I'd love it if we could both stay all day and help out, but you know Mother will be furious if we're late.'

'As soon as the bottle is ready, we'll say goodbye.'

'But first we have to give Parisa her picture,' Samira reminds me, checking her watch. 'What if you do that while I change Sara? I saw Parisa in the hall a few minutes ago.'

I find Parisa, talk with her, comfort her, give her the picture. This all comes so naturally to me that I feel born to care for children, nurture them, make them feel safe. If I had my way I'd spend whole days at the orphanage. This is what I want my life to be. Not always here, but in my own home, raising kids, enjoying their lovely ways. This is me.

It's possible to walk home from the orphanage without passing the boutique. It's very possible. But I take Samira along that route. Why? Because I'm the fool I am. And in fact Samira's head and heart are so occupied with the day's experiences that she barely notices where I'm leading her. I give no indication of having anything special on my mind, and nothing special is going on in my heart – except that it's pounding like an African drum. Why am I doing this? I have been with innocent children. I have enjoyed their embrace. I have felt my heart melt as I cuddled them. So why am I doing this? Because, Allah forgive me, I want to.

As we reach the shop I glimpse at my sister. Her gaze is on the ground, lost in thought. I glance in through the window. He's there, he's there. But he's speaking to a young woman – a customer, no doubt – and she is smiling at him, and he's smiling at her, as he well might, since she's about to purchase something. A white-hot flush of anger sears through my heart and into my throat. Have I ever felt such virulent rage in my life? I have not. I don't know which of them has made me so angry, the smiling young woman or the shopkeeper. But I know who I want to pound with my fists – the young woman. Dear Allah, it has come to this! I am treating the shopkeeper as if he were mine, as if he has made a sacred oath to stay loyal to me for life. This is passion. And it is madness.

Do you see, Doctor? Do you see the truth about me? I have been kept in such a state of ignorance that I have grown to adulthood without knowing one-millionth of what I should know about the world, about love, about men, about my own heart. And yet I am a woman nonetheless. The rage I feel is a woman's jealousy. The possessiveness I feel, without the least justification, is that of a woman who has claimed a man for her own and demands that he honour her by never looking elsewhere. I have a woman's pulse, a woman's passion living side by side with the ignorance I grew up with.

I glance into the shop again, and this time the shopkeeper lifts his gaze and sees me. He ceases to pay the least attention to his pretty female customer. His eyes seek mine. What do I let my gaze reveal? My disappointment with him, that he should be smiling at that other woman? My acknowledgement of all that I hope for in whatever relationship develops between us? I cannot say. But I certainly reveal something, because he comes out of his shop, stands on the street and raises his hand. I should be looking ahead. I shouldn't notice that he's raised his hand. I shouldn't notice, all over again, how extraordinarily handsome he is.

But I do look back. I see him wave. And my white-hot anger gives way to rapture. Without a single worry that someone might see me and report my behaviour to my brothers or father, I smile at him. Yes, I loosen my chador slightly and smile at the man who is colonising my heart.

That night, I take *The Prophet* from the wardrobe, light a small candle, and read: *Then said Almitra, 'Speak to us of Love.' And he raised his head and looked upon the people, and there fell a stillness upon them. And with a great voice he said, 'When love beckons to you follow him, though his ways are hard and steep. And when his wings enfold you, yield to him.*

I feel as if Gibran is speaking directly to me. And I plan to listen.

The Doctor

One evening in the summer of 1996, I am lying on a cot in the
military hospital, in a room set aside for doctors to rest between
crises. I feel an exhaustion that reaches right into my bones but I am
unable to sleep. I have a book I'm enjoying, *Julian* by Gore Vidal,
an amazing author, but it lies open on my stomach while my mind
follows desultory trains of thought to one destination and another.
I find myself thinking of my marriage, of the exasperation I often feel
with Azita, of our differing priorities, hers being the household and to
a certain extent her prestige within the broader family, mine being my
writing, which means much more to me than my career as a surgeon. It's
my writing that most sharply reveals the divergence in the values that
guide my wife and me. My works of translation mean status to her, but

to me they are creative expression, nothing to do with status. Finding the right phrase, the right sentence in which to render in Persian what is written in another language; drawing on the poetry in this ancient language of ours so as to convey the poetry of an observation made in the much more modern language of English – that's the thing that lifts me up and gives life meaning.

For Azita life is about belonging, being merged with the dreams and ambitions of her wider family, being the envied wife of a doctor and writer. But belonging means nothing to me. I am a Jew. In my heritage, in my very nature, I am an outsider. It's true that I yearn to see our country of Iran embrace sanity and civilisation, and in that sense I do in fact want to belong. But even if Iran and the mullahs and the Revolutionary Guards and the Basij – the whole regime – converted overnight to reason, even if they all adopted tolerance and generosity and gave up persecuting young women, I would still be an outsider. I would look around and say, Good, but then I would resume my life as a Jew, as one who cannot belong in Iran, ever. Other than under the Pahlavi dynasty, which ended in 1979, Iran has never been a safe place for Jews, unless one goes back to 2500 BC when Cyrus the Great was ruling a tolerant Persian empire. But that would be like comparing ancient Egyptian civilisation to modern Egypt.

My thoughts have a tendency to help me reconcile myself to the life I lead, to the wife I married to please my mother, instead of marrying the woman I loved. Oh, that's something I haven't mentioned before, the fact that I didn't marry the woman I truly loved, the woman who preceded Azita – the intelligent, wonderful Mahshid. I loved and admired her intensely, but alas, our fiery love was not acceptable to my mother, and it was my mother who controlled my life in that regard. Mahshid was my father's first wife's niece, and in Iranian culture, marrying a girl related to your mother's competitor is a blasphemy.

My mother pointed her finger at me when she found out about my secret love. 'Over my dead body you will marry that girl!' And a couple of weeks later she had found my future wife, through the ridiculous ancient process of asking friends and neighbours if they knew a 'decent girl'. Thus was I forced, out of cowardice, to betray Mahshid.

The phone beside me in this sweltering room rings piercingly and in an instant my thoughts pack themselves away. My aide, Nemati, tells me that I have two very sick soldiers in Emergency. 'You'd better come right away.'

I toss my book onto the rough military blanket and take the steps down to the emergency room two at a time. The military hospital is American-built. It seems ages ago that the United States was a bosom friend of the brutal, despotic regime that preceded Iran's present brutal, despotic regime. The Americans gave us this hospital and mountains of weapons and a stern injunction to stop the spread of communism in the Middle East. The Shah said, 'No problem.' The Americans said, 'And sell us your oil.' Again: 'No problem.' Politics aside, though, the Americans built a fine hospital. I seem to spend as many evenings within its thick walls as I do at home. In some ways it's more peaceful than my own home, and on quiet nights I can spend time doing what I love, which is writing my latest book, *Battle of the Gods*.

Pushing through the swinging metal doors of the cramped emergency room, I see two young soldiers with their heads lowered into buckets, vomiting their hearts out. The buckets are already at least a third full of something yellow and vile, so putrid-smelling it almost makes me vomit myself. Nemati tells me the soldiers both started vomiting two hours ago. One of them has taken off his shirt, and the other's uniform is splattered with vomit.

I put my hand on the one closest to me, the shirtless one, and ask, 'Have you two had any diarrhoea?'

He shakes his head, and the other manages a weak moan in response. I begin examining them. Both are very pale. I roll up the trousers of the shirtless soldier and see pinpoint red spots on his legs. Turning to the legs of the second man, I find the same thing. Gently I press my finger against the spots. They don't disappear, a sure sign of internal bleeding.

'What have you been eating?'

The shirtless soldier manages to stop vomiting long enough to say, 'What we all ate – ragu.'

'Anything else?'

'We were patrolling in the bush. We were hungry, so I found some mushrooms. The kind we have in our village.'

I tense, already suspecting the worst. 'When did you eat them?'

'A few hours ago. Do you think they were bad? They tasted all right.'

I have seen mushroom poisoning once before, when an entire family ingested wild fungi in an omelette, a deadly experience. There isn't an antidote. These young men could die in a matter of hours, and even dialysis wouldn't help. They need to be in intensive care under constant monitoring. Dehydration will shut down their kidneys soon and they'll go into seizures, followed by liver damage and then heart failure. Their chances of survival are remote.

'Nemati, call an ambulance!'

Moving even as I bark out instructions, I search for veins, but their blood vessels are already collapsing from dehydration. For the thousandth time I wish the hospital had airlift facilities. The closest general hospital is in Mashhad, two hours away. There's little I can do until the ambulance arrives, except monitor the soldiers.

Thirty minutes later I watch the paramedics load the soldiers into the back. They will be dead before morning.

I go back to my cot on the second floor feeling sick at the waste of it all. During the Iran–Iraq war, the government was so quick to praise young soldiers as martyrs, so ready to name streets and squares and lanes after them. But they can't even feed these conscripts enough to prevent them foraging on the forest floor for poisonous fungi.

I'm in my private surgery a couple of days later when a call comes through from my wife's twenty-year-old cousin, Pejman. After exchanging the traditional pleasantries, he pauses for a few seconds, then tells me he has a problem.

'I really need your help. When will you be in Mashhad again?'

'In Mashhad? I'll be there a week's time for Mr Qolizadeh's seventh. I'll find time to see you.'

The seventh and the fortieth days after someone's death are highly significant for Muslims, and I'll be attending Azita's grandfather's final funeral ceremony with her.

'I don't think this can wait that long. Can I come to Quchan in a couple of days for a quick chat?'

I take out my appointment book and scan it for an opening. 'Wednesday afternoon? Can you come to my surgery?'

'Yes, of course.'

I give him the address, but before hanging up Pejman asks me to keep the conversation between us private. I run my hand through my hair. Let it be a financial problem, please. Or some embarrassing medical problem of his own. Just not a request for another termination.

The next day has been scheduled for a visit to Arash's sister's primary school. Of all my responsibilities as a doctor, this is one of the most rewarding. Working quickly, I check every child's heart, listening closely for the specific murmur that signals rheumatic fever, a serious condition in Iran. I'm stunned by the number of murmurs I hear, and frustrated that these children don't receive the treatment they need. Fortunately no epidemic has broken out, although lice are a problem.

I spend longer on anyone with specific symptoms. The most common is coughing, but some children have skin conditions, and an alarming number suffer from depression because of issues at home. Although I can't counsel them, when I encounter a child who is too quiet or has other signs of depression, I refer them to Mrs Jafari, a psychologist friend of mine who's willing to help victims of violence or neglect at home. Like me, she provides her services for free. Aware that she can't see every child suffering from depression, I select the most severe cases. But choosing is a difficult process, and I know that if the abuse is severe, counselling can't always help. Far more than counselling will be needed, but under Iranian law, psychologists and doctors cannot interfere in 'family issues'.

On this visit there are more than eighty children who I'm sure are clinically depressed, far more than Mrs Jafari could possibly fit into her schedule. Of all the ailments, depression in girls makes me the most furious. The laws of the Islamic Republic could almost have been drafted with the object of causing mental breakdowns in girls and women. I drive home seething. Arash tries to calm me down.

'You can't do everything. Without your visits, things would be much worse. Can't you let that be enough?'

I slam my open palm against the steering wheel. 'It's not what I can or cannot do that upsets me. Those poor little girls have no chance as long as our country lets men do anything they want in their homes – and nobody can oppose them.'

I could say more. I can't stand to think how many of those girls have mothers whose husbands beat them and who have no way out. The law won't let them apply for a divorce, or do a damned thing to keep the men away from them. No matter how badly battered and mistreated she is, a woman can't get a divorce unless her husband is declared psychotic or jailed for a long time. And even then a divorce takes years and the woman receives almost no financial support. She loses her children. So many little girls, seeing that there's no hope for their mothers, have to ask themselves what hope there is for them. A woman under physical threat can't even call the police, because the police will probably side with the husband. For God's sake, legally a woman has to have her husband's permission to leave the house. An educated woman can't get a job if her husband wants her to stay at home.

I know this, all Iranians know this, and yet there's nothing we can do about it. I'm a doctor but I feel powerless to help. I see the sadness in those little girls' eyes and it goes straight to my soul. I know exactly why they're depressed and I know that until the laws change, there's nothing I can do for them. I have a daughter and I won't let this happen to her.

That's the full text of the rant I want to unleash. But Arash has heard it all before.

Arash shows Pejman into my office the following afternoon. I haven't seen him for over a year, and during that time he has left his thin boy's body behind and become a strong, sturdy man. He has graduated from high school near the top of his class, but his family is not well off and his father needs him to help with his business digging wells on farms. The two spend a few weeks at a time in remote areas of the country, labouring from dawn to dusk under the relentless sun, then return to Mashhad for a couple of weeks' rest. The work is exhausting but it has made Pejman muscular and deepened his skin colour to a rich brown.

The minute I see his face I steel myself. An unwanted pregnancy is the only thing that brings that expression of dread.

'Doctor Karimi, thank you for your time.'

'Please, just call me Kooshyar. You're my relative.'

Pejman turns the corners of his mouth up in an attempt to smile, but his eyes are too troubled to convince me the smile is genuine. 'As you wish.'

I gesture to a chair. 'Make yourself comfortable and tell me what's going on.'

He sits stiffly on the edge of the chair, his long square fingers tapping the arms of it in an uneven rhythm.

I pour him a glass of water. 'Pejman, you can tell me anything. I'm a doctor and I hear unusual stories every day. Everything between us stays confidential, so feel free to tell me what has happened.'

Taking a deep breath and exhaling with a prolonged sigh, he says, 'Okay. Here goes. I've been seeing a girl named Hedia, a geography student who goes to the University of Mashhad. She's a wonderful girl. I love her with all my heart.' He pauses and rests his head in his hands for a minute before continuing. 'I really want to marry her, but I can't.'

I am sure now that he has come about a termination.

'I've been seeing Hedia in secret for the last few months. A couple of weeks ago, we had . . . We, um, we happened to have . . .'

'Sex?'

He nods, avoiding my eyes. 'Yes. And, um, she's very distressed about losing her virginity. We don't know what to do. I'm really sorry for her. So sorry that —'

I interrupt, trying to avoid revealing any trace of impatience in my voice. 'Why don't you marry her?'

Pejman raises his head and meets my gaze. I see the misery in his eyes. 'Because her father won't give her to me. He wants her for an educated man. He is an engineer and her brother is a medical student. They won't marry her to an uneducated man who digs wells.'

'Have you tried to ask for her hand?'

'I asked my mother to call the family. She doesn't know that Hedia and I have been seeing each other, she only thinks I've seen her on her way to university and that I like her. But her family didn't give us a chance to go to their house and ask for her hand. They already have someone in mind and are pushing her to marry him.'

'Who is he?'

'A university lecturer.'

'Okay, how can I help you, Pejman? Is there something more?'

'More?' He draws his brows together and looks for a moment like a little boy trying to understand that his beloved grandmother is dead and he will never see her again.

I ask quietly, 'Is she pregnant, Pejman?'

His eyes open wide and he shakes his head. 'Oh, no.'

'That's a relief.'

Again he taps his fingers, hard and fast, on the chair. 'But it's almost as bad, don't you see? I don't want to destroy her future. She'll have to marry this man and if . . .'

'If what, Pejman? Please, don't be shy.'

'If he sees she's not a virgin, you know what will happen. So I'm hoping, I'm wondering, if you would be kind enough to fix her virginity.' Leaning forward, he hurriedly adds, 'I don't know if that's possible, but I've heard that it is.'

As I adjust to this request, he says, 'I'll pay the cost, whatever it is.'

I rise from my desk and stand by the window, looking down at the cars on the street below. 'Pejman, I want to be honest with you. Yes, it is usually possible to repair virginity, and I'm able to do it.'

'Thank you, Doctor Karimi!' Pejman jumps to his feet and joins me by the window, his hand already reaching out to shake mine.

I take a step away from him. 'I didn't say I *will* do it.'

His hand falls limply to his side. 'But you're my only hope, Doctor Karimi. You know what happens to a girl who loses her virginity.'

'I know very well. But there are consequences.'

'What consequences?'

'I could get hanged for it. Did you know that?'

He leans his forehead against the window and closes his eyes. 'I knew it was dangerous, but I didn't know it was that bad. I know most doctors won't do it. That's why I came to you, because you're a relative.'

As important as relatives and friends are in the Middle East, I know a close relative would understand if I refused to do something so risky.

'Please, Doctor Karimi,' says Pejman, turning his head to face me again.

I see tears in his eyes. I don't signal any response to his plea. I am waiting, I think, to see if it's in me to say no to him. Because I should. Tens of thousands of girls in Iran either fall pregnant out of wedlock or lose their virginity before marriage each year. Am I to give myself the task of saving all of them? I wouldn't suggest that I am the only abortionist in Iran. Other doctors perform terminations, sometimes regularly, more often only in special cases – for the mistress of some high official, for example, or because a very large sum of money is being offered. When I say tens of thousands of girls I am making an educated guess, based on Iran's population of sixty-six million and the numbers who come my way. But I am more likely to be under-estimating than over-estimating. We are talking about human beings and their appetites. Men and women will fall in love inconveniently, or surrender to sexual passion; men will violate women. I would guess that most who become pregnant in this way attempt to perform the abortion themselves, or go to some amateur abortionist, or someone who sells them folk remedies, or advises them to harm themselves in ways that may bring about the evacuation of the uterus. Many of these attempts no doubt succeed, perhaps killing the woman at the same time. In other cases, the couple will be compelled to marry, however inappropriately.

Then there are those girls and women who are quietly murdered, whose deaths are never investigated, since no police inspector is going to pursue a case that requires the state prosecutor to dispute the word of a male. A father or brother need only say, 'Her throat was cut because she dishonoured the family,' and that will be that. Or the boy or the gang of boys who have raped a girl will say, 'She took off her chador and begged me to fuck her.' End of case.

There is another reason why unwanted pregnancies do not always reach the stage of termination, whether by a doctor or by a baby butcher, and it is this: only a minority of Iranians are interested in revenge and honour killings, in casting out the daughter who is with child. In the majority of families there will be anguish, yes, there will be shouting and tears and extravagant expressions of disappointment. But the daughter's throat will not be cut. She will be kept at home to give birth, and the baby will find its way to an orphanage, or it will be raised within the family. And the daughter will live. Even with the medieval mentality that prevails in Iran, most parents love their daughters. We never hear of those loving mothers and fathers who live through a period of anguish, then forgive.

Pejman reaches out and touches my shoulder, the gesture so small I barely feel any pressure. 'I'm sorry. I shouldn't have asked. Forgive me. I'll leave now.'

By some trick of the light, his face takes on the appearance of one of the soldiers who ate the poisonous mushrooms. He's nearly the same age; he's another young man who's made a catastrophic mistake. Even with all my skills and access to medicine, I hadn't been able to help the soldiers. Pejman I can help.

'Call me next week,' I tell him, 'when I'll be in Mashhad with my family. I'll see what I can do.'

He grabs my hand. 'I'll never forget this, Doctor Karimi. Never.'

He'll never forget? I predict he will. Not completely, but his gratitude will diminish in intensity over the years. I don't care.

'Give me a call on Thursday on my mobile phone.'

Pejman calls me on schedule, although not at the most convenient time. Azita and I are in the kitchen in Quchan, and I have no intention of letting her hear this conversation. I take the phone into the backyard for privacy.

'Doctor Karimi, are you coming tomorrow?'

'Yes, and it'll be the only chance I have to help you. Do you have a safe place?'

'We can use my place.'

'Are you sure it's safe?'

'If it can be done in the afternoon, yes, it will be.'

The funeral ceremony is in the evening. 'That's ideal. I'll see you at one o'clock.' Pejman gives me the address, and I hang up and head back inside.

Azita looks up from the stew she's stirring. 'Who was that?'

'Arash calling about one of my patients.' I open the refrigerator and take out a pitcher of water to avoid looking at my wife, but I can feel her suspicion. Neither of us says a word.

The next morning, while Azita is bathing Newsha, I pack the car for our trip to Mashhad, tucking my medical bag and other supplies at the back of the boot. Aside from Newsha's cheerful chatter and predictable questions about how much further we have to go, the journey is quiet, but I dread the surgery ahead of me. I glance frequently into the rear-view mirror to watch my animated daughter and wonder how I could possibly risk our futures in the way I'm planning to. Who am I helping, really? Who am I harming? Maybe if a few more women were publicly stoned, or beaten to death by the men in their family, the international community would demand the barbarism stop. Maybe instead of helping women, I am keeping them in peril.

But then, who am I to decide that women should martyr themselves? And that is exactly what I'd be doing if I stood by and let them face death. I am in the privileged position of being able to provide some comfort and relief to desperate women who can find no assistance elsewhere. Really, I should rejoice that I can help those few that I do, but if I had the power I would reach out to every suffering Iranian. This is a Third World country. It is possible to find examples of dire poverty here equal to the worst anywhere on earth. Tehran and Mashhad are huge, teeming metropolises, but Iran is essentially a nation of villages, and in those villages many people have a way of life that has not changed in five thousand years. If you happen to drive through one of these villages, risking the suspension of your fancy vehicle on a road designed for goats and donkey carts, you will see people aged before their time by the sheer grind of holding body and soul together; women in hijab so severe that even their noses are covered, with a leather apparatus that extends to their eyes, leaving two tiny holes for sight. These women will be mothers to three or four children out of a dozen they have given birth to, the rest having been taken by any of a score of diseases that run riot in rural Iran, including tuberculosis. You will see limbs set crookedly by the itinerant bone-setter who goes from village to village; or toothless men who may have had every diseased tooth in their heads wrenched from the jawbone by an amateur dentist who, like the bone-setter, plys his trade over a broad area. You will see mullahs who did not wait for the Islamic revolution to dole out laws fashioned by desert-dwelling tribes thousands of years earlier – an eye for an eye, a tooth for a tooth, literally. And you will see children who have never known a classroom, standing in the only garments they possess, gazing at you in your shiny vehicle as if you were a creature from another planet.

I don't mean to suggest that Iran is inhabited only by the wretched of the earth; people in the villages will still smile. But God help them if an epidemic of typhoid or meningitis breaks out. They will die like flies, and mostly without much complaint. I am sometimes seized by a longing to become the messiah of my nation's poor, to travel about healing by touch, spreading joy wherever I go, so that these people cry out, 'It is the man of miracles, it is Kooshyar Karimi, beloved of the poor man!' This fantasy of deliverance passes in a minute or so, and I become once again the Jewish doctor from Mashhad who courts the noose.

I feel Azita watching me from the passenger seat but can't bring myself to quell her suspicions. Unreasonably I become angry with her, as if my predicament is all her fault. When she asks if something is bothering me, I snap, 'Since when do you care how I feel or what I'm thinking about?'

She folds her arms across her chest and stares out the window, her face turned away from me. She will never fight with me in front of our daughter, even to defend herself.

'I'm sorry,' I say, touching her shoulder, but she shrugs my hand off.

I wish I could share my worries with her, but how many women would agree to their husbands performing illegal surgery? To risking their future? Our marriage may not be a bed of roses, and Azita can be an irritating woman, but her resistance is not unreasonable.

Mashhad is where I grew up, the location of a thousand vivid memories, many of them painful. It's a big, grubby city with one extraordinary building that redeems the squalor, the shrine of Imam Reza, the eighth Imam following the Prophet. All of Mashhad is considered a shrine in fact, a holy city, and is the destination of pilgrimages by Shiite Muslims from all over the world. It is also Iran's intellectual capital, the home of most of its greatest poets, both contemporary and ancient, including Ferdowsi, the most famous poet of all, Persia's national bard.

It is the home, too, of a great many crooks, gangsters, con artists, standover men, homicidal maniacs and drug lords. Holy Mashhad and Gangsterland Mashhad live cheek by jowl, reflecting the reality of Iran, and of the wider world: beauty and glory around one corner, and a bit further on, salivating cretins stropping their blades on leather belts. It's a city with a pulse, which is the most important thing. Out of the madness of the fanatical mullahs, the psychopathy of the bad guys, and the creative craziness of the poets, something greater than the sum of its parts has built itself.

Azita had lived in the upper-class part of town, while I grew up in real Mashhad, where my left-hand friend was a burglar and the right-hand one a member of an underground opposition group. Both were executed years later, leaving deep scars on my heart for two very different reasons.

We drive into Mashhad with Azita, so far as I can judge, relishing the family side of the funeral rites. A Persian funeral is not quite the same thing as a Western one. Here people are nuts about getting together with countless relatives to eat and eat and eat and lament. It's a ritual that predates Islam, and gives expression like nothing else to the foundationally social Persian soul.

Azita's father's house is already crowded with people from across the country. Hundreds of family members of both genders and all ages have come to attend the evening funeral. Mr Qolizadeh was the oldest man in the family, and tradition dictates that every living relative be at the ceremony, but most would have come anyway. He was a kind, loving, generous man with an open mind and a big heart.

While I greet people, shaking hands with those I don't know well, kissing the cheeks of those I do, Newsha runs out to play with the other children and Azita joins the women in the kitchen. It must cost a fortune to provide two huge meals for so many, and I momentarily feel sympathy for Azita's father. Of course he would never complain, since offering elaborate food is a way to show respect for the deceased. As I inhale the aromas of vegetable, meat and fish dishes, each seasoned with exotic spices and fresh herbs, I lament that I will miss at least one of those meals. I can already smell *khoresh-e fesenjan*, a delicious dish of meat cooked in a creamy walnut sauce, and I know my wife will help make *ghormeh sabzi*, a subtle concoction of lamb, herbs and lemon that takes hours to prepare. Pomegranates, apricots, plums, stuffed grapes and dates, pistachios, walnuts and almonds fill tables set against walls. Pitchers of orange drink and tea are everywhere.

I quietly excuse myself, telling one of the older male relatives that I have to see a sick friend of my father's.

'May Allah grant him a speedy recovery.'

'Thank you for your good wishes. I will tell him.'

I drive to the address Pejman gave me. To my surprise the building is a modern three-storey house. Pejman has assured me we'll have privacy. 'I have the basement floor to myself. My family lives above me and there are tenants above them, but nobody will disturb us.'

With the engine still running to keep the air conditioning flowing, I call Pejman on his mobile phone. 'I'm here,' I announce.

'I'll buzz the door open for you. Please just come in.'

He greets me on the other side of the door, keeping his voice down. 'Thank you so much for this. Hedia is waiting for you. Shall we go to her now?'

In the bedroom sits a nineteen-year-old of stunning beauty. Her face is a perfect oval, her skin flawless, her eyes fringed with long, thick, curling lashes. Her full lips are heart-shaped. I greet her, smiling in an effort to put her at ease.

Hedia rises, her manteau opening to reveal a pair of jeans. Her pink shoes match her loosely tied pink scarf. 'Hello, Doctor,' she murmurs, her head lowered in either shame or respect, perhaps both.

Setting my bag on the floor I say, 'We don't have much time. Are you prepared for me to examine you?'

She nods and I ask her to remove her jeans. She hesitates, arms tensing at her sides. I reach over and pull a blanket off the bed. 'Here,' I say. 'You can cover yourself with this.'

I turn my back to afford her a modicum of privacy. 'Let me know when you're ready.' I open my bag and put on a pair of gloves before turning again to her.

'Will this hurt?' she asks nervously.

'No, but before I can do anything I have to examine you to see if it's possible to restore your virginity.'

'So you mean it might be impossible to repair?'

'Let's be positive. I can tell you in a second.' I walk to the bed and ease the blanket over her knees. 'Relax.'

Females in Iran usually go to female doctors, even for a routine illness, and I know she'll be shy about my close inspection of her genitals. Examining her hymen is especially intrusive. I put my hand on both sides of her labia minora and pull them up so I can look into the orifice of her vagina. I can see the remains of her hymen and I'm encouraged to see that it's a good size. The shape and size of the hymen is unique to each woman. Some are crescent-shaped and so flexible they don't rupture even during sex; only childbirth will tear them. Some women have a very small, thin tissue that is almost non-existent. Others have a network-shaped hymen with holes in it, and a small fraction of girls are born with an unperforated hymen that has to be surgically cut to allow menstrual blood to flow. Most commonly, a hymen is a semicircle that covers slightly less than half the vaginal opening. Since Hedia's hymen is a good size and has only recently been ruptured, I'm confident I can repair it.

'I think I can do it,' I say with a smile.

'Thank you so much!'

'I'll give you a tiny needle with a local anesthetic to numb the area, and after that you won't feel anything. I'll need Pejman to help me with this.'

Hedia's eyes meet mine for a long moment. They tear up and her lips tremble as she grapples with her emotions. Finally she nods, the movement barely perceptible. She's accepting the intense embarrassment of a stranger feeling about in her vagina while Pejman witnesses it.

I open the bedroom door and find Pejman pacing up and down the small hallway outside. 'I need your help,' I tell him.

Reluctantly he shuffles into the room. His eyes immediately go to Hedia, who has lain back down with her eyes closed. He takes a step towards her but I put a hand on his arm. 'You'll need to wear gloves.' I take a second pair from my bag and hand them to him.

'I'm so sorry, Hedia,' Pejman whispers, touching her shoulder with an intimacy that shows they love each other deeply.

A tear slides down her cheek. She reaches up and puts her hand briefly over Pejman's before wiping the tear away.

'You can talk later,' I tell Pejman. 'We have to get started.' I show him how to pull the labia up gently while pushing backward at the same time to give me access to the hymen.

'Sorry, darling,' Pejman says softly, doing as I've instructed with trembling hands.

I drain local anesthetic into a syringe, asking Hedia if she's allergic to anything. She shakes her head, her eyes still closed as if locking her shame deep inside where no one can see.

'This will sting just a little.' I give her two injections at the edge of her vagina. After waiting briefly for them to take effect, I reach for a pair of fine scissors and begin cutting the edges of her hymen.

'What's happening?' Pejman whispers when he sees blood.

'The blood's a good sign. The more bleeding, the better chance of healing.'

I ask Hedia if she feels any pain.

'No,' she says weakly.

I use sterile gauze to wipe the blood so I can have a better view. 'It looks good.' Deftly I take a pack of catgut suture from my bag and open it. The hymen will need no more than three stitches; two would probably be plenty. I adjust the bleeding edges until they are directly opposite each other, so they will heal properly. I insert the needle and complete the first suture.

As I begin the second, a loud voice calls out, 'Pejman! Where are you?'

What in God's name? My heart lurches as Hedia's legs jerk in response.

'Don't move,' I whisper.

'It's my father,' says Pejman, terrified.

'Stop him from coming in here!' I couldn't have been interrupted at a more critical moment, but there is no way I can continue with Pejman's father likely to come into the room in search of his son.

As Pejman reaches the door I hiss, 'Take your bloody gloves off!'

He yanks them off and drops them on the floor.

'I'm scared,' Hedia whimpers, her face drained of colour.

'Ssh.' I'm listening to Pejman's father through the closed door. Sweat streams down my face – small rivers of fear. Pejman's father is an extremely traditional man and if he discovers what's going on here, all three of us will suffer horribly. He won't listen to any explanations. Fury will rule and he'll act swiftly. Worse, all the relatives gathered for the funeral will hear about it immediately. Not only will they be incensed about the illegal surgery and Pejman's sin, but they will never, ever forgive us for ruining the funeral. There is no telling where the rage would lead.

Pejman's conversation drags on but I can't make out a single word. Is his father demanding to know what's going on?

Hedia lies motionless as I stand over her with a needle holder and forceps in my hands, staring at the door, knowing it could be thrown open any minute, and Pejman's father come flying across the room at me.

Finally the voices stop, and a minute later the door opens. It's Pejman, alone. His underarms are stained with sweat despite the air conditioning. 'Oh Allah, that was close,' he wails.

Hedia tries to push herself up on her elbows. 'Stay still,' I tell her. Then turning to Pejman: 'How did he get in?'

'I have a second door to my place and he has a key for it. He wanted me to go to the chemist to buy his medicine, so he just walked in.'

Extraordinary! I told Pejman I needed complete privacy and

absolute secrecy, and he neglects to tell me that his father could well walk in on the procedure.

'Is he gone?' asks Hedia.

'Yes. I told him I'll get his medicine in a few minutes, so we have to hurry. He's in a bad mood and will come back if he doesn't see me leave soon.'

I continue, my hands unsteady from the stress, with a surgery that requires a hundred percent precision. I am insane. Pejman is insane. This country is much worse than insane.

Finally I put a pad on Hedia and begin replacing my supplies in my bag. 'No running or swimming or jumping for a week,' I tell her.

She's in a sitting position now. 'Doctor Karimi, I don't know how to say thank you.' She's too shy to look at me.

I squeeze her shoulder gently. 'That's fine,' I tell her. To Pejman I say, 'I need to leave without anyone seeing me. Especially your father.'

Pejman takes me through a side door, going out first himself to make sure nobody is around. Before I get into my car he thanks me again and reaches into his pocket to pay me.

'Don't worry about that. You can give it to me later. You will be at the funeral, I assume?'

'Of course, we'll all be there. But please, it's better if I pay you now where nobody can ask why I'm giving you money. It can never compensate you for the risk you've taken, but I have to pay.'

I know Pejman doesn't have enough money to pay the normal fee, which is a hundred thousand toman. 'If you feel it necessary, I'll accept five thousand toman.'

He counts out the money and I reluctantly accept it.

I take my time driving back to Azita's father's house. I'm not ready to face a house full of people dressed in black. Parking in a circle of shade under an old cedar tree, I get out of the car, lean against the trunk and light a cigarette. In my pocket I feel the wad of bills Pejman gave me. Growing up in the slums taught me the value of humanity, and I have learnt that money holds no true value in itself. As my heart rate returns to normal, the expression of relief on Hedia's face comes back to me. She hadn't been exaggerating when she took my hand and said, 'You have rescued me from things too horrible to imagine.'

I put the cigarette out and get back in my car. Yes, I've done the right thing, and my conscience is at peace, but do I have the nerves for this? For the sake of a clear conscience, I practically have to bleed from the ears with dread.

Leila

In her habitual grudging way, Mother gives me permission to visit the library once more. Always and forever, such a song and dance about a half-hour trip to return a book. You'd think I was asking to walk naked through the bazaar. And yet, as reluctant as she is to let me out, she is perhaps just a little more ready to concede than on other occasions. Instead of listing a dozen chores for me to complete before I head off, she simply gives up and says, 'Go then.'

'Maybe you'll see your sweetheart again,' Samira whispers teasingly. I know I am blushing furiously, and I know that she can see right through me, but still I vehemently deny any feelings for the mystery man.

'He's not my sweetheart!'

'Oh, he's not? Is that why every night, when you think I'm sleeping, you sneak his book out of the wardrobe and read it by candlelight?'

'It's the library's book. It's *The Prophet*. It has nothing to do with . . . with that man. Samira, don't encourage me to feel things I have no right to feel.'

Listen to me, Doctor. No right to feel. Remember Gibran's words in *The Prophet*? *When love beckons to you, follow him, though his ways are hard and steep. And when his wings enfold you, yield to him.* The truth is, I'm torn between duty and passion, as so many people are. Surely in your life, Doctor Karimi, you've known this struggle between the two – between what your heart yearns for and what your head says you cannot have?

I put on my black chador, imagining what it would be like to walk outside without one, without even a scarf covering my hair. When a breeze blew, my hair would be swept this way and that. What would it be like to know such freedom?

I have *The Prophet* under my chador and I can hear those words whispering to me: *When love beckons to you, follow him . . .* I want to yield to love, to this passion seething inside me. I want to follow ways that are hard and steep.

But oh Allah, I think I want even more to never have seen the man in the shop, to never have looked into his eyes. I want to be the quiet, shy, well-mannered and obedient girl I have always been. I want to be . . . nobody. I am not strong enough for passion, for the dark eyes and full lips and gentle manner of this man whose boutique I am approaching even now.

Doctor Karimi, do you regard this passion in me as immature? Does it seem to you, as you listen to me, what you'd expect from a girl of thirteen, rather than a woman of twenty-one? I cannot point to very much in defence of myself, to be sure, but please don't make me ashamed of what I felt. I have paid for it – who knows that better than you? If you wish, you can think it was all to do with my being kept locked away from the world, but that would not be the whole truth. At times I have torn at my own face in hatred of what I felt. I have rained abuse down on my own head. But Doctor, that love, that passion, it was in me to feel that way, it was waiting; it was helped along by books, and by the strange brain in my head that made me want to be something other than a dutiful daughter.

Don't stop at the boutique, I am telling myself on that day. Nothing good will come of it. I force myself to dwell on the images of punishment I have seen over time, on television, in the newspaper, some in the street – a hideous collage of beatings, floggings, stonings, shamings and abandonment of women who have pursued romances. I compel myself to gaze on these images again and again as I come closer to the boutique.

Don't stop, don't stop, don't stop, please just keep walking, please, please, please . . .

My head is bowed low and my eyes are pinned to the pavement, but I know he is there.

And he is. He's leaning against the wooden frame of the door, lighting his cigarette, hands shielding the flame from the wind. When he looks up his eyes meet mine, recognition blooms on his face; he smiles and my body ceases to be a body, ceases to be equipped with limbs and joints and a torso housing organs, and becomes the universe itself, a cosmos of light and warmth. And the cosmos that is me merges with the galaxy that is him. For two or three seconds, or perhaps ten, we are held in the embrace of Allah.

Then his gaze is briefly caught by some movement to his left and the enchantment is gone. What is left is agony. I think, If I can't have him, I will kill myself. If I am never to kiss his lips, better that I die.

And all those images of punishments that were meant to fortify me against spells and enchantment, they mean less than nothing.

I walk on to the library, but I know that something has changed in me. I am going to suffer. It will be worse than anything I have ever known. Doctor Karimi, there in the street on that day, I passed from paradise to the certainty of a hell awaiting me, and I did not have it in my power to alter a thing.

The house is unusually quiet as I step into the courtyard. There is no trace of either my sister or mother.

'Samira?' I call. I wander to each room, peering in for a sign of my family. Hearing hurried footsteps behind me, I turn to see Samira running down the hall, a smile illuminating her face.

'Ssh!' she whispers, a finger to her lips.

'What's going on? Tell me!'

'Mrs Nasiri's here.' She pauses for dramatic effect. When I look at her blankly, she adds, 'She's talking to Mother.'

'Is it . . . about you?'

Samira wraps herself in her own arms. 'Yes,' she squeals. 'About me and Saeed.'

'Allah! Truly?'

Clamping a hand over my mouth, she whispers, 'Don't let her hear you.'

So that was why Mother had allowed me to go to the library. She wanted me out of the way.

Samira is wearing her best skirt and blouse, and her hair, freshly washed and dried in the sun, hangs loosely around her shoulders. In our traditional family, she is not allowed to wear makeup until she is married, but the joy and excitement that radiates from her has made her more beautiful than cosmetics ever could.

We sit in the living room while we wait, whispering to each other, imagining what is going on in the other room.

'What do you think they're saying?'

We both know that negotiations of this sort resemble a business deal. Is your daughter a good investment? What is to be gained? What is to be the cost?

'Mother is probably telling her what a fine cook you are. And she's sure to mention your sewing and dolls.'

'What else?'

Samira knows 'what else'. Our mother has rehearsed the 'what else' for years, hoping for this very opportunity. But Samira wants to hear it spoken aloud.

'She'll tell her how capable you are of looking after the house and that you're good with children. She'll say how you go to the orphanage just to be near kids, and because you're kind and good and want to help them. Then she'll say how obedient you are.'

I speak the last words without thinking, only realising once they are out that complete obedience may not sound like a desirable character feature. But Samira takes it as a compliment. There is this small difference between my sister and me: she is entirely given to accommodating, to pleasing, but I have developed a resentment of my role as the eternal good girl. I want to be the girl who runs through the bazaar to the boutique, the girl who says to the shopkeeper, If you love me, take me in your arms.

'What else is Mother saying?'

'That everything will be perfect. And Mrs Nasiri will agree it's a good match. Saeed will come over with his parents to meet you and our parents, and then they'll set a date for your marriage, and you'll live together happily until the end of time.'

Samira's expression registers the joy of everything I'm telling her. She's like a child listening to a fairy story, ready to swoon when the princess and the prince enfold each other in their arms.

'It goes without saying that you do want to marry him?'

My sister takes a moment, retreating within herself as if to retrieve the answer from some secret vault inside. So strange. She is swept along by the happily-ever-after power of the courtship story, and yet perfectly content to say this: 'I'm nearly thirty and still living with my parents. That's embarrassing, to say the least. I see the look in other women's eyes when I meet them. They have children already, and no longer see me as someone they can talk to about their lives. Besides, until I get married, you have to be here too. You need your own life.'

'Don't agree to marry him because of that! Because of me!'

Samira smiles at me indulgently. 'Of course not, dear. I'm only saying that an agreement would solve a lot of problems.'

You see how it is, Doctor Karimi. Samira has fashioned a work-able reconciliation between the giddy joys of marriage and the practical benefits of wedlock. But not me, not Leila. Passion has me in its iron grip, and will never let go. Love is the soaring mountain; simple common sense is a soft undulation that would barely rate the description of a hill.

An hour passes with my sister and I sitting in tense silence. Then we are jolted by the sound of our mother's voice calling Samira to the dining room. Her hands shake as she tidies her hair and walks through the doors to meet the woman who may well be her future mother-in-law.

I want to be at my sister's side, but have to content myself with imagining the scene that unfolds. Samira will greet Mrs Nasiri, who will be sipping her tea from fine china at the dining table and studying Samira's manners. Samira will carry more tea and fresh fruit to Mrs

Nasiri, as is the tradition, and Mrs Nasiri will ask about her education and whether or not she wants to have children. Samira is being interviewed for a job, in effect; all her efforts and inspiration will be devoted to making the most favourable impression possible.

Mrs Nasiri will speak about her son. She will tell Mother and Samira his age, how he earns a living, and where he lives. She'll praise him highly, no doubt claiming he is kind, caring, and of course very good-looking. If all goes well, when Mrs Nasiri has finished painting a picture of a man any woman would be happy to marry, she'll rise to leave, and with a smile promise to have a chat with her son and let us know the outcome.

When I finally hear the door close behind Mrs Nasiri, I run out to join my mother and sister in the kitchen.

Mother is speaking excitedly, fussing over Samira. 'In my heart, I feel very good about this! Oh Leila, can you believe it?' She closes her eyes and puts her hands together in prayer. 'Allah, please make this marriage happen, please let my dream come true, please give Samira the gift of a family.'

It's a sleepless night for my sister and me. We lie clasping hands excitedly. If I am honest with myself, I don't feel any great joy over this potential union. Samira has seen Saeed before, without paying much attention to him. It was not love at first sight. She tries to recall his face, but beyond knowing that he has dark hair and eyes like every man in Iran, she draws a blank. How can I share her excitement when the man she may be promised to is a complete mystery? This is my one hope: that Saeed will love her as she deserves to be loved.

'This is maddening,' Samira admits. 'And maybe pointless. What if he comes to meet me and decides he's not interested? What if the moment he sees the scar on my cheek, he decides that mine is not the face he wishes to wake up to each morning?'

Samira is in a constant state of insecurity about the scar that runs across her left cheek. It is the result of an accident when she was six, and running home from the shop with a tiny goldfish in a plastic bag. She had bought it for *Nowrooz*, the Persian New Year celebration. 'You must be very quick or the fish will die,' said the shopkeeper, and just near our doorway she tripped on the kerb and fell. The doctor who sutured her face at the local hospital warned my anxious father that a scar would remain forever, and even though it's not deep, it has almost ruined her chances of marriage.

I want to say something scathing about men who can't overlook such a tiny blight, but then I recall how devoted I am to the glossy hair and firm jaw and lustrous eyes of my shopkeeper. If he'd been a pudgy guy with buck teeth and a squint, I may never have noticed him. We are all shallow, Doctor Karimi, some more than others, but beauty stirs us like nothing else on earth.

'Don't worry,' I say to my sister. 'He would have to be a fool not to want you.'

My father is fond of saying that love grows after a marriage, and is a matter of practice. 'Train yourself to love your husband, and you will,' is his belief. He makes it sound like a matter of discipline. I can't bear to think of marriage in that way. It makes me feel nauseous.

Four days pass before Mrs Nasiri returns. My mother ushers her into the dining room, closing the door behind her. Matchmaking is a time of high excitement in Iranian families, for both mothers and daughters. It's one of the few occasions when the predictable yields to the fresh and novel. The excitement probably has its roots in tribal life, going back thousands of years, and maybe has something to do with reinvigorating the family, making it stronger. Sons and daughters find mates, babies are born, the family and the tribe are enriched.

The protocols are very important. Mrs Nasiri, having made her initial visit, is now back with her verdict on the fitness of my sister for marriage to her son. She will have made countless inquiries about Samira's character, far and wide. Some people will have said, 'Yes, a fine young woman, good-natured, nice smile.' Others will have said much the same thing then added, 'Pity about that scar on her cheek.' This is when all those years of behaving in the proper way in public will pay off for Samira. Nobody will say, 'I saw her with her hair exposed one time – shocking.' Nobody will say, 'She looks at men, the hussy.' Mrs Nasiri will call in on some wise old woman of the town who has seen a thousand courtships ending in a thousand marriages, and this wise old woman will say, 'Yes, in my opinion, this Samira you talk of will make a good wife for your Saeed.' That will clinch the match.

Mrs Nasiri departs. Mother calls for Samira, and for me. She says, 'Yes, Saeed will visit us in one week.'

This means that the meeting has gone well, that Mrs Nasiri is happy for the courtship to proceed. Samira and Saeed are engaged.

Samira almost swoons with relief and happiness. Twenty-nine years old, and at last a bride. She says, 'I don't believe it! I don't believe it!' She has to sit and fan her face to prevent some sort of emotional meltdown. 'Oh dear Allah, I hope he likes me when we meet. Please tell me he'll like me, Leila.'

'He'll adore you,' I tell her. And he will. Mrs Nasiri would not have let things go this far if she thought her son would reject Samira. 'He'll look at you and see a queen.'

'Will he, Leila? Are you sure? I've waited so long for this, I can't bear to miss out again.'

My sister is not in love with Saeed. She barely knows what he looks like. She is in love with marriage. Not for its own sake, but for the freedom it will give her, and because it will release her from the cold grip of pity. It is as if she has been stalled for ten years in the role of daughter, treated like a child. She is desperate to move to another stage of her life. As soon as Samira is married, my mother will never again talk to her as if she is ten years old, never again forbid her to do this or that, never again instruct her in posture and decorum. She will never say, as she does now, 'Don't smile in the street, silly girl.' It is freedom that has made my sister giddy. She has drawn in just two or three breaths of the air of liberty and it has lifted her into the clouds.

'What should I wear?' Samira asks me on the day of her meeting with Saeed. She pulls one skirt after another out of the wardrobe, one blouse after another, studying them for a few seconds before putting them on the bed.

'What does it matter? You'll have your white chador on. All he'll see is cloth. And remember what Mother said. Don't act excited to see him. Look at him as if he's one of a hundred suitors you're choosing between.' I use an English expression I've come to know: 'Stay cool.'

'Gool?'

'Cool. It means . . . it means, like nothing surprises you. Like you're always in perfect control of your emotions. Cool, not hot and flustered. Okay?'

'But I'm not gool. I'm . . . how do you say it?' Samira is looking for her own English word. 'Crazy,' she says. 'I'm crazy!'

I pull her by her hand, make her sit on the bed and look me in the eye. A surge of sadness has risen in me and tears are running down my cheeks. Soon my beloved sister will be gone. I'll be alone in this prison with nobody to share my joys and sorrows with.

Samira puts a hand to my cheek. 'Sweetheart, what's wrong?'

'Nothing. Nothing.'

She knows, but can offer no solace other than to say, 'Your day will come, Leila. It will. I know it in my heart.'

In the main living room, Father and Mother wait expectantly for Saeed and his parents to arrive. Samira and I watch through a window. Samira is no longer overflowing with joy and delight. This is the moment of truth. She is about to set eyes on the man with whom she is likely to spend every day of every year for the rest of her life. If he turns out to be a block of wood, then it will be with a block of wood that she makes her life.

We take seats beside our parents. We can't be caught watching through the window when Saeed arrives.

The doorbell rings. Majid answers it, and ushers the Nasiri family into the living room. Saeed and Samira take their first proper look at each other. And I have my own first look at Saeed too. He's of average height, a little overweight. Receding hairline, well-trimmed moustache and beard. His nose is on the large side, making his small eyes appear even smaller. He is well dressed in a black jacket, grey pants, and crisp white suit. He isn't ugly, but he isn't attractive either.

Our parents take their seats as Mother gestures for Samira to make tea. This tradition is upheld in all marriage arrangements. The prospective bride must show her ability to cook and brew tea while also displaying her manners and skill as a hostess.

Samira's face is blank as she rises with me in tow. I follow her to the kitchen where she stands staring absently out of the small window above the sink. I don't know what to do with myself. Do I hold her? Do I speak? What can I possibly say? The bubbling of the stovetop kettle is the only noise in the kitchen, apart from the low echoing of words and laughter that stream down the hall from the living room.

'This is it,' Samira murmurs, more to herself than to me. Her eyes haven't left the small landscape visible from the window. The kettle whistles. She makes the tea and when it is brewed she solemnly pours it into delicate china cups; then with great care she arranges the sweets and pastries she has baked on a silver platter, and cautiously loads it all onto a tray.

The protocols of the day don't allow me to return to the living room with Samira. I have shown myself, proving that I am not some grotesquely malformed relative of the bride-to-be that would be a horror to have in the family, and now it's my task to disappear while the two families chat. As Samira prepares to carry the tray into the living room, I tell her that all will be well, that she and Saeed will be happy together. She nods, without conceding anything, and leaves me alone in the kitchen.

I must encourage my sister, I must support her. But in truth I do not think of her engagement to Saeed as being equal in intensity of feeling to my secret and unannounced 'engagement' to the shopkeeper. Where is the passion in Saeed? He seems to me dull and uninspiring.

I learn from Samira later that night that Saeed works long hours as a taxi driver. 'He's not a very rich man,' she says as we sit cross-legged on her mattress, braiding our hair, 'but he says he likes his job and works hard. *And* he promised that his wife will be provided with anything necessary for a comfortable life. He's not too fussy either. He said he could tell I was an excellent cook and will look after the house.'

And my response? 'He sounds nice.'

'I was so nervous, you have no idea. I kept thinking he was going to be rude, or aggressive, or really traditional. But after tea he sat beside me, and when I finally dared to take a little sideways look at him, he had this shy smile on his face. It was a really nice smile, tender and sweet. I relaxed after that, he just didn't seem as scary anymore.'

She's pleased with her suitor – or pleased enough.

She says, 'He said he didn't want me to leave the house without asking his permission. That he wouldn't mind me visiting friends or family, but I would have to ask first; he doesn't want me walking in the streets if it's not necessary. I told him that was all right, I'd expect any man to feel the same way. He said the last thing he wanted me to know was that he hopes for children very soon. That he's getting old – he's forty – and doesn't want to be a grandfather to his children. He's been married before, you know. His wife was a witch. Oh Leila, I'd adore having a man who was more modern in his tastes than Saeed, of course I would, but if I wait for a man like that I could be waiting forever. I'll have a bit more freedom, so that's good. Not a lot, but a bit. I told him that we must treat each other with respect, and he agrees with that. And I said I don't want to be hurt by my husband, I don't want to be hit and abused. He said he'd never do that. So I should settle for what's been offered. At least it's safe.'

Safe? Who can get excited about safe? I don't say that, of course. I smile, and nod my head.

'That was all. Everybody clapped and cheered and wished us great happiness and prosperity. You can imagine the rest. Mother was proud to talk about my complete *jehaz* and how it includes a rug and china and silverware and a TV and stereo and all kinds of linens. I'm a bargain!'

I wrap my arms around my sister and hold her tight. Please Allah, I think, let every minute of Samira's life from here on be blessed. Let no harm ever come to her. Let no pain cross the doorway of her new home.

And I let her go.

The Doctor

Hamid is an uncomplicated young man, or so I believe him to be. I say 'believe' because I hope that here too I will be forgiven for telling his story from the inside, so to speak. Hamid was raised to be obedient to his parents and to the state, and he is, or he has been up until now. He has never acted in any way that couldn't have been predicted. At times he has felt something like pride in being so predictable. He has made do without political convictions, without dreams, without any vision of a larger world. But lately something has changed. Discontent, once a complete stranger to him, has taken up residence in his imagination and begun to bicker with his thoughts, has begun to contradict him, and has fashioned a message that it whispers to him all day long, all night long: There must be more to life than this.

It has made him realise, as he didn't before, that he is sick to death of the routine of his marriage. His wife was chosen for him, and he went along with his parents' wishes. Yet if he had his time over again, he would be as complaisant as he was the first time around, he knows it. He might yearn for the adventure of a real romance but it will have to fall in his lap, because he is too timid to go out and seek it.

There are millions of Iranian husbands just like Hamid, tyrannised by their own imaginations. And it's not only their wives they are tired of; life itself is an ordeal to them. They are male Emma Bovarys, aware every day of that whisper: There must be more to life than this.

Until recently, Hamid has accepted the sedation of the familiar. His modest home, modest wife, modest child, modest store and modest car make of him a modest man. There are no quarrels, no arguments, no desires he can't overcome. His remedy for discontent is to remind himself that he is better off than many other husbands. His wife is not a harridan; his son is unusually obedient, almost reclusive; his work is not an insufferable burden – he should count his blessings. And he does. Oh, but that longing, that longing! If the chance came along, timid as he is, he might just find the wherewithal to seize it. Or not. He doesn't know.

He entertains dangerous fantasies. He imagines dousing his store in petrol and striking a match. He pictures himself taking a heavy wrench to his car, smashing and denting and crushing it, destroying it completely. He wants to run to the coast of Iran, leap into the ocean, swim to the far side of the world, struggle to shore in a new land, begin a new life. And that new life will begin with a new woman, some creature of rare beauty who will adore him from the instant she sets eyes on him. She will say, 'Hamid, I am forever yours. Undress me. Make love to me. If you spurn me, I will die.'

Is it wrong, to long for love? Is it wrong to wish with all of one's heart for life to be as vivid as it can be? Surely it's heroic to strive in this way? To seek what is just beyond reach? To strain until one's fingers can touch it, and then strain even more, until one's reach and one's grasp are the same?

As if by some distinct sign from Allah, Hamid meets her, the creature of rare beauty with a longing in her eyes. On that summer afternoon, with the heat growing more and more intense, the joyless music of the faltering fan vainly rotating beside his desk, he sees a young woman through the window of his shop. She is wrapped in a standard black chador, face veiled, body hidden, eyes averted – there is no reason for him to be so inexplicably drawn to her. But he is. And though his wife is resting upstairs, he knows he will speak to the woman. He will overcome every scruple, disregard every caution of his culture and faith, and he will speak to her.

A slender arm extends from the young woman's chador. She is holding out a colourful treat. A little boy sits mesmerised in front of her, eyes darting nervously as he snatches the sweet and scurries off like a frightened mouse. Hamid watches as she withdraws her arm back into her chador, and he notices that a book has fallen to her feet. It lies there in the dust, but she remains unaware of it, her back now turned to him. And he can read the title from where he has gone to stand, just inside the doorway of his shop: *The Little Prince*.

Stepping forward, he picks up the book. The young woman whips around, only now sensing his presence, and he can hardly conceal the jolt that shakes him as her eyes meet his. A rich honey-brown, they burn with curiosity and alarm.

He holds up the book, striving to appear casual. 'This is a good book. *The Little Prince*. One of my favourites.' He chances another look into her eyes. Her stance has been relieved of some of its tension, though she remains stiff and on guard.

Receiving no reply other than the shy averting of her eyes, Hamid continues. 'It's not like a children's book at all,' he says, tapping the cover with his finger. He extends it to her, watching as her eyes follow the line of his exposed arm with acute caution.

'Thank you,' she says softly, 'thank you very much.'

Her voice is a bewitching melody. He wants to hear it again. He wants to see her eyes again too, explore their beauty and allure. Her eyes and her voice – just for a moment they are all that exists.

That night, he lies in bed beside his wife enjoying vivid fantasies that form by themselves. The young woman lifts her eyes to his and holds his gaze. She smiles modestly, averts her eyes, then lifts her gaze once more, unable to help herself. She slides her chador off her hair, lets the long chestnut locks fall over her shoulders. She is still smiling. She says, 'Hamid . . . Hamid . . .' He wants to kiss her lips. He will kiss her lips. She says again, in a murmur, 'Hamid . . . Hamid . . .'

All that he longed for, yearned for, despaired of ever finding. Will he ever see her again? He prays silently: Let her return. Let her return.

His wife stirs in her sleep. He waits while she resettles herself.

Let her return. Dear Allah, let her return.

Leila

My family's home is buzzing with activity, Doctor Karimi, as you might well imagine. A date has been set for the wedding of Saeed and my sister, with Saeed's father agreeing to pay the expenses for the party. Even my brothers are happy, partly because they will no longer be responsible for Samira and won't have to be constantly on the lookout for ways in which she is dishonouring her family – not that she ever did any such thing – but more because she is showing herself to be worthy of respect, by having at last found a husband. Being brothers to an unmarried sister who is getting on in years is humiliating. People might begin to wonder if she has some secret vice, one that might spread through the entire family.

There is a great deal to do before the wedding, and time moves with alarming speed for the first time in my life. There are flowers to arrange, a feast to prepare, a dress to find, jewellery to buy, hair to be styled. We have to hire a wedding dress, because of the high cost, but the one Samira sets her heart on is stunning and elegant regardless. It has a long white glittering train that follows the gown like running water. The intricately sewn patterns of white beads and gems twinkle and reflect the light of the store as Samira stares at herself in the change-room mirror. Mother has stopped herself from crying twice already, but seeing her daughter finally wearing her wedding dress causes the dam to break. I have to hold my own tears back as I watch Samira, who is mesmerised by her reflection. How foreign and uncertain this must all feel to her, how unrecognisable she must find herself wearing a dazzling gown and not a black chador.

A few days before the wedding, the engaged couple spend the afternoon in jewellery stores looking for rings. Samira tells me about it later. 'Mother and Mrs Nasiri walked ahead of us to give us a chance to chat,' she says. 'You can't imagine how strange it is to walk beside a man who isn't a brother. I was holding on so tightly to my chador, I don't know if I'll ever get used to being in front of him without one.'

'Do you think you'll talk about those things when you're married?' I ask, drying the dishes and placing them on the shelves.

Samira giggles. 'I'll find out, won't I?'

While I'm sweeping the living room the day before the wedding, I feel two soft arms wrap around my shoulders from behind. I inhale my mother's comforting scent of herbs and fruit and find myself melting into the unexpected embrace. My shoulder grows damp from her tears, and her breath comes in stutters.

'Leila, if Allah wills it, you'll go to your own husband's house soon,' she whispers, squeezing me tightly once more before releasing me. By the time I turn to face her she has already wiped the tears from her cheeks. She reaches into a pouch concealed at her side and pulls out a handful of money. My eyes widen at the sight, never having seen so much cash in my life. To my shock, she places a fistful into my hand.

'I want you to go out and buy yourself a beautiful dress, Leila. It is such a special day, for all of us.'

'Oh Mother,' I gasp, 'I can't take this much money. It wouldn't be right.'

She hushes me, nudging me towards the door. 'Go, go. We can't have you in an old dress at your sister's wedding.' She winks at me – winks! I've never seen her so carefree and happy. 'Do your shopping quickly,' she says. 'We still have a lot to do here.'

I walk briskly along the bazaar's main street. At least fifteen different shops sell women's clothing, most of them run by women. A display of beautifully coloured gowns catches my eye, and I wander into the promising store. There are so many lovely clothes to choose from, so many bright tones, textures, sequences and ruffles. I try on at least a dozen outfits, feeling like the girl I imagined myself to be in my fantasies, free, independent, stylish. Whisking through expensive fabrics, the staff of the store waiting on me hand and foot, I finally settle on a soft, flowing white skirt with tiny pink and blue flowers sprinkled across it. I love the way it spills so beautifully to the ground.

With my purchase in hand beneath my chador, I venture into the maze of stores once more to find the perfect blouse. As each display disappoints me, I begin to feel weary for the first time that day.

I know a store you've yet to visit, says a treacherous voice in my mind. I quieten it, hurrying through the bazaar. I am acutely aware that the boutique I am avoiding – the boutique I am in truth avid to visit – is only a few blocks away. I change direction, spoiling any chance of ending up where I have no right to go.

Allowing my feet to navigate, I permit my mind to wander. I don't know why I do this. I haven't let a single subversive thought pass through my head in weeks; it's too dangerous. Maybe it's because I've been walking so long, maybe all the freedom of today has made me reckless, maybe I simply don't have the energy to keep the thoughts locked away anymore, but the very moment I release control, the images come flooding in. His hands, his eyes, his lips, the languid way he leans in the doorway of his shop. I have never been so confused and yet so sure. I halt midstep, looking around at my unfamiliar surroundings. It seems I have wandered too deeply into the labyrinth. Lost in a sea of black chadors and rushing pedestrians, I am completely alone with myself and the clearest thought I have ever had rings like a bell in my head.

I want to see him.

And suddenly I know exactly where I am. Disappearing into one of the winding side streets, I walk faster and faster. My chador flaps around me with the speed of my progress. I dodge carts and taxis until I can see the boutique window. Crossing the dusty road in a few quick strides, I step over the threshold before I have time to change my mind. A little bell chimes to signal my arrival. I close my eyes.

Footsteps approach me. I turn and look at the face and form of the man who has made such a wreck of me.

He smiles, and it is a smile of genuine delight. 'You again,' he says softly.

Dear Allah, he's so beautiful! Have I dared to think that? I can't help myself. But Leila, don't say it aloud.

'I'm looking for a shirt,' is what I manage to say.

'I have some lovely ones that might suit you. Why don't you take a look?' And he adds, his voice acting on me like balm, 'What's the occasion, if I may ask?'

I dare to glance at him again. He is stunning in a black shirt with fine grey stripes. 'My sister's wedding.'

'Well then, congratulations to your sister. My name is Hamid, by the way.'

The word seems like a spell. I murmur it to myself, then offer my own name.

'Leila,' he repeats. 'How . . . how beautiful.'

For a space of three or four seconds we say nothing. It is almost as if we have taken a vow by exchanging names. For Hamid to say 'How beautiful' is an unheard of intimacy between an unmarried woman and man, and really, I should run from the shop and never return. But I do not run. No power on earth could make me.

'You had a shirt I admired a month or so ago. It had —'

Before I can finish my sentence, he steps across the room and holds up a shirt that looks like it belongs to a princess. Pure white silk, the collar and sleeves accented with lace as delicate as a spider's web.

'How about this one? White goes with anything.'

The beauty of the garment is enhanced by the beauty of the man displaying it to me. I want to embrace the shirt and the shirt-seller, but I command myself to calm down. 'I don't know. I want to make sure I can afford it before I try it on.'

'Don't worry about the price. Let me show you the fitting room.' He walks to the other end of the shop and opens a door. He hands me the shirt as I step past him, and closes the door behind me.

I feel uneasy taking off my clothes knowing he is just on the other side of the door. It seems far too intimate. I remove my chador, begin unbuttoning the shirt I'm wearing, then stop. He is too close. I feel as if I'm sinning just by undressing. I hold the white shirt up in front of me and appraise the look. No, too stark. I want something with colour. Like the blue shirt I'd seen before.

I put my chador back on and hesitantly open the door, squeezing the shirt against my chest as if it were a shield that could protect me from harm. To my relief, Hamid is behind the counter.

'How was it?' he asks, looking up.

'It's not quite what I'm looking for.' I put the shirt back and skim the racks for the blue shirt. Not seeing it, I decide to go. I feel more uncomfortable by the moment. I should go, and go now. But I feel such reluctance to take myself out of the reach of the shopkeeper's charm.

'You don't happen to have the blue shirt that was in the window a few weeks ago, do you?'

Hamid says, 'I most certainly do.' He disappears into the back of the shop and returns with the shirt. 'I knew you liked it, so I kept one for you.' He holds it out to me.

'Oh,' I say, 'it's more beautiful than I remembered.'

'I'm sure it'll fit.'

I take the shirt and return to the fitting room. I make sure the door is closed, take my chador off once more, and hold the shirt against myself. It is lovely. I decide to try it on. I check the door again to make sure it's shut tight, then take my shirt off, put the new one on, and study my reflection in the mirror.

'Oh,' I whisper. 'The most gorgeous shirt I've ever worn.'

I slip the skirt I've just purchased out of its wrapping and hold it to my waist. The combination is perfect. I put the skirt back in its package, put my own shirt back on. Lowering my chador over myself, I leave the fitting room.

Hamid, back behind the counter once more, asks me if I like the shirt.

'I do,' I reply, and dare to look straight into his eyes.

He holds my gaze for longer than any man has ever looked at me before and extends his hand. 'Let me wrap it for you,' he says. 'You have good taste.'

'But you didn't tell me how much it is.'

His voice is so soft I have to lean towards him to hear. 'Leila, it is yours,' he says.

'No, no, please, I must pay for it! You've already given me a book, and this is too much, to give me a shirt as well. I *must* pay.'

Hamid smiles and makes a gesture of resignation. 'If you insist. But no more than two hundred toman.'

Doctor Karimi, you can see the situation I'm in, can't you? You are Jewish, but you know our culture inside out. Can you see? I'm engaged in a conversation with Hamid when I barely know him. This is what would be thought of as a great wickedness. I shouldn't be having a conversation of any sort with him. I shouldn't be in his shop alone with him. It's as if part of my being has leapt ahead weeks and months to a time when I kiss his lips, allow him to caress my arms, my neck, to uncover my breasts and kiss my nipples. The very fact that I don't hurry from the shop with my chador held close to my body and tears running down my face is proof that I will accept much greater wickedness than simple conversation. Whatever love is before it is love – before it is given that name – that is what has me in its power. Even as I struggle to behave decently, I am imagining my mouth on his.

I feel the softness of the shirt against my fingertips. I know it costs three times what Hamid is asking. Should I accept his ridiculously low price or find a reason not to buy it?

'Okay,' I say. 'Thank you.'

He wraps the shirt with great care and hands me the parcel. 'All yours,' he says. Then he comes from behind the counter and walks me to the door. 'I hope your wedding party is everything your sister wishes for. Goodbye, Leila.'

'Thank you. Thank you so much.'

Will I say his name? I think, Leila, you have your parcel, go!

'Thank you, Hamid.'

I hurry from the shop, amazed at my boldness.

In its life, our house has never glowed and sparkled as it does today, Samira's wedding day. My mother, my sister and I have scrubbed every surface, brushed spiders' webs from every last corner, moved cupboards to sweep up the sort of dirt that hides away for years, polished the cutlery, rinsed and dried glasses until they gleam like crystal. The house and backyard are decked out with tables and chairs, candles, streamers, all illuminated by coloured lights. An Iranian wedding is one of the few rituals of the Persian people that has not yielded to the piety and parsimony of the mullahs. People still expect to enjoy themselves at a wedding. They expect to laugh and clap and tell jokes and raise glasses of juice to toast the bride and groom. And they expect to eat until they fall into a coma and have to be carried home with a smile on their face.

We have enough food to satisfy each guest's appetite five times over. Because this is what the guests will remember: that the family of the bride did not stint on food, and that the kitchen was not idle from the first minute of the festivities to the last.

My mother, Mrs Nasiri and Samira have visited the beautician together to have their hair shampooed and shaped, their eyebrows plucked, their cheeks treated with mysterious products that remove wrinkles and blemishes. Afterwards, Samira hurries off to the dressmaker to be fitted into her wedding gown, and when she returns, her chador covering her, she pulls me into the bedroom to show me what has been achieved. When she lifts her chador, I don't know whether to applaud or fall to my knees in praise. She is astonishingly beautiful in her wonderful dress. On her wedding day, and at hardly any other time, an Iranian woman can show off her face and figure without any risk of being thought a harlot. Samira has very distinct curves to reveal at her wedding party.

I say, 'Oh, Samira! My dear sister, nobody at the wedding will equal your beauty. I adore you. Everybody will adore you. Saeed will think himself the luckiest man on earth.'

We embrace and weep. The world is changing. We are not two sisters at home anymore. We are sister and wife. I feel a grief that I can't give expression to. Samira will go to her own home with a husband. I will be left with a passion for a man I might never see again.

I am waiting with a heart that aches in such a complicated way for my Aunt Sediqa to arrive at the wedding. To hold her in my arms, to be held by her, is the only balm I can think of for this maddening distress of mine. I can't say to her, Oh Aunt, my sister is leaving me alone in this house with a passion I can't control, but it will help just a little to see the one person on earth who might begin to understand.

She arrives at last. I run and hug her the instant she steps over the threshold.

'Look how gorgeous you are,' she says, clasping my hands in hers. She has more grey hair since the last time I saw her, but other than that, there is no trace of the challenges she faces as a divorced woman. Aunt Sediqa works in a hospital as an assistant nurse, earning just enough to pay her rent and household expenses, but she never complains and is nearly always cheerful.

It is now the task of my mother and Aunt Sediqa to prepare Samira for her entry into the room where the ceremony will take place. They fuss around her, smoothing her dress, making tiny alterations to the fall of her hair, offering endearments. Then they lead her in. First- and second-degree female relatives fill both sides of the room, but the only men allowed in the house at this time are Saeed and the mullah.

Samira takes her place beside Saeed in front of the *sofreh aghd* *. Ten women hold a white net over their heads. Aunt Sediqa rubs two big sugar cones against each other, sprinkling sugar dust on the couple's heads as a symbol of happiness in their future life. Everybody listens silently as the mullah reads verses from the Koran and instructs the couple that a woman must obey her husband and a husband must respect his wife. At the conclusion of the ceremony there are claps and cheers. My own personal prayer to Allah is that He grants my sister a good life with her husband. And I beg Him to give them many healthy, happy children.

Finally the fathers of the bride and groom are invited into the room. Father kisses Samira's cheek and puts a gold necklace around her neck. He says what every father says at this point in the wedding service: 'My daughter, Samira, go to your husband's house with your white chador and may you never come back unless in your white shroud.'

Mother gives Samira a bracelet, and holds her for one final moment as tears flow unchecked down their faces. Then it is my turn to give my sister a gift. I step forward and offer a small gold coin Aunt Sediqa gave me four years ago on my eighteenth birthday.

'But Leila, this is your favourite thing in the world.'

'No, sister. You are my favourite thing in the world.'

Samira looks into my eyes. I think she can see the trouble there, mixed though it is with my love for her. I think she can see that something new and powerful has come into my life, into my heart. But just at this moment she isn't free to sit me down and question me, console me, advise me.

'Beloved sister,' she says. 'Forever my beloved sister.'

---

* The elaborate floor spread used in traditional Persian weddings

The Doctor

It's a hot July evening in Mashhad, the fortieth day of observance of the death of Azita's grandfather, and with the exception of a few of the closest relatives who are still truly grieving, the mourners are eating and gossiping in the living room. I have been back and forth between Quchan and Mashhad a few times while Azita has been assisting her family with the funeral. I have said all I can say about Mr Qolizadeh's death. I am not about to give myself over to extravagant displays of grief – wailing and weeping, striking my chest with my fist to show how distressed I am. I liked the old man and I feel sad at his passing, but that's as far as I'm prepared to go. I'm sitting by myself in a secluded spot trying to read, but the heat and the clamour of traffic outside makes it impossible to concentrate.

If I can't read, maybe I can make myself useful to my wife. I find her with the others in the living room, covered from head to toe in her black chador. After almost six weeks of this semi-hysterical ritual of lamenting she seems to me aged beyond her years, her face pale and drawn with dark circles under her eyes. In her unattractive state, I feel a greater tenderness for her than when she's carefully made-up and dressed in something stylish. She asks me to find our daughter and give her some attention. Her father has complained that Newsha is being a nuisance.

'She's upset by the women crying,' Azita says. 'She doesn't understand what this is all about. And she wants to know where her great-grandfather is.'

Newsha clings to me fervently when I locate her on the floor among the mourners. I am moved, as I always am, by my daughter's beauty and innocence. And as usual when I'm in a susceptibly tender mood, I think of the child we didn't have, Azita and I, the child we aborted before we were married. I am not sentimental about terminations; I don't dwell on the spark of life in the foetus I am aborting. But nor am I indifferent to the foundational tragedy. The tiny foetus, if allowed to live, becomes a Newsha, with all her beauty and charm. It is never a happy outcome, a termination; it always saddens me. Indeed, if I were practising in a Western country and a woman came to me saying that her pregnancy was a little inconvenient, I would probably tell her to find some way to cope. In a society established on barbaric premises of sin and punishment, I am cast in a role I would never adopt in a rational, tolerant world. I must believe this about myself, or I could never look into Newsha's eyes and enjoy the love overflowing in my heart.

Azita and Newsha are to remain here in Mashhad for a few days more, while I must return to work at the hospital in Quchan. But first

I have to call in on my brother Koorosh, who has phoned me about some delicate problem. He didn't explain anything on the phone, but his evasiveness makes me sure I am about to be asked to terminate a pregnancy again. He said the 'problem' doesn't concern him, that he was asking for help on behalf of a friend.

I am to meet Koorosh at his mother-in-law's apartment rather than his own house. I arrive before him and enjoy a cup of tea with his mother-in-law, and then Koorosh turns up with his wife, Mariam. And it is Mariam, it transpires, who is making the request. As soon as her mother has excused herself, Mariam gets right to the point. Her parents have a maid, Nesa, and Nesa has a daughter by the name of Najma, sixteen years old. A few months ago, Najma had been unwise enough to go to the house of a boy she had come to know, and there she was raped by him and two of his friends. They had lured her to the house for just this purpose. Under Iranian law she was guilty of inciting rape merely by entering the house. Now she was pregnant. Her father was no longer on the scene, but Najma had a brother who would be free to cut her throat were he to find out. Najma, for her part, was planning to forestall her brother's retribution by taking her own life.

The conversation always reaches the same point whenever abortion is being proposed. I alone, the person will tell me, can save the girl or woman from death, or abandonment by her family and consignment to the streets as a prostitute, a lifetime of humiliation and dire poverty. But of course it is a very dangerous thing for me to do, so if I cannot bring myself to . . . well, they will understand. Whatever the order of words employed, they always add up to the same thing, with the person encouraging me to put my head in the noose waiting stony-faced for my decision. Usually they add, while waiting, 'And you may be sure, Doctor, that we will never tell a living soul.'

It makes me wish I had become an engineer, or a dentist, or the man who sells melons and mangos and bananas in the bazaar. I have to say, it is possible to get a little fed up with the whole business.

But what to do?

'I will have to examine her first,' I say to Mariam.

'Oh thank you, Kooshyar, thank you, thank you, we will never forget you. Nesa blesses you, Najma will owe her life to your kindness.'

My brother Koorosh has been watching me all this time with a fixed expression. He is quite sure I will agree to the request, after a certain amount of anguished hand-wringing. He knows me inside out. And I love and respect him dearly and deeply.

I perform the termination in a bedroom of Mariam's mother's apartment. Najma looks exactly like the victim she is – haunted, confused, skinny, pale, struggling through the worst nightmare she has ever experienced, wishing to be rid of the baby and yet horrified at what she is doing. The fear in her eyes burns intensely, and behind the bright flame of her dread there is a quieter one of shame. It glows unwaveringly, a pilot light of self-loathing and degradation. I know it will burn long after this ordeal and the thought makes me sick with sorrow.

The initial injection of Prostodin brings on bleeding after an hour or so, and of course cramps and searing pain. The poor child can barely believe what her body is doing. It is as if she has handed herself over to a torturer. She groans, she shrieks, she wishes she were dead. A neighbour from downstairs knocks on the door to inquire in a worried way about all the screaming. Mariam's mother explains that it is only the television – her son-in-law has turned up the volume, the silly fellow, but nobody listens to her when she complains, you know how it is . . .

The further injections bring on more bleeding, then the evacuation of foetal matter, the full miscarriage. Najma's screams shock the daylights out of Nesa, Mariam and Mariam's mother. They have no experience of this sort of trauma. They look at me, trying to judge if things are going normally. What they're surely thinking is that the girl is dying. Agony of this sort could only be followed by death, couldn't it?

I remain calm, outwardly. 'All is as it should be,' I tell them. Inside, I'm seething with emotion. Najma's screams are as hard for me to bear as they are for her mother.

Finally it is done. The baby is gone. Nesa thanks me in the most heartfelt way. Najma too attempts to convey her gratitude. Mariam and Nesa help her down the stairs and take her home. Najma's brother will never know what's happened. I am left with Mariam's mother.

She says, 'Kooshyar, you have done a good thing, a brave thing. That child will bless your name forever.'

I smile and nod as I pack up my instruments. But what I'm thinking is this: Fuck this country and fuck its laws that protect men who can do that to a child like Najma.

And this: Please God, no more days like this. I can't take any more.

Leila

You have a brother, Doctor Karimi – you have spoken of him in our conversations. I don't know how close the two of you are, but if you love him as I love my sister Samira, you'll know the grief that flooded my heart when I awoke the morning after the wedding with her gone. For so many years she was the moment of happiness I enjoyed in the first minute of each day. Oh, how can I explain it? We completed each other. We were individuals, yes, but it was Samira who provided the finishing touch to my human existence, the one who breathed confidence into me. And to have her gone – I was like one of those people who has lost a limb but can still feel pain there, all the nerves that once made the limb move having not yet accepted its absence. All the nerves of my heart craved for Samira to turn to me and say, 'Good morning, darling.

Did you have a nice sleep? What did you dream of? Tell me everything.'

Aunt Sediqa has stayed on after the wedding and it is to her I go after I've washed and dressed. She knows at a glance the troubled state of my heart. With my head against her breast I let my tears flow.

'We did everything together, but now it's only me. Who will I talk to?'

Aunt Sediqa says, 'You can call me and write to me. Maybe we can even convince your parents to let you visit once in a while.'

'Leila! Where's the tea? Where's breakfast?' Ali bellows from the kitchen. My sensitive brother, so full of understanding.

Mother is brimming with happiness. She has fulfilled one of the immemorial duties of a Persian mother by seeing her eldest daughter wed, and out of the family house and into her husband's home. Finding a husband for me will be her next mission. Then, once both daughters are married, my parents can put money aside to help Ali support his own family.

Aunt Sediqa returns to Mashhad the next day. The house is bleak, the doors and windows battened against the cold. There's no warmth from the sun, no birdsong. I open *The Prophet* and turn to the passage about joy and sorrow. *When you are joyous, look deep into your heart and you shall find it is only that which has given you sorrow that is giving you joy. When you are sorrowful look again in your heart, and you shall see that in truth you are weeping for that which has been your delight.*

It is especially hard to appreciate wisdom at the time it would be of most benefit. Decades after the struggle, yes, maybe then. But of what use is wisdom to the suffering?

The following morning, I ask permission to return my book. My mother snaps, 'Come and help me clean the basement. You and I have to do the work of three people now, and you want to run off to the library? Ridiculous.'

So I work away beside my mother in the basement for two days, aching for the reward of a thirty-minute visit to the library. When I make my request once more she looks at me in a worried way, as if she has come to think of reading and visits to the library as a type of perversion.

'Why are you so interested in books? It's not a good thing for a single girl to go out all the time.'

All the time? Dear Allah, thirty minutes a fortnight.

Appealing to my mother's high regard for money and duty, I say, 'But when I took the book out I agreed to return it on time. If I don't I'll have to pay a fine.'

She pauses to think through the implications. Then: 'I'll have Majid return the book tomorrow.'

I could weep with frustration. I desperately want to see Hamid again, even if only for a few seconds, but if I pester my mother about going out she'll only become more stubborn about it.

That evening after dinner, Mother gives the book to Majid and asks him to return it. He accepts the task with bad grace.

'Why should I return her stupid book?'

'Because you're the youngest one,' says Father, ending the conversation.

Later that night, I take *The Little Prince* out of the wardrobe, close my eyes and picture myself in Hamid's shop, his smile when I lift my eyes and meet his gaze. The pleasure I've conjured is so intense it invites a corrective. A voice whispers to me, What a naïve girl, fantasising about a handsome man in a shop. Do you think you're anything special to him? He talks to all the women like that. It helps him sell things. You're an immature girl from a boring family with nothing to offer him. You'd bore him to death.

From my mattress I can see my lovely blue shirt on a hanger.

Hamid has touched that shirt, saved it just for me. I go to the closet and press my face against it, drawing in deep breaths until I find a trace of his scent. Then I return to my bed and open *The Little Prince* to the chapter about the fox. After reading it I decide to be patient, as the fox advises the little prince to do. Every day I'll think of Hamid, and in some mysterious way he will know my thoughts and think of me too.

But what if he needs more than my thoughts to remember me? If I don't go back to see him, he might decide he's mistaken in thinking he matters to me. I have to let him know how I feel. How? A letter. Writing to him will be safe.

I search in the wardrobe for paper and a pen and return to my mattress to write. But before I put pen to paper I pause. What if he laughs at me? No, if he is that kind of man, would he think *The Little Prince* a great book? Would he have saved the shirt for me? I must be honest. I write:

Mr Hamid

This letter is from Leila. I've been to your shop a couple of times and you gave me a beautiful book, *The Little Prince*. The last time I was in your shop was about a week ago when I came to buy a shirt for my sister's wedding. You gave me an excellent price on the blue shirt. I want to tell you how much I appreciate your kindness. I'm a single girl, and I pray every day. I know it's a sin for me to talk to a man. I have never touched a man in my life, and I feel guilty writing these lines to you. But all I want to say is that since my sister has gone to her husband's house I have been lonely. I took *The Little Prince* out of its hiding place tonight and read my favourite part and thought of you. Please forgive me if I'm too forward. I don't know what's happening to me, but I have to confess I cannot stop thinking of you. I believe in my heart you are a special man. I live at 22 Shahid Hoseyni Street, and my phone number is 2223467. If you want to call, please ring between ten o'clock in the morning and two in the afternoon. If my mother or a man picks up the phone, don't say anything. I'll wait for your call for the next seven days. If you don't call, I'll understand you don't want to talk to me and I apologise for offending or harassing you. That is not my intention.

Allah be with you.

Leila

I read through what I've written and blush all over my body. This is a love letter! One of those impassioned cries from the soul that women have been addressing to their lovers for a thousand years, and longer. Look what I've said – 'I have never touched a man.' That's as good as saying, 'But I want to touch you, I want you to touch me.' It's an invitation to lovemaking. And yet I know I won't retract a single word. I'm a torch of desire even as I bow my head in shame.

I fold the paper and hide it in the wardrobe, and the next day, while my mother is preoccupied in the yard, I tuck it into an envelope, put a stamp on it and address it to Hamid's shop. As soon as my mother leaves to buy vegetables, I'll sneak out to mail it. There's a mailbox only five minutes away.

But my mother remains in the yard all morning. Maybe she'll leave after lunch. I can only pray and hope, as I always do. When the men come home for the midday meal I continue to peel the potatoes. As I finish the last one and put the paring knife down, Ali storms towards us waving something in the air.

'What is this?' he bellows.

Oh Allah, he's found my letter and is going to kill me! He shoves my copy of *The Little Prince* under my nose.

With astonishing nonchalance I say, 'Samira left that for me.' Then I realise that my letter was right under the book. By some miracle he hadn't seen it; he must have been blinded by fury. But what if his anger drives him back to tear the room apart, to see what else I'm hiding? He'll kill Hamid. He will find him easily; the envelope is addressed to him.

'Samira's book?' says Ali, grabbing my arm and forcing me to face him. 'This is a kid's book.'

I shake my head. 'No, it's a famous book that has been translated into many languages.' My mouth is dry, my face pale.

Ali leans in so close I can smell his breath. 'Why do you look so frightened?'

I stare up at him, unable to answer. But even in the midst of my dread, what goes through my mind is: Why do you think you have the right to question me in this way? Why do you think it's acceptable to behave like a baboon, ranting and snarling and baring your teeth?

He storms away and I go after him. By the time I reach him he's rifling through my wardrobe, tossing things on the floor without any compunction.

'What are you looking for?'

'My Year Twelve certificate. Mother said she put it here a couple of years ago.'

'Let me help you. I saw it when Samira and I were straightening things up.'

Ali's search has advanced to the shelf where I've stashed my letter. I pick up a stack of thick folders from the top shelf and set it on the floor. Squatting over the pile, I choose the thickest one and hold it out to my brother. 'Here, I'm sure it's in this folder.'

This is a lie, but my trick works. Ali steps away from the wardrobe and takes the folder from me. I have to hide the letter before he starts searching again. I can see it quite clearly now, but how can I conceal it with him a few feet away?

My fingers race. Finding the certificate is my only hope. As I reach deep into the back of the wardrobe, Ali roars behind me, 'This is rubbish!'

And then I see what I'm searching for, the certificate sticking out of an uneven stack of papers. 'Here,' I cry, pulling it forward and thrusting it at him.

He seizes it and walks out of the room, making no effort to thank me. Only my relief saves me from shouting at his back, 'Manners of a pig!'

I follow behind him. I know him too well to think he's forgotten about the book he found in the wardrobe.

'What's Samira's phone number?' I hear him demand of Mother.

'It's there in the book.'

I go after him into the hall and pick up a vase, as if to give the flowers in it fresh water. Then I wait out of sight to listen.

'Hello, Samira, it's me, Ali.' He asks her about the book, and I can tell from his response that she's told him it belongs to her.

Hanging up, he strides past as if even to glance at me would require more respect than he could possibly muster.

'I talked to Samira on the phone yesterday,' Mother tells me a few days later as we sit on the rug repairing a mattress. 'She's so happy. Saeed is a generous man. He even bought her a new dress.'

A few minutes later we realise we are out of thread. Mother pulls herself to her feet to go and buy more.

I've been waiting for this moment for three days. I run down the hallway to my room and retrieve the letter. I stand staring at it as if it were about to speak to me, admonish me. Fool of a girl! How old are you? Twenty-one or twelve? Your grand passion is a dangerous fantasy that could end with your throat being cut. Grow up now. Avoid the hell awaiting you.

Yes, it could use those words, with some justice. But I am ready with words of my own: Am I to endure this forever? The abuse of my boorish brothers? My father's refusal to allow me to attend university? Am I merely to avert my eyes and accept every blow aimed at me? Am I to tremble because my brother has discovered a book in my wardrobe, an innocent book, not the Kama Sutra but *The Little Prince*? Am I to be denied my rightful dignity? Remain a prisoner for life?

I hurry to the mailbox, glance around to make sure I am not being watched, put the letter to my lips then push it through the slot.

Love, more than anything else, is long periods of waiting. Is that your experience, Doctor Karimi? What I desire with all my heart is to be in Hamid's shop once more, but I have to wait. It will take two days for my letter to reach him. If he responds the instant he reads it, I'll have a two-day wait. But he might wish to think things through before he calls. One day of thinking? Two? Two days at the most, I decide. Then he will call me. So that makes a four-day wait. Or the letter might reach him in one day, and he might call without a second's reflection, which means the phone could ring any minute.

But I'm being preposterous in my impatience. The letter could not reach him in a day. And he couldn't be expected to call the instant he's read it. No, I must find the patience to wait four days.

Oh, but the waiting is an agony! I want to go to bed and sleep through all that time and wake just as the phone rings. It is too much to expect me to wait four days. It is inhuman. 'Please Allah,' I whisper in my room, 'if I have ever pleased You, let Hamid ring me now. Or if not now, within the hour. This is my prayer.'

I'm in the yard helping Mother water the plants when the phone's shrill ring breaks the silence. I almost drop the watering can in my rush to answer it.

'Hello, darling, how are you?'

'Oh, Grandmother Robabeh, it's nice to hear your voice again.' That's what I say, but what I want to shout at her is, 'Go away, ring another time. Please!' I discipline myself to chat briefly, then hand the phone despondently to my mother. She talks for forty-five minutes. What if Hamid is trying to get through? Mad with longing, I find a task for myself trimming the long branches of trees touching the roof. It's two in the afternoon when my mother hangs up the phone. There will be no call from Hamid today. I find a private moment to go to my room and scream into my pillow.

He doesn't ring the next day. I hold my head in my hands in despair. He doesn't care, he thinks I'm a stupid girl. I should kill myself now. What is the use of life to me? I am sick of myself, sick of Hamid, sick of my family, sick of life, sick of love, sick of waiting and waiting and waiting.

No call the next day either. Nor the next. The sheer exhaustion of living with a passion like this in your heart! It's as if it's a disease, trying to kill me by overthrowing my body's defences. *I want you dead*, it whispers. *That's how you honour passion, by dying of it.*

Every scenario plays through my fevered mind: Hamid chuckling quietly to himself as he reads my declaration of love; Hamid calling a friend into his shop to say, 'You must read this, it's hilarious, a foolish girl who came into my shop imagines she's in love with me.'

My humiliation deepens with the passing of each day. I look in the mirror and see the pale, pinched expression of an unattractive girl who has allowed her imagination to run away with her. I have heard of girls at pop concerts in the West who become hysterical with desire for male singers. These girls scream and weep and write extravagant letters to their idols. That's the type of naïve self-indulgence that has overtaken me. I should have remained cool and aloof, keeping my feelings private. Oh Doctor Karimi, everything about passion is painful. How can we explain our hunger for emotional chaos of this sort? Should we not run from it as we would from the plague, avoiding the weeping, the heartache? It is almost as if we ask a man holding a whip to bring it down on our soft flesh until we bleed and writhe. And yet one word from Hamid, one glance, one tender caress, and it would all have been worth it, every blow of the lash, every drop of blood.

By the seventh day I no longer listen for the phone. I am resigned to acceptance of my folly, or I believe I am. When Majid comes home and sits down for lunch, saying, 'Hurry up, I only have twenty minutes,' I ignore him. He's just another insensitive man who believes he can treat me like a slave. That's a new development: I have begun to see all men as natural tyrants. Certainly all Iranian men. I have the examples of Antoine de Saint-Exupéry and Kahlil Gibran as men of tenderness and sympathy outside Iran, but my years in this country have not provided me with a single man to match them.

'Leila, get your brother something to eat,' my mother yells at me. I dish up some chicken and rice and set it on the floor in front of him.

He scoops up a big mouthful. 'I'm so hungry I could eat a horse,' he says, rice and juice dribbling down his chin. He disgusts me. I turn away, afraid I'll vomit, and just as I reach the kitchen the phone rings.

'I've got it,' Majid says, jumping up. 'Hello?' He waits for a response. 'Hello?' He seems to be listening to someone on the other end. Is it Hamid telling him about the letter? My heartbeat changes from the moribund rate it has adopted over the past couple of days to a rapid, clamorous thudding. I look for somewhere to run.

Majid says, 'Wrong number,' and returns the phone to the cradle. He mutters, 'Stupid man.'

After days of telling myself I'm a pathetic fool for ever expecting Hamid to ring, in one second I'm hoping with all my heart that it was him on the phone, Hamid who loves me and wants to hear my voice. And immediately I despair of myself. If there is one lesson I should take from this catastrophe of mine, it is to listen to my head. I have a good mind, I know I do. Do some justice to your wits, Leila (so I scold myself), by making use of them. Your heart is a dunce. Your head is much more reliable. The call was a wrong number. Hamid does not love you. What hope for you, if you are forever ruled by your heart? Or indeed for the world? A revolution with a great many vile features was brought to this country by people who were ruled by their passions. Passion is a donkey.

Yes, those are the very words I use, Doctor. I chastise myself for hours. But passion laughs at mere common sense. It knows it will win. And in bed that night I throw myself from side to side, looking for comfort. I picture Hamid phoning to say, 'Leila, I intend to come to your house and talk in a most serious way to your father. I wish to be accepted as your suitor. I will say to your father, Honoured Sir, I saw your daughter in my shop the other day and I was moved by her modesty and the light in her eyes. Honoured Sir, I have made inquiries and am told that your daughter is unmarried, as I am. I want to do everything in the proper way. Will you accept me as a suitor for your daughter's hand?'

The next day, my mother wakes me early. 'Your Aunt Parvin is coming for dinner tonight and we need to get an early start.'

I barely finish my small breakfast of tea and orange slices before Mother puts me to work sweeping, washing, cooking and dusting.

By noon the house sparkles, but she's still not satisfied.

'Wipe the windows. But use old newspapers, not a towel. The towel will streak the glass.'

'I know, I know,' I mutter under my breath. Next to cleaning the basement full of spiders, doing the windows is the chore I hate most.

'And daughter, start at the top and work to the bottom.'

I pull a chair close to the window and climb up to begin. I've just commenced when the phone rings.

'Get that, Leila,' my mother yells.

I sigh and climb back down to pick up the phone.

Nobody answers.

'Hello?' I repeat.

'Leila, is that you?'

I drop the spraypack of glass cleaner. It's him, oh Allah, it's Hamid. And I can't think of a single word to say.

'Can you talk?'

'Yes. Yes, I can talk.' My mouth is painfully dry. My hands tremble so violently I have to hold the phone with both hands.

'I got your letter,' he says. 'I called the other day but a man answered. I was scared to call again. I didn't want you to get into trouble.'

'Thank you,' I murmur. So it *was* him. And he hadn't given up at the first sign of trouble.

'Listen, I'm going to give you the phone number for my shop. You can call me anytime you get a chance.'

He gives me the number, but I'm so anxious I have to ask him to repeat it. My mother will come in any moment to find out who I'm talking to. 'I've got it, Hamid.'

There's silence until Hamid asks, 'Why don't you say anything?' He sounds amused, and I giggle nervously.

'My mother is too close. I can't.'

'Okay, I understand.' He lowers his voice. 'Your letter was lovely. Honest and real, and I want you to know I feel the same about you.'

My legs give way. I sink to the floor. 'Thank you,' I say softly.

'I want to say more, but it sounds like you can't talk right now. Call me when you can, Leila?'

'Yes, Hamid, I'll call you.' I'm about to hang up when he stops me.

'Leila . . . don't go. I just want to hold the phone while you're on the other end.'

'But say something,' I whisper. 'Please, say something.'

'I wanted to say that . . . I wanted to say that you're beautiful, Leila. So beautiful.' Then he hangs up.

I keep holding the phone after the line disconnects, unwilling to let go.

'Who was that?' my mother calls from the kitchen.

'Another wrong number,' I shout back, but my joy spills over and becomes laughter of pure delight.

My mother walks in and looks at me with her head to one side. 'And what's so funny about that?'

'Nothing, Mother. The person had a funny accent, that's all.'

I leap back onto the chair to continue cleaning the windows. All the magic has returned to the world. The colours I can see – just the drab greys and browns, the mild blue of the sky, the sketchy white clouds, the neighbour's green curtains – seem like the colours of a carnival. My body is weightless. I am certain that if I wished to I could ascend gracefully to the ceiling. Oh, the ache of the smile on my face, I can't subdue it. Little giggles of the most wonderful happiness I have ever known keep escaping my lips. Hamid thinks I am beautiful! In the thousands of years of human history, has there ever been such joy in the heart of a woman? Never in the universe!

My mother returns to check my work. 'That window is clean, Leila.

Do you want to wear the glass away? What are you doing?'

'Sorry, Mother.'

'Wear your nice dress tonight. Kazem is coming too.'

I say nothing. She knows I can't stand my cousin. He is twenty-nine and owns his own business, but he's still as obnoxious as he's been all his life. He has no respect for women and treats them with contempt.

'Did you hear me, Leila?'

'Yes, I heard you. But you know I don't like Kazem. He says ugly things about women.'

'Leila, you're a mature girl now and old enough to know that love follows marriage, not the other way around. I didn't like your father either, but we got married and we have been happy.'

'Marriage?' I'm horrified. 'Who's talking about marriage? To Kazem? That's impossible!' I pick up the chair and stomp into the kitchen.

'Watch your tongue, daughter. You'll do what we decide is best for you. Don't you forget that.'

Kazem? Marry that toad? I'd rather be dead. I know who I want to marry. And I know who wants to marry me. The difference between Hamid and Kazem is the difference between fresh sparkling water that quenches your thirst on a hot day and a stagnant pool coated in green slime.

But I dutifully dress nicely under my chador. Not for Kazem – for Hamid. He's the man I will be thinking of when I sit down to dinner. When Kazem looks me up and down in that disgusting, groping way he has, as if he's removing my clothes with his eyes, I'll be holding a dialogue with Hamid in my heart.

Kazem's mother, my Aunt Parvin, constantly praises her grotesque son, his handsome form, his accomplishments. What can I say? I see him for what he is. I want to stand up at the dinner table and say, 'Aunt Parvin, if you think this grunting little pig you have given birth to is handsome and clever, I pity you with all my heart.' But I say not a word. In the silent intimacy of my conversation with Hamid, I say a great deal.

My brother Ali asks Kazem how his business is faring, and Kazem takes the opportunity to tell us all that he's insanely successful, about to buy a new apartment, and hopes to marry.

Ali asks, 'Do you have someone in mind?'

'My mother's been suggesting your sister Leila. I don't know. We'll see what Allah plans for us.'

I burn with anger. What, am I to be discussed as a candidate for marriage with this oaf as if I were some sort of mute beast?

'I have to attend to something,' I say, excusing myself from the table. I go straight to my room, bury my face in my hands and groan. Then I pray, not to Allah but to Hamid. 'Come to my father's house, my beloved. Come and ask for my hand. If Kazem asks first, I will be compelled to marry him. And on my wedding night, I will cut my own throat and bleed to death thinking of you.'

At last I hear the front door closing behind Aunt Parvin and her repulsive son. A minute later, my mother throws my door open and stands with her hands on her hips. 'Daughter, you shame me. Hiding yourself in your room while we have guests!'

'I don't like to be around Kazem. He's a pig.'

My mother gasps at my temerity. She hurries to my mattress and squats down beside me. Her black eyes are full of menace. 'Listen to me, Leila. If they ask for your hand and you refuse, you'll destroy the whole family. Is that something you want to do?'

I shake my head miserably.

'You'd better not. Look at me, daughter.'

I lift my gaze and face my mother's threat.

'I'm warning you, here and now. Your father and I will make a decision. And you will abide by it. Do you understand me?'

When I say nothing she seizes my chin and holds it tight. 'Do you understand me?'

'Yes, I understand you. But I still say Kazem is a pig.'

She looks as though she wants to lift her hand and slap me hard, but she regains control of herself and sits back, studying my face. 'Say your prayers and ask Allah to help you be a good daughter, worthy of our love and respect.'

I am more aware than ever of the meagre few minutes I have alone in a week. I'm always in the house, and my mother is always nearby. For unmarried young women in Iran, it is an obligation to remain within sight of at least one parent on a daily basis. If we were permitted to get about freely, who knows what horrifying habits we might adopt. We might smile wantonly. We might flirt with a man, a sin to make the angels weep and the portals of paradise topple. I have thought a lot about the profound mistrust of the appetites of women and men that lies at the foundation of Islam, and it seems to me that my faith, along with many others, I am sure, is a faith of denial.

Four days pass between Hamid's phone call and any opportunity I have to call him back. I pray for my mother to go out on some errand for half an hour and leave me alone. At last, on the morning of the fourth day, she takes herself to the market to buy tomatoes and rice.

I rush to the telephone, making sure I'm in a position to see through the window should she return sooner than expected, take a deep breath and dial. He answers on the second ring.

'Hamid? It's me, Leila.'

'Leila? Hold on a second.'

I can hear the phone being placed on the counter. I hear a woman arguing with Hamid. 'If the shirt isn't for sale, why do you have it in your window?'

'It's the last one in the shop. I can't sell it until I can order more. If you want to place a special order —'

'Forget it,' the woman says. 'I'll shop somewhere else.'

I shouldn't have called and taken him away from his work. Now he's lost a sale. As soon as he picks the phone up again, I apologise. 'Oh Hamid, I'm so sorry I phoned when you have business to attend to.'

'Don't worry about business. I want to talk to you, Leila. How have you been?'

'I've been well. How about you?'

'Good, too. Working hard.' His voice is light. Happy, even.

'Are you smiling?' I ask.

'Yes, why do you ask?'

'I can see it. I can see your smile.'

Hamid laughs at that.

'How can you be so relaxed and cool?' I ask.

'It's my nature. Aren't you relaxed?'

'I'm so nervous I can't think straight.'

'Why?'

Is he being disingenuous? 'Because . . . well, because I'm a girl, and this is the first time in my life I've ever . . .'

'Ever what?'

'Ever had a conversation like this with a man.'

Hamid lowers his voice. 'Don't worry, everything's going to be all right.'

'How can you be sure? Do you know how dangerous this is for me?'

'Yes, I know exactly how dangerous it is. But Leila, don't worry.

Everything will be all right, I promise you.'

I jump in alarm as I hear the door open. 'I have to go,' I whisper.

'No, wait —'

'I can't. I have to go.' As I hang up the phone I hear him call out, 'I miss you!'

I dash into the kitchen and open the oven, pretending to be checking on the eggplant casserole.

I stay awake for hours after I go to bed, playing the conversation over and over in my head. There's so much I want to talk to him about. I need an hour on the phone with him, two hours. I toy with the idea of asking Hamid to ask my father to marry me, but I know I could never do that. It's up to the man to make that move. But if he comes to ask for my hand, I'll jump into his arms.

I reach Hamid on the phone again a week later, when Mother goes out for a *rozeh* with women in the neighbourhood. The women will have tea and listen to a mullah preach. At the end of the *rozeh*, everyone will make a *nazr*. I know my mother's *nazr* will most likely involve me and marriage. She asks if I want to go with her but I tell her I have to finish sewing the sheets. This is a lie, but my mother accepts it.

Once she's gone I dial Hamid's number and on the third ring he picks up. He's been waiting for my call for days, he tells me.

'This is the first chance I've had.'

'Your first chance?'

'Hamid, I live with my parents and three brothers. I have no freedom. I can't pick up the phone whenever I wish.'

'A big family. And where's everybody now?'

'My father and brothers are at work, and my mother has gone to a *rozeh*. She'll be back soon, but I have a few minutes.' I pause, then add,

'I'm sorry I had to hang up like that last time, but my mother came in. If she knew I was talking to you . . .'

'I understand. You have to be very careful.'

We make small talk, but even this inconsequential stuff is sheer delight to me. Such a volume of longing dwells in me for this type of intimacy; it's like a vast dam of emotion, and now I have opened the floodgates just a fraction. Little by little, the tenderness of his voice leads me on from small talk to confession.

'All I can do is think of you. Every moment of the day, I live for the chance to call you. Please don't think I'm silly for telling you this, Hamid.'

He doesn't reply immediately, and a sudden panic takes hold of me. 'I'm sorry. I shouldn't have said that. It was too forward, and now you'll think I'm strange.'

'No. I was smiling too hard to speak. I feel exactly the same way. From the first day I saw you with your orange lollies for that little urchin, I liked you. I wanted to know all about you. That's why I bought the book for you. Leila, I think about you constantly. Constantly.'

'Thank you,' I whisper, and a type of slow ecstasy spreads through my veins. Such happiness had seemed impossible, and now here it is. Nothing I have ever read about love has prepared me for the joy of it. I think, This is what life means. This is the one great thing we are meant to understand. This is everything, everything.

Hamid has a plan. He thinks it is too risky for me to keep coming to his shop. Someone will notice the frequency of my visits. He wants me to come to his house.

'Hamid, how can I? My father and my brothers would beat me half to death just for talking to you on the phone. If they knew I went to your house, they would murder me. Truly, they would murder me.'

But he has such convincing things to say about the plan. We will be able to talk for hours without interruption. 'So many things I want to tell you, Leila. How can I tell you them at the shop, with customers coming and going and watching us suspiciously? And Leila, my heart will burst if I can't speak to you in a private way. I'm not exaggerating. My heart will burst.'

'Hamid, this is so dangerous, really so dangerous.'

'Coming to my shop is even more dangerous, Leila. Am I never to talk to you for more than five minutes? How can I live like that?'

I'm standing on the edge of an abyss. The far side is not close – but I could leap it if I tried. Or I could fail and plunge to my death. Such a leap calls more for faith than physical strength. I close my eyes for a few seconds and summon all my courage.

'This may be the most foolish thing I've ever done, but yes, I will do it. Give me the address. I'll come to your house.'

'Oh Leila, it's such a relief to hear you say that. To sit and talk to you, to see your face, the light in your eyes, your beauty – this will be heaven.'

He gives me his address and asks when I will come. I don't know, of course, but I promise to come as soon as I can. I hear his long sigh of release. I feel as if I have become some sort of stringed instrument resting on the ledge of an open window, and Hamid's sigh is a warm breeze that passes over the strings and creates a low, soulful music.

His final words before my mother's return forces me to hang up are, 'I bless you, Leila. I bless you.'

Through persistence, I win my mother's approval to go to the library for a new book. She finds a dozen excuses to keep me at home but I patiently overcome each one. She says that Majid will get me a book, and I point out that he wouldn't have the faintest idea what I read.

He'll come back with a story about serial killers, I tell her. Then she says that if people see me visiting the library so often they'll think I do nothing but read.

'So often?' I exclaim. 'Four times a year? Is that often?'

She says, 'Whenever you feel like reading a book, you should pray to Allah to make the desire go away.'

What I want to do when I hear her say this is go to the window, open it wide and scream for an hour. But instead I say, 'The stories I read would please Allah in His heaven. He would say, Look at that child reading *The Little Prince*. How this delights Me.'

'Do you dare to put words into the mouth of Allah? Daughter, you surprise me!'

'Mother, Allah wants me to read. He told me in a dream.'

'Is that true? Well, I have also had a dream,' my mother says. 'I dreamt that a snake came into the garden and bit you. You became so sick I thought you would die. I will go to the dream reader and ask her what this means.'

'But can I go to the library? For a short time? Please?'

She casts about for new reasons to deny me – it's too windy outdoors, I might get run over by a car, it could start raining. In the end she relents. I conceal my delight.

I hurry to the library through a flurry of yellow and brown leaves falling from the plane trees, and a cool breeze tossing the fabric of my chador about, rushing against my cheeks. I quickly choose a book that will justify my visit, *The Little Black Fish* by Samad Behrangi.

Mrs Salimi endorses my choice. 'A wonderful story. Sad, though. Have you read this writer before?'

When I say no she tells me this book will be a good start. 'You'll love it, Leila, I'm sure.'

The whole transaction lasts less than two minutes. I hurry from the library to Shahid Goli Street, to Hamid's house. It's a very plain dwelling, painted white like most others in the street. The door has been left ajar for me. I push it open a little further. Hamid is standing at the end of a short hallway.

'Come in, Leila,' he whispers.

I close the door and walk towards him with a smile. It's as if I could stroll straight into his arms, hold his face in my hands and kiss him. But I don't, of course. I take small, timid steps, only just daring to lift my gaze and stare straight into his eyes. He's stylishly dressed in a light brown shirt and grey slacks. He smells of patchouli and lime.

'Leila, you look beautiful. The wind has made your cheeks red, and your eyes are sparkling.'

We both laugh, but softly. There's more romance in the moment than either of us could do justice to, though I know that if he tried to kiss me I wouldn't resist. I *want* him to kiss me, but at the same time I want him to feel too shy for that yet. I've only discovered in the past few weeks how astonishingly simple and so crazily complex love can be. I crave contradictory responses from Hamid – boldness and shyness, daring and caution. I want him to be both eloquent and tongue-tied by emotion. I wish he'd lift my scarf off my hair, but I also need him to show a sincere respect for my modesty. And another strange thing: although I am a novice at romance, I still feel as if my heart and body know exactly what to do. That's the simple part. The complex part is that I would run a mile if he said, 'My dear, I am so aroused by your beauty that I can barely control myself.' What I desire of him is patience, endless patience. I want him to go to my father, speak meekly of his wish to marry me, and then, months later, when he is ready, take me in his arms on our wedding night. I will wait for him.

He leads me into a large room with light streaming in through windows that reach almost from wall to wall. Gauzy curtains cover the glass. Hamid gestures for me to sit down on the sofa and I hesitantly lower myself. I'm not used to furniture – we sit on the floor in our house – and I shift to get a better grip on my chador, making sure it covers me completely.

'Would you like coffee or tea?'

'No, thank you.' I would love a drink, but I'm too shy to accept one.

Hamid smiles. 'I'm going to have orange juice. Could I get you some too?'

It seems impolite to say no to everything he offers, so I nod, and watch him stride into the kitchen. I know my mother would gasp at the modern style of this place. She wouldn't let herself dream of owning anything as beautiful as the white cabinets and shiny chrome appliances. Everything in the house is sparkling and new, like in the slick American magazine I saw at Aunt Sediqa's.

'Relax a little, Leila,' Hamid calls from the kitchen. 'Say something.'

I feel that I'm disappointing him. 'I'm fine,' I call back. 'It's only that I've never been here before and, well, I don't have much time. I just came to say hello.'

He comes back with the juice, puts my glass on a side table and lowers himself casually into a chair. 'Did you go to the library?' he asks.

I take the book out of my chador and show him.

'*The Little Black Fish*,' he says, taking it. 'Such a sad story. It's about a little child. In fact, it's about our lives. I think Samad was one of our best writers. It's a shame they killed him, like so many other bright people in this country.'

'Samad Behrangi was killed?'

'Oh yes. Assassinated.'

I would like to know more but I'm too shy to pursue the subject. Women are not meant to comment on such things. 'You know so much about books,' I say instead. 'My father and brothers have no use for them.'

Hamid smiles. 'I confess I love reading. It relaxes me and I learn from it. It's odd, I'm a businessman but I love literature. I always wanted to become a writer or open a bookshop, but my fate was to own a boutique and sell clothes.'

'When do you have to go back to your shop?'

'I have plenty of time. One of my friends is looking after it. I had him there on hand in case you phoned. And you did.'

I yearn to spend the entire afternoon with this charming, softly spoken man. We have so much to talk about, so much to learn about each other.

Hamid hands the book back. 'If you go home without this, your mother will know you were up to something.' Then he says, 'Leila, what are your plans for the future?'

I take a cool sip of juice. Is he going to talk about marriage right here and now? What will I say if he does? But I'm jumping way ahead. I'd better just answer his question.

'I'm not sure what I'll do.'

'You must have some kind of plan? You're a smart girl and so pretty. I don't want to embarrass you, but you are so beautiful it's impossible not to mention it.'

I've blushed crimson, and I struggle to change the subject back to my plans. 'I'd like to go to university and become a teacher, but my parents won't let me.' Then I dare to add, 'I'm hoping that when I get married, my husband will allow me to study. I adore children and I'd love to teach them.'

Hamid adopts a thoughtful expression. 'You know,' he says, 'it's a very sad thing how strict so many of our people are. It's almost the twenty-first century. Women all over the world have the same freedoms as men, but here in Iran we still suppress women, rob them of liberty. It's tragic.'

Doctor Karimi, you could not possibly imagine how shocked I was to hear Hamid say this. The very sentiments my heart was so familiar with. When my brothers bullied me in their coarse way, I consoled myself with these same thoughts. Oh, dear Allah, to have a husband who treated me as an equal!

And yet images fill my mind of government spokesmen on television warning against dangerous liberal radicals who seek to plunge a dagger into the heart of the Islamic republic. Surely the government will uncover Hamid's beliefs and hang him in public. I want to caution him, remind him that people have been put to death for saying such things about the rights of women, but I am afraid he will think me uneducated, a country bumpkin.

'It's late,' I say, getting up from the sofa. 'I have to go.'

'Already?' Hamid's shoulders droop with disappointment. 'I wish you could stay, but I don't want you to get into trouble.'

He rises gracefully and waits for me to go down the hallway. At the door I hear him behind me. He says, 'This is for you,' and when I turn he offers me a single red rose. 'Take it, please.'

The scent overwhelms me. I reach out as if under a spell and for a second Hamid's hand touches mine. Just that brief contact of skin on skin arouses in me the passion I feel when I am alone and picture Hamid's face, his hands, his lips.

'Thank you,' I whisper. I lower my head and as I slip outside I lift the flower to my nose and inhale its heady perfume. I have never before drunk in the aroma of anything so intoxicating. Then I hold it under my chador, pressing it against my heart, and all the way home I go over every word, every look, every gesture of our time together. I can still feel his touch. But I realise I cannot bring the rose home. There is no possible way to explain it. I find a quiet nook, take my book out from under my chador, carefully peel the petals off and let them fall between the pages.

The house is empty when I reach home. I go to my room and remove my chador, open the book and press my face to the petals. Then I transfer them to *The Little Prince* and put the book near my bed. I lie down with my head on the side so I can see it.

I say it aloud, the words so sweet they're like warm honey in my mouth. 'He is my love, my love.'

The Doctor

Another one.

I have come to know when a patient intends to ask me to perform a termination. There is always a hesitancy, an attempt to say what must be said in a roundabout way. The expectation of the patient is that I will grasp the nettle and say, 'Oh, you're talking about a termination.' The patient may or may not be the woman who hopes to have her pregnancy ended. I may find myself talking to a friend, or the friend of a friend, or the father of the baby, or a friend of the father, the uncle, the brother, the cousin . . . And as soon as I pick up the signals, decipher the code, I feel sick. My thoughts on the matter are still conflicted, despite my commitment to help whenever I can. And it's a worry to me that so many people approach me to ask about a termination. They would not even hint at the procedure unless they felt fairly confident of the outcome. Any doctor could have them prosecuted. So why ask me?

I tell those I help that they must never, never implicate me, never say a word about what I've provided. But they do, they tell others. I'm sure they don't go about referring by name to this cooperative Doctor Karimi who aborted their mistress's baby, their daughter's, but one day a friend will mention that he has been forced to look for a doctor who performs a certain procedure, because his brother, his father, his son, his uncle has been foolish and made a girl pregnant, and now they both face terrible consequences. And I am becoming known as an abortionist. The police don't know, or I would have been arrested by now, but by the looks of things quite a number of people do. And one day, the police will know too.

This time it's a Mr Najarian, an unsmiling fellow in his mid-fifties with a neatly trimmed grey beard, grey hair, black suit, white shirt. He seats himself opposite me, responds without much enthusiasm to a few words of greeting. He is in a controlled state of distress.

'And what brings you here to Quchan, Mr Najarian? You are not one of my regular patients.'

He puts a hand to his mouth and coughs nervously, clears his throat. He turns his gaze to the window, then back to me.

'I have a special request for you, Doctor Karimi. A woman is . . . in trouble.'

In trouble. How many times a year in Iran, or indeed all over the world, is a pregnancy spoken of in this way? Nothing in nature is more consistent with survival than pregnancy, and while I don't mean to deny that a pregnancy is often wonderful news, just as often it's 'trouble'. The foetus knows nothing about it. It strives for growth, it feeds, it sleeps, it extends its limbs, it thrives in the paradise of the uterus. Only out in the dangerous world is it grieved over, resented, hated, feared. Najarian's expression of distaste blended with dread tells me I am about to hear a story from the dangerous world. He might be the father. He might have been fooling around with a servant, with a neighbour's daughter, with his wife's niece, with his own daughter. The sex may have been consensual or it may have been rape.

'Go on,' I say.

'I have a hotel in Mashhad. Fifty people work for me. One is a middle-aged widow named Samaneh. She's just a cleaner.'

He puts his hand to his mouth and coughs once more. 'Samaneh has a daughter. Her name is Esmat and she's only fifteen. The silly girl has been seeing a man and now she's pregnant.'

'Indeed?' I say.

'Doctor Karimi, you're our only hope. She can't keep this baby.'

'Why not? She can marry the man. Many girls marry at fifteen in Iran.'

'Doctor, please understand. The man is old, and he's already married. He isn't going to marry Esmat. She is desperate. If her brother finds out, he will kill her.'

I shake my head. 'Mr Najarian, you know terminating a pregnancy is illegal. I apologise, but I'm afraid I can't help you.'

Putting his hands on my desk, he lowers his head. He wants to convey his helplessness, and also his respect for my position as surgeon. 'I know the law. But if we can't fix this, the girl will kill herself, or be killed by her brother.'

This man can, I think, detect in me the character of someone who can be persuaded against his better judgement. Or at the very least, he can see that I am not obdurate. And I, in turn, can see in him a man fully capable of deceit. I don't believe his story. It is quite possible he's a police agent, attempting to entrap me. Such things happen. Or it may be that he himself is the father of this child. He reminds me Mullah Hassan, the sheikh of our mosque in the slum, the religious leader of the whole community. Mullah Hassan was an expert at two things: praying to Allah and molesting little girls. The former was his badge of honour, but of the latter it was forbidden to speak.

'Mr Najarian, what makes you think I could help this girl with a termination? I've never done anything like that.'

He sits upright in his chair once more. 'Doctor Karimi, please don't be offended, but I know about you. I know you terminated a ten-week pregnancy for Akram Basiri more than a year ago in Mashhad.'

I betray nothing, but Najarian has caught me off guard. I remember the woman he's referring to. She came to me with her fiancé to terminate her pregnancy before their marriage. The couple were in exactly the same situation Azita and I had been, and I didn't turn them away.

'Akram is my niece,' says Najarian. 'She gave me your name.'

'I see.'

'Doctor, I've come a long way. Don't send me back to Esmat with bad news.'

I accept that Najarian is not a police agent. But why is this wealthy man so concerned for one of his cleaner's daughters? I ask him as much.

'Doctor Karimi, I'm a devout Muslim. I'm paying for the cost of this procedure. I want to assure you that everything stays between us. You don't need to worry about anything.'

'I feel sorry for the girl,' I tell him, 'but no, I can't help.'

He takes a deep breath. He closes his eyes for a few seconds. Then: 'Doctor Karimi, please. I'm begging you. This girl will surely kill herself unless you help her. Her mother won't be able to live with herself if her daughter takes her own life. She's a good, hardworking woman and has asked for my help. Please, prevent this tragedy. She is a human being!'

He's laying it all bare. If I asked him to get down on his knees and kiss my shoes, he would. I'm moved – I admit it – by the change in him. He came here with his pride intact, now he's begging.

'This is what I will do,' I tell him. 'I will give it two days' thought. Call me after that.'

'Doctor, can I take back better news than this? Please?'

'Two days.'

His eyes are overflowing with tears. 'Doctor, I beg you, don't forsake this foolish girl. I beg you.'

'Two days, Mr Najarian.'

He nods, wipes his eyes with his fingers. 'Very well, then. Two days. I thank you, Doctor.'

He knows that I will say yes. I know it myself. Why do I insist on the two-day wait? To convince myself that I am about to make a sober judgement after weighing up all the risks? To show myself that I cannot be swayed by what may be no more than a sob story? Why bother? An old man weeps in front of you, and you put your head in a noose to ease his suffering. Why pretend you are about to use your mature judgement? You have no mature judgement.

Ambiguity of motive plagues me. Do I take these risks simply to convince myself I'm a good person? Perhaps I have some sort of martyr complex working away in the deepest recesses of my subconscious. Perhaps I expect to be caught one day and tried, then marched to the scaffold where I will stand radiating the white light of the pure-at-heart even as the noose is slipped over my head. I don't know, I don't know. A few months ago, I was asked to restore the virginity of a girl who had surrendered to her passion for a young man even though she was promised in marriage to another, much older man. She feared that this man who was to become her husband would discover she was no longer a virgin and spurn her, leaving her family covered in ignominy. I did all I could, but the surgery failed and the girl took her own life. I grieved for days. I find it next to impossible to say no to anyone who faces such pain, such ruin, but maybe it would take greater strength of character to say no. After all, do I expect to change the politics of such a hidebound regime as this one that rules Iran? There is no chance of me making even a minute difference in that way. Should I not simply accept that fact? Would that not be the mature thing to do?

When Najarian calls me two days later, I tell him I will see Esmat. A cry of relief comes down the line. 'Doctor Karimi, I bless you!' I tell him to bring her to my house in a week's time, and again he gives a cry of relief.

I have told my wife about Esmat, and that I will be performing a termination here in our home. I do not normally tell her when I'm about to do such things: she assumes that I've done only two or three in the past, and gotten away with them for various reasons. But I cannot do this one at the patient's house, my preferred option, and my private surgery is too risky for an illegal procedure (there are other offices in the building, and patients can arrive at any moment), so I need to do it at home. That left me with no choice but to confide in Azita. She was furious, raging about my irresponsibility and selfishness, and wrung from me a promise never to perform another, considering how dangerous it would be for her and Newsha if I were caught. Azita would be not much more than a beggar for the rest of her life. Even her family would likely disown her.

On the day I see Esmat, Azita takes herself off with Newsha to visit relatives. She doesn't want to be anywhere near the place.

Najarian arrives on time with Esmat. I am surprised to see her mother, Samaneh, with her. I'd imagined that part of the reason the termination was so important was to keep Esmat's condition a secret from Samaneh. But there's no time to ponder this.

The first step is awkward for everyone. I need to make sure Esmat isn't more than twelve weeks pregnant. Women have lied to me about this in the past, to convince me to go ahead with the termination. Esmat, shy and embarrassed, holds her head down. I lead her to the room I've equipped with a gynaecology bed and a spotlight. I ask her to lie down and she doesn't move.

Samaneh steps forward and speaks firmly to her daughter, not without sympathy and concern. 'Do what he says. He's a doctor. We talked about this.'

Hesitantly Esmat lies down, clutching her chador around her. Najarian watches nervously. I wish he hadn't come into the room with them, but it would be disrespectful to ask him to leave. I feel Esmat's abdomen through the fabric and am relieved to find she is clearly less than twelve weeks. I tell her mother, 'She's too thin to handle much bleeding. She might end up requiring oxygen and special medications that I don't have here.'

Najarian responds for the mother. 'She'll be fine, Doctor.'

Now Samaneh grabs my arm. 'Doctor Karimi, my daughter is strong. She can handle it, please just help us.'

The termination will be started by injecting Prostodin. Severe abdominal pain and vomiting will follow as the uterus contracts and stops supplying blood to the foetus. I'll have to inject Esmat almost hourly until she starts bleeding and miscarries. Some women need intravenous fluids because the medication can cause a serious drop in blood pressure. Many faint from the pain and bleeding, and as if that weren't enough, the vomiting causes severe dehydration but the patient can't drink anything, because fluids only increase the vomiting.

It's a hideous procedure to experience and to watch, but it's generally safer than dilating the cervix, scraping the uterus with a curette, then suctioning the embryo from it.

'Is your daughter allergic to anything?' I ask Samaneh.

'She's allergic to penicillin, honey, eggs, and some other medications that I can't remember.'

I think, Okay, that's it. I won't proceed. I once gave Prostodin to a forty-year-old married woman who almost died from anaphylactic shock, even though on that occasion I had the right medications on hand and the woman was strong. I can't take such a risk with someone's life again.

'I'm sorry,' I tell them, 'but I can't help you. I have something that would make Esmat miscarry but I can't use it without knowing if she's allergic to it. If she is, she could go into shock.'

Najarian steps closer and takes my hand in his two hands. 'Please! She'll be fine.'

'Mr Najarian, we're talking about her life.'

'Is there any other way, Doctor?' Samaneh pleads.

'I can use a curette, which means opening her cervix, but it's difficult in Esmat's case.'

'Why, Doctor? Could she die?'

I am encouraged that at least someone is concerned for poor Esmat's life. 'This is her first pregnancy and her cervix is closed, so I'd have to sedate her to open it. I'd have to use devices that are painful, and sedating her without any oxygen or resuscitation equipment is almost as dangerous as injecting her with Prostodin.'

Najarian interrupts again. 'She can handle this, Doctor. Pay no attention to how thin she is. She is very strong.'

I shake my head. 'No, I can't take the risk.'

Najarian reaches into his pocket and takes out a wad of cash. 'Here,

Doctor. This is seventy thousand toman. Please, do it.'

'No, I'm sorry.'

'Please do it,' whispers Esmat from the bed. 'I'll be okay.'

I turn to her. She is sitting clutching her black chador around her thin body. She looks so vulnerable, and her eyes are so desperate. Her lips tremble as she tries to smile at me bravely.

Here's the situation: if I go ahead, Esmat could die. If I don't, she will very likely kill herself. I go to my cupboard and select emergency injections, syringes, intravenous fluid and cannulas.

Najarian can't contain his relief. 'Thank you, Doctor, thank you, thank you.' He removes himself to the living room.

The procedure becomes an emotional marathon. I tell Esmat what I intend to do, detailing each stage. She listens as if I'm describing the mechanics of a lunar landing. When I explain the evacuation of the uterus by means of suction, she grasps what I've been talking about for the first time and a look of horror replaces her blank incomprehension. She and her mother have followed my instructions to the point where the wretched girl is lying on the bed with the lower part of her body naked. But the suctioning of the foetus from the womb is too much for her. She leaps up, searches about wildly for some avenue of escape, then crouches in a corner, heaving with sobs.

Her mother says, 'Child, this is our last chance!'

Esmat shakes her head. Samaneh tries to haul her up from the floor, without success, sobbing herself by now. I hang back, half hoping the girl will get her way and they will all go home, relieving me of any further responsibility. Every so often I utter a few ineffectual words of caution: 'If you can't go ahead with this, it might be for the best . . .'

Then Najarian storms in from the living room, seizes the sobbing Esmat and carries her to the bed.

'There is no other way,' he hisses. 'Silly girl! Are you tired of your life?'

I attempt to intervene but he is in a transport of rage.

'Okay, no more!' I shout. 'She's not ready for this. No more!'

Najarian turns to me, his expression divided between terror and fury. He plunges his hand into his pocket and brings out that great wad of banknotes again. 'Eighty thousand – take it!'

'Put your money away. This is a nightmare. Can't you see how frightened the girl is?'

But he presses the money on me, pleading. I refuse, and refuse, over and over.

Then Esmat speaks up in a small, agonised squeak. 'Do it. Do it, please. I trust you, Doctor. Please make it stop.'

Najarian, Samaneh and I stand silent. Esmat is still weeping, her shoulders jerking with the rigour of her ordeal.

Najarian speaks first. 'You heard her, Doctor. Please do what you must.'

Samaneh, pale with distress, nods her head. 'Please go ahead, Doctor. I beg of you.'

Against my better judgement I commence the procedure. I put a sphygmomanometer cuff around Esmat's right arm to check her blood pressure. I take the cap off a cannula and tie a tourniquet around her left arm. She manages a small smile, doing her best to be brave as I insert the cannula into a vein.

'Now I'm going to put in the speculum and have a look,' I explain. I rub gel on the speculum and slowly insert it, aware it will be quite uncomfortable for a fifteen-year-old who has never given birth before. 'You're doing fine,' I tell her, sounding far more confident than I feel. 'Now I'm going to give you some medication to relax you. Don't fight it, just relax.' I know she could go into respiratory arrest with this drug, in which case I will lose her.

Sweat trickles down my forehead. I've been in many dangerous situations before, but sedating a patient at home is one of the most stressful things I have ever attempted. When Esmat falls into a light sleep I check her blood pressure and listen to her heart rate. I monitor her breathing carefully. Everything seems well within normal range.

Excusing myself, I leave the room to get a drink of water while the medication takes effect. In the hall I find Najarian pacing nervously.

'How is she, Doctor?' he asks anxiously.

'Fine for now. I've sedated her and will do the termination in a few minutes.'

'Thank you so much, Doctor,' he says one more time. 'I think I'll get going. I have to be home before eight tonight. My family's waiting for me. I have to drive back to Mashhad. Samaneh will take Esmat back.'

What the hell? This man has brought them all the way here, has all but forced Esmat to terminate the pregnancy despite considerable risk, is willing to pay a large sum of money, and now he's leaving them to find their own way back to a city nearly 150 kilometres away?

'Go, then,' I tell him.

'A thousand thanks, Doctor. I can't tell you how —'

'If you're going, go.'

Back in the room, I check Esmat again. She is still doing fine, by some miracle. I put on a fresh gown and sterile gloves, preparing mentally for the first and most difficult stage of the procedure. It will also be the most painful one for Esmat, and requires intense concentration on my part. If I slip up, or move too suddenly, severe damage and heavy bleeding will result.

I work in silence. Samaneh seems to be struggling in some way herself. Finally, quietly, she says to me, 'Esmat . . . she's a good girl.' Her words are like an offering. I extract my instrument, turning to face Samaneh with a reassuring smile.

'I'm sure she is. Pregnancy happens to many good girls. It's human nature to want to be united with someone you love.'

'There was no love involved,' she says, shaking her head sadly. She hesitates, her words dying in her mouth several times before she manages to tell me what she evidently must. 'I lost my husband two years ago. He was a labourer, so already we were poor. I had to start working. I was lucky to find a job in the hotel.' She pauses again before pressing on. 'Soon after I began there, he came . . . and asked to arrange a *sigha* with me.'

'Who?' I ask. According to sharia law in Iran, when a man organises a *sigha* with a woman, he can sleep with her for a specified time, from a very few hours to many years, as agreed upon with her. All he has to do is pay the sum of money, also agreed upon in advance, and she belongs to him for the duration. It's a type of legally sanctioned prostitution. Women rarely enter into it willingly.

Samaneh clenches her sleeping daughter's hand more firmly, drawing in her chador tightly and averting her eyes. A defensive posture.

'Samaneh, who?'

'That bastard, Najarian.'

I nod in sympathy. Such a degrading position to be placed in.

I return to the procedure, quickly checking Esmat's breathing.

'I had to,' Samaneh continues, as if she must justify herself. 'He threatened to fire me otherwise. I have four children to feed. What choice did I have? He gave me only two hundred toman a week under the *sigha*, but I had to agree.'

Two hundred toman is barely enough to buy a pound of meat.

'Then one day he saw Esmat, and he liked her.'

I halt what I'm doing and look at Samaneh. I know where this story is going.

'First he asked me to agree to a *sigha* with her, but I refused. For weeks I refused! Finally he became vicious. He said he would ruin my life. He would tell the whole town that I stole from his hotel, after he'd given me a job out of the goodness of his heart. He said I would never get work again. I couldn't let my children starve. We had no choice. He took my poor daughter. She cried every night. I'll never forgive myself.'

Samaneh is sobbing now, deep breathless sobs. When she regains her composure she continues her story. 'He has a wife and five children and seven grandchildren. He's terrified his wife will find out about this. That's why he was in such a hurry to go back to Mashhad.'

I apply my next instrument, and then the next one. The sedation is wearing off and Esmat is getting restless, jerking with pain. By the time I reach the last instrument, she screams.

'Relax now, you'll be fine,' I say soothingly. I don't like to see her in pain, but I'm encouraged that she's alert.

After forty-five intense minutes of effort, I've dilated her cervix to about one centimetre. That is enough. I begin the final part of the procedure, the suctioning, twenty minutes of it.

'Almost finished,' I assure Esmat. I wish I could ease her pain, but giving her more medication is too risky.

Suddenly a big flow of blood rushes out, staining her thighs. This is not part of the procedure. It's catastrophic. What have I done? I continue to suction the blood, but the bleeding is getting more severe by the moment. Have I ruptured her cervical canal? So much blood is spilling out that I can't see the speculum inside Esmat anymore. I stand up to get a kidney dish to put under the stream of blood. The suction alone can't handle it.

'Is everything all right?' Samaneh asks. She's worried, and why wouldn't she be, my gown covered in blood.

'Yes. She's fine.' I manage to place the kidney dish under the blood, and keep suctioning. I knew there'd be bleeding after the removal of the placenta, but this is far more than there should be. Worse, Esmat is quiet. A grave sign. I check her blood pressure: 86 over 50, far below the normal level. She is in shock. Be calm, I tell myself. Be calm.

'Is she okay?' Samaneh asks, certain now that something has gone terribly wrong.

'Her blood pressure's down. I have to give her more IV fluid.' I turn the drip up to the maximum and a constant flow of normal saline surges into Esmat's vein. But I know that even if this improves her blood pressure, I must slow down the bleeding or I'll lose her. I reach inside and take the speculum out. It's full of huge blood clots and tissue.

It is said that every ship's captain has a haunting dread of his vessel's hull striking something that should not be where it is – a rock, a reef, an iceberg. That is the enduring nightmare of his profession. The greatest fear of every surgeon is the unanticipated flow of bright red blood; this is our reef, our rock. The blood is life itself.

Keeping the speculum out of Samaneh's view, I put it in the kidney dish and leave the room to empty it into the toilet. As I hurry back to Esmat's side I feel a cold breeze on my body and realise I'm drenched in sweat.

The sheet beneath Esmat is covered in blood, and more continues to stream out of her. I put the kidney dish back under her and check her blood pressure: 80 over 45. Her life is faltering. She isn't strong enough to handle much more bleeding.

'Why isn't she moving anymore, Doctor?' Samaneh whispers. 'Why is she so still?'

'She's weak. I'll fix this.'

I rush to my cupboard and grab an ampoule of Dinoprost. For a long moment I hold my breath. What if this is another drug she's allergic to? It's a gamble, but I'm out of options. If her blood pressure declines further, she'll go into a hemodynamic coma and die in a few minutes. And if she has an allergic reaction to the Dinoprost, she will die in a few minutes. I close my eyes and pray to my Adonai. Instantly I recall the Star of David I carved as a boy on the wall of our house in the slum, when I was feeling how brittle my Jewish existence was in volatile fundamentalist Iran. Esmat and I share the same uncertain fate at this moment. Prayer is the only solace, even though it doesn't change anything.

I inject two milligrams into her right arm. Dinoprost works quickly to contract the uterus, which in turn reduces the bleeding. But it also contracts the stomach and causes severe vomiting.

'Esmat! Esmat! Open your eyes!' She can hear me, but she's too weak to respond. I take her limp hand. 'Squeeze my hand.' I feel a pressure so light I almost miss it, but she has heard me. She is trying to do what I tell her. She is trying to fight her way back to life.

The IV fluid is almost half gone. I grab another bag and tie the tourniquet around her other arm. I search for a vein, but her low blood pressure has caused most of them to collapse. Finally I locate a small one and insert the second cannula.

Blood enters the tube. I establish the second intravenous line and set the bag of normal saline to the maximum flow. Now she has a two-line infusion. I check her bleeding and I'm encouraged to see it is diminishing.

'Open your eyes, Esmat! Don't go to sleep! Talk to me!'

Five minutes pass in excruciatingly slow degrees. Samaneh rubs Esmat's shoulders, saying nothing. She has no doubt that her daughter is near death. The bleeding slows further. I check the blood pressure again: 90 over 62. Thank Adonai! I love Dinoprost! I love the man who invented it.

Turning to Samaneh, I say with a smile, 'She's safe now.'

Five more minutes pass before Esmat opens her eyes. Then without warning she vomits a huge amount of liquid. I pull her into a sitting position and ask her mother to hold her. I dash to the kitchen for a plastic container, run back and put the container under her mouth. I have to make her more alert. 'Open your eyes! Talk to me! I mean it. *Speak.*'

'I'm okay,' she manages to whisper.

She wants to lie down but I can't let her. The risk of aspirating the fluid into her airway is too great. I ask Samaneh to hold her upright while I remove the first bag of fluid. Esmat weighs too little to be given any more fluid. If her blood pressure drops again, transfusion will be the only option and that will be impossible in my house.

I carry the empty bag into the bathroom and take off my blood-stained gown. Catching my reflection in the mirror I'm startled to see the bags under my eyes. Only a few hours ago, when I'd showered and shaved, my eyes were alert. Now they're drained and lifeless. I splash cold water on my face and go back to Esmat.

Her blood pressure is now 102 over 84. She is out of immediate danger and I sit with her as she regains her strength. Samaneh holds her in the patient way of mothers the world over, with no thought of her own comfort, with prayers for deliverance forming on her lips. If I were to tell Samaneh that she had to sit holding Esmat for another ten hours, she would obey without a sound. This is the daughter she gave birth to fifteen years ago, and now, by a bleak twist of fate, she has been compelled to help her rid her own womb of a baby. It's been a life-and-death struggle to save her daughter not from typhus or cholera or some virulent strain of influenza, but from pregnancy. The three of us have been through all this to avoid the consequences of a man's lust. But dear God, it has been worth it. I look at Esmat, so young, yet finding the courage to endure this nightmare, and I look at Samaneh, the eternal mother, holding her child to her heart, and I think, Kooshyar, it's been a good fight, blood and tears notwithstanding; we're on the side of the angels.

'She's ready to get dressed now,' I tell Samaneh, and leave the room to give Esmat some privacy. Now that the procedure is complete and she is out of danger, her modesty will return.

I slump onto a chair to wait. I know that Esmat will bleed slightly for another few days, and that she still faces the risk of another major bleed or serious infection, even sepsis. She'll have to watch for any sign of infection, one of the major causes of death in a termination.

When I hear Samaneh call out, 'She's dressed now, Doctor,' I return to the room.

'Thank you,' Esmat says in a quiet, embarrassed voice. She is a painfully shy girl. It's sickening to think of her in the hands of the vile Najarian.

I smile at her. 'You're going to have some bleeding for the next few days, which is normal. I have to give you one last injection. This one is antibiotics to prevent any infection.'

I give her the shot in her arm, then write prescriptions for more antibiotics and fill out a form to request an ultrasound. I scribble my mobile phone number down and hand all the paperwork to Samaneh. 'I want you to call me any time she feels feverish, has severe pain, or starts bleeding a lot again. Okay?'

Samaneh nods.

'I also need your phone number so I can check up on her.'

'Doctor, we don't have a telephone.'

'I need a number, Samaneh.'

'I can give you Najarian's mobile number, but if you call him, make sure his wife isn't around or he can't talk.'

'I'll be careful.' I hand her a pen and paper. Embarrassed, she confesses she can't write. She tells me the number and I write it down. 'And how are you going to get back home?'

'We'll get the last bus to Mashhad.'

'Do you have money to get the ticket? For Esmat's medications? For her ultrasound?'

Samaneh nods after each question. Then she says, 'You gave my daughter a new life. I don't know how to thank you. Allah protect you and your family.'

'The next few days are crucial. You have to give her lots of fluids and salt, and meat if you can. Red meat to bring her iron level up.'

Samaneh and I help Esmat to her feet. She is weak and still in pain, but she can walk with her mother holding her arm. Before they leave the house I squeeze some money into Samaneh's hand. Watching them go, I think briefly of Najarian back at home with his wife and children and grandchildren, greatly relieved to have his problem settled. He'll soon begin to be attracted to Esmat again. He has a legal right to have sex with her. In about two or three weeks he'll ask Samaneh if her daughter is sufficiently healed for intimacy to resume. Samaneh will say, no, she is still recovering. Najarian will ask again a few days later. Again Samaneh will say no. Najarian won't ask a third time. He'll simply say, 'She is ready.'

I go to my bedroom and drop down onto my bed, light a cigarette and take a deep drag. My mind is made up. If a desperate woman comes to me, whoever she is, I'll do it. I can't be bothered any longer with my ambiguities. Maybe I do crave to think of myself as the saviour of Persian women. Good for me. I don't care anymore about my motives.

Leila

It's late afternoon. Mother shouts from the living room, 'Hurry up, they'll be here any minute.'

'Almost done,' I call back. My mother always wants to make sure things are perfect for guests, but why is she so nervous tonight? It's only Samira and Saeed coming for dinner. Mother has never gone out of her way before to serve exactly what my sister wants, but now that Samira is married she has her mother's respect. Or is it that Saeed will be with her? Either way, I'm amused to see my mother acting like this. I'll have to tell Hamid about it.

I have slipped into the habit of viewing my life through Hamid's eyes. When I cook I wonder if he would like the dish I'm preparing. When my father and brothers talk about business I try to remember what they discuss so that I can ask his opinion. And of course when I read I imagine discussing the book with him. I have married Hamid in my soul and now I'm living my life with him. It's a joy to me. I relish all the homely, everyday aspects of the marriage I've conjured up almost as much as my fantasies of kissing and touching. Almost, but not quite. Those fantasies can become so intense that I have to lean against a wall and close my eyes and wait for my heartbeat to return to normal. I have no way of knowing if this physical arousal is normal in women. I could ask Samira, but how? 'Sister, I imagine Hamid kissing my breasts and I come close to fainting – is it the same for you with Saeed?' She would think I've lost my mind.

Throughout dinner, Saeed and Samira steal small, smiling glances at each other. The affection between them is like a current. They make sure my mother and father don't see their secretive messages, but Samira doesn't hide them from me.

After we've eaten, when my father and Saeed settle down to discuss things in the way men do, I have a chance to spirit my sister away to my bedroom to chat with her in private. This is the first chance I've had to ask her about her marriage night, her *hejleh*. I say, 'Tell me everything. Everything!'

Samira looks away and blushes. 'Oh, I couldn't do that,' she says.

'You must. Everything. Was Saeed gentle with you?'

'Well, if you must know, yes, he was very gentle.' She looks away again, this time in a type of reverie.

'Well?' I insist.

'Well what?'

'What did he do?'

'What do you think?'

'Sister, don't drive me crazy. Tell me properly.'

Samira smiles and pats my cheek. She's already much more mature than she was a month ago. I'm just a child to her now. 'Okay,' she says. 'You'll be a bride yourself before long, so I suppose I can tell you. We were lying on the marriage bed almost naked. Can you imagine! I barely knew Saeed, and here I was naked beside him. And we kissed. I was scared half to death, and I kept thinking, What do I do next? And then we – we, well, you know. We did it.'

'Oh, Allah! What did it feel like? You have to tell me.'

'What did it feel like? It hurt. Well, it's supposed to hurt. That wasn't a surprise. Mother told me it would hurt the first time. And it did. A lot. You know what I was thinking about, more than anything? I was thinking, Dear Allah, make me bleed so that Saeed can see I'm a virgin. And sister, I bled and bled. I was so relieved.'

'Does it still hurt?'

Samira closes her eyes for a moment and a huge smile spreads across her face. 'No, sister, it doesn't hurt anymore. Just the opposite. Oh Leila, it's heaven. I can't tell you how beautiful it is. It's heaven. And I scream so loud, but not from pain. From pure, pure pleasure. I'm almost ashamed to speak to you about it. And he wants to do it twice, three times each night. He feels my breasts and kisses me and in ten seconds I'm on fire. I amaze myself. I want him to touch me deep, touch me everywhere, I don't want him to stop.'

I'm devouring every word. My mind teems with images of Hamid. I'm so aroused it's almost like pain.

Samira says softly, as if she can read my thoughts, 'Have you seen him again? Your shopkeeper?'

Blood rushes to my face. For a moment I'm breathless. 'Yes. Yes, I have. His name is Hamid.'

Samira grabs my hands. 'How did you get out of the house to go to the shop again?'

'Will you keep this secret? Swear you will!'

'Sister, your secrets are safe with me. I don't have to tell you that.'

I told her everything, in detail. On hearing that I went to his house, Samira lets out a tiny scream and stares at me as if I've just dropped to earth from the moon.

'Don't worry. He's a gentleman. I was only there for a few minutes and nothing happened. But wait until you see what he gave me.' I jump up and take my book from the wardrobe. 'Look,' I say, displaying the petals. 'From the rose he gave me. Oh, Samira, it smelled like paradise.'

She puts her hands on my shoulder, ignoring the petals spread out in my palm. 'Leila, please, what you are doing is very, very dangerous. You *must* be careful.'

'I am. But . . .'

'But what?' I read the concern on my sister's face.

'Samira, I think I'm in love. I think of him constantly. His voice, his eyes. Every minute, every day.'

'But this is *haram*, Leila.'

'I know, but maybe we can get married. I haven't touched him. I won't do that.'

'Then tell him to come and marry you.'

'I can't just say that. I've let him know my elder sister is married, and I'm available for marriage, so —'

The door opens and our mother walks in. 'No more talking. Samira, you should look after your husband now. Leila, come and help me make dessert.'

We follow her into the kitchen. We don't have a chance to talk again until we say our goodbyes in front of everyone. Samira whispers into my ear as we hug farewell. 'Be careful, darling. Don't take foolish chances.'

Almost a week after Samira's visit, I finally have a chance to call

Hamid. My mother has gone out to do some shopping, but she'll be back in twenty minutes or so. I keep one eye on the door as I dial and our conversation is brief, but tender. I tell him I think of him each time I smell the rose petals.

'I keep them in the book you gave me. I like to think it makes the little prince happy while he's away from his planet and the only flower that grows there.' I feel I know Hamid so well I can afford to speak like this with him.

He laughs softly and teasingly. 'I can't say things like that myself, Leila. But I love to hear you say them.'

The next week, while I'm putting thick tape around the windows to stop the drafts, Samira calls. Mother answers, and I continue to work while listening to her side of the conversation.

'Don't forget to have a nice dinner ready any time Saeed comes home. And when he first comes in the door, don't talk about annoying things. If there's a problem, wait until after he's had time to rest. Men work hard and they need to have peace in their home. If you bother him with complaints and worries or ask for things, he'll think you're selfish. He'll look for a new wife.' She pauses, lowering her voice. 'And if you want him to buy something for you, always ask in bed before you let him touch you.'

Having said goodbye to Samira, she hands the phone to me and heads into the backyard to take down the laundry.

'Samira,' I say, 'you have to help me get out of here. I miss Hamid terribly, and I think he's trying to find a way to tell me he loves me.'

'You think so?'

'I'm sure of it.'

'Maybe next week I'll ask Saeed if I can visit the orphanage, and I'll ask Mother to let you come with me. But you have to be very cautious, Leila. Remember, men are not like us. They want different things.'

'Does Saeed want different things to you?'

'Sometimes. I'm training him. I find ways to make him take my feelings into account. But you haven't had the chance to train Hamid.'

Mother raises no objection when Samira asks her to let me come to the orphanage. The day before we plan to go, I call Hamid and tell him I can meet him at his house, and suggest a time. He says, 'Leila, I can't wait. I'll count every minute until I see you.'

I finish reading *The Little Black Fish* that night, so I can discuss the book with him. It's a sad story, as he said. A curious baby fish with black scales that lives in a small river wants to see the world. She decides to travel, and swims against the current, seeing for the first time other fish of great beauty, and all sorts of wonders. But in the end an ugly fat fish eats her. I'm making the story sound simpler than it is, Doctor Karimi, but that's the basics of it. In Iran it's always read as a political allegory, as I'm sure you know.

Next day, Samira and I buy lollies in the bazaar, and distribute them to the kids, to the usual clamour of delight. I greet little Ali and Salmeh and cuddle baby Sara, thrilled to see her tiny hands opening and closing as she reaches for my face. Then I excuse myself, leaving Samira to read stories to the children, and hurry off to spend fifteen minutes with Hamid. I'm a little sick with guilt for spending such a short time at the orphanage, but my need to be with Hamid is so strong that I've overcome any feelings of selfishness by the time I reach his house.

The door is ajar, as it was last time. I step inside and call, 'Hello?'

Hamid appears in the hallway, smiling happily. 'Leila? Come in, come in. I've been dreading you would change your mind.'

He holds out his hand to me. Shaking a man's hand is a grave sin.

But not to accept his would be rude, and isn't being rude also a sin? Besides, I want to feel the contact of skin on skin. His hand holds mine firmly, then he covers it with his other one, all the time smiling at me with such tenderness. A wave of pleasure rushes through me.

'Make yourself comfortable while I get a drink for you. Apple or pomegranate?'

I seat myself on the sofa, and even though this is only my second visit I feel almost as if I belong here now. Will this be my home soon?

Hamid pours two glasses of apple juice and joins me, but this time he sits beside me instead of taking a seat across from me. This is an escalation of intimacy, but it is welcome. I think of Hamid as my husband in all but name. The boundaries of our relationship have been redrawn in my mind, in my heart. Had he sat beside me on my first visit, I would have blushed crimson and probably run away. Now I'm saying to myself, It's okay, Leila. He loves you, you love him, years of married life await you. As long as we don't touch, nothing truly sinful has happened. Try to relax, silly girl.

'It's getting so cold,' Hamid begins. 'Maybe I should have made you tea?'

I say, 'No, this is perfect.'

'It seems like years since I saw you last.' Then, in a voice deep and low: 'I want to tell you something, Leila.'

I turn to him so that I can meet his gaze. 'What is it?'

Reaching out he touches my cheek, a liberty so brazen I should stand and run from the house. But I don't.

'I don't know how to say it,' he says, running his hand through his hair. 'It's silly, I know, but . . .'

'Nothing you say is silly to me. Please, tell me.'

Hamid raises his glass to his lips and takes a long drink of juice. He turns away for a moment to set his glass on the table, and then, turning back to me, says softly, 'I love you, Leila.'

Those words, Doctor! I'm left staring at him, at his lips, his mouth, the place from where those words issued. It's as if I have to concentrate to properly grasp their meaning, as if they are echoing over and over. A great silence seems to fill my being. Hamid and I are facing each other at the very centre of the universe, with stars in the billions, an infinite number of galaxies, glittering around us. There is no one else, just him and me. I have imagined hearing those words for weeks, but nothing has prepared me for the magic of this moment.

But just when I most need to speak my mind, declare what's in my heart, the stern figure of some nameless mullah rises before me, a representative of my faith, my culture, my family. To respond with those same words to Hamid would make me a harlot, a woman without any moral core. In addition, I am too shy to utter them.

Moving closer, Hamid takes my right hand. I don't resist. My hand fits perfectly into his, as if every part of us is made for each other – hands, hearts, souls. But his smile has vanished, to be replaced by a look both haunted and hunted. He slides his other hand over mine. 'I don't know what's happening to me, but I can't stop thinking of you. I think of your beautiful, beautiful eyes. I stare off into space when I'm at my shop, waiting for your call. I jump every time I hear the phone ring, hoping I can hear your voice, even if only for a few minutes.'

Speak, Leila! If ever in your life, speak now. And I do. 'I feel the same way. I think of you every night. I sleep with the rose petals under my pillow and wake up dreaming of your eyes.'

Hamid takes my arms with both hands and draws me close. I gaze into the fathomless depths of his eyes and he again tells me he loves me. Now I can say it. The mullah has shrunken in size. I am free of fear. 'I love you too.' This love between us comes from above. This is what Gibran talks about. It isn't sin. It is beauty in its purest form.

'Close your eyes,' Hamid whispers.

My eyelids close. I did not know that lips could be so soft. I move my mouth against Hamid's. I drink him in. Waves of pleasure surge through me. He presses me to his chest. The weight of his body floods me with a new response, one I have never known before and could not have guessed at. It is hunger. Desire has always had a fairytale quality in my imagination – the thrill of fingertips brushing the smooth skin of my wrists, my throat; exquisite sensations, but not truly sexual. The hunger I now feel is rougher, stronger. I want to be engulfed by Hamid, annihilated, torn from the place I occupy on earth and flung full-length down some hallway in heaven, then pressed down where I lie by Hamid's body, pressed with such force that my breathing will stop, and I will die in his arms and be reborn.

He moves his hands to my back and then slips his arms around my waist, drawing me closer still. As he kisses me, I hold him against me avidly. I want to be devoured, but I also want to devour him. Then without warning, he releases me and falls back against the sofa. He drops his head into his hands. 'I'm sorry,' he stutters. 'Leila, you're so beautiful, I got carried away. Please forgive me.'

Forgive him? Forgive the most glorious moments of my existence? The feeling of floating like an angel? And more than that, the hunger that he's brought to life in me? I say, quite mildly, 'Really, it's all right.' I wish he'd raise his head and look at me again. Please do that, you beloved man. Please look me in the eyes.

Then I notice the time on the clock. 'Oh dear, I'm so late!' I fix my chador around me. 'My mother's going to kill me.'

I head to the hallway, Hamid close behind.

'Will I see you again?' he asks.

I turn my face up to him. I want nothing more than to remain here with him for the rest of my life. 'Yes,' I say. 'Yes, Hamid.' While

I'm still able to exercise some will, I run out the door.

By some miracle, my mother isn't at home when I get back. All the excuses I've prepared wilt away as I support myself against the wall, catching my breath. Then I hurry to the bathroom, pull my scarf off and look at myself in the mirror. Have Hamid's kisses left indelible marks on my face? Of course not, but my guilt is such that I expect to see the scarlet outline of his lips all over my cheeks, my neck.

I wander about the empty house, reliving the sound of Hamid's voice, the strength of his hands as he held me by the shoulders. And I think of the way he suddenly stopped and reproached himself for going too far. I hadn't wanted him to stop, not in the least.

Long, lonely days pass without a chance to be with him once more, but finally, in mid-December, while I sweep the backyard, Mother sets out for the bazaar to find the good-quality rice she prefers. I put the broom away the minute the door closes and go to the phone.

After two rings a woman answers. I hang up instantly. Who could she be? I'd seen a woman in the shop a few months ago. Maybe she worked there. I'll ask him.

Or maybe I dialled the wrong number in my haste? I call again, and again the woman answers, again I hang up. I shouldn't have done that. I should have just asked for him. But no. No one can know about me until he comes to talk to my father. He may not be ready yet to tell anyone.

I go to the bathroom to shower and relax under the flow of hot water. I dry my hair and clean the shower. Almost half an hour has passed and still Mother isn't back. Maybe I should try calling Hamid again. Maybe he was outside for a smoke.

I dial again, with the same result. It's tying me in knots. There must be a perfectly good explanation. He can't be at the store every minute it's open. He'll have business outside the store too.

My hand flies to my heart as another possibility enters my mind. What if he's sick or hurt? What if he's in the hospital? I'd never know.

Please, Allah, I pray. Let him be safe and healthy. Please, don't take him from me.

Days pass in severe anxiety. I can hardly sleep. When *The Little Black Fish* is due back at the library, Mother finally gives me permission to return it. I tiptoe into the hall and call the boutique. One ring and he picks up the phone.

'Hamid, I am about to go out to the library,' I tell him quickly, and he says at once, 'I will be home, waiting for you.' I hang up, just before my mother comes back.

I keep my library visit short, staying only long enough to politely ask after Mrs Salimi's health and to pick out a book. Then I hurry to Shahid Goli Street, humming to myself.

The door is open as usual. I run the last few steps. Hamid is waiting in the hall.

'Leila! You're more beautiful than ever.' He closes the door behind me and I follow him into the living room. Everything is in its place, as always. I wonder if he has someone come in to clean for him or if he keeps things neat by himself. I tingle at the thought that soon it will be my job to look after these things and cook for him, doing whatever he asks of me.

'Look what I have today,' says Hamid.

I turn around to see that he's holding a black book with the title *Kelidar*.

'Is it good?' I ask.

'It's exceptional. Critics say this is the best novel written in a century in Iran.'

'Who wrote it?'

'Mahmoud Dowlatabadi. A great writer. I'll give it to you when I finish. But what am I thinking? I haven't even offered you something to drink.'

'I don't have much time today, I'm afraid. I have to go very soon.'

Hamid sighs and puts his hand to his head. 'It's always like this,' he says. Then he takes my hand and leads me to the sofa. He sits down and tugs me gently to sit beside him.

'It won't always be like this,' I tell him. 'But today I told my mother I'd be quick about getting a new book from the library. If I'm late she won't let me out for weeks. Maybe not for the whole winter.'

'It's as if you're a prisoner,' says Hamid, with what I take to be genuine sympathy.

Doctor Karimi, I want to be as candid as I can be about what follows. I feel in my heart that you are the only man on earth I can reveal these things to. But please, look away from me a little, while I confess. For the sake of my soul. I am ten minutes away from being raped, ten minutes away from something that any girl raised in my culture dreads more than death itself. And Doctor, if I could go back to that day, and if the voice of Allah called to me, 'Leila, choose now, a death of terrible agony, or what awaits you at Hamid's hands,' then I would say without a second's hesitation, 'Death, I beg of You, death in whatever way You decide.'

Hamid says, 'Surely when you get married you'll have more freedom.'

'I hope so,' I say, knotting our hands together. Is this it? Will he ask me now if I would consider marrying him?

But instead he leans away from me and asks, 'So, what book did you choose today?'

I take the book out of my chador. *'Talkhoon,'* I say quietly. I hope he doesn't sense that I want the talk of marriage to continue. I'd hate to seem pushy but, as you know, that is what I want more than anything on earth, Doctor.

'Another sad story,' he says.

'Is there anything you haven't read?' I ask, smiling affectionately.

'There are many books I haven't read, but I read this when I was fourteen. It's about a girl who falls in love and ends up with a broken heart.'

Tears spring into my eyes. Is he trying to warn me? Am I too traditional, too backward for a man like him? I flinch when I feel his hand go around my shoulder. But only for a second. He moves closer to me, whispering, 'Leila, your beauty is simply astonishing. I can't tell you how much I adore you.'

And my rather boring response to this? 'Thank you, Hamid,' as if he were doing me a favour instead of speaking words of love. What I want to say is, 'If you think me beautiful, enjoy me.'

When I don't move away, Hamid eases my chador off my head so he can see my hair. 'Black silk,' he says softly, and his lips touch my cheek even as he speaks.

I have never let a man other than my brothers see my hair. The feeling is very strange, almost frightening, but I have no urge to resist. He moves his hands through my hair, kissing it, letting it flow through his fingers like water. His scent intoxicates me, his breath warms my face like sun on a winter's day. I long to reach out and touch his hands but I can't seem to move. He puts a hand under my chin and gently lifts my face. We gaze into each other's eyes. Then he kisses me, his lips so soft it's agony to imagine ever being without their touch. His fingers caress my cheeks, then trail down to my neck. The sensation is more than I can bear, and when he moves his hand to my breasts I do nothing to stop him; nor when he reaches under my chador and unclasps my bra, not even when he cups in his hand first one breast and then the other. I press my own hands against his chest, uncertain whether I want to pull him closer or push him away. This is all wrong, an unpardonable sin, but he is so strong and yet gentle at the same time that I can't resist him.

He eases me back onto the sofa until he is on top of me, my chador around my waist. Sliding his hand over my stomach, he reaches for my underpants. I can't catch my breath. I press my legs together, but when he touches me just below my navel I want to scream out in pleasure. I loosen my legs, not knowing what will come next, but wanting to find out, my body calling out for more. And yet at the same time I try to pull back from him, saying, 'No, Hamid, no.' He keeps touching me, making me moan with desire. He undoes his belt, his lips still on mine, and with one hand works his trousers off. I try to stop his hands from moving over me again. I need to slow things down. Doctor Karimi, it is as if a war is being waged inside me, one side shrieking, 'You want this, you know you do!' and the other side screaming at him, 'Go away! Leave her be!' Before I can twist out from under him, I feel something hot between my thighs. All at once and completely I know what I want. There are no longer two sides struggling for possession of me. I want Hamid to stop.

'*No*, Hamid! I want you to stop – *now!*'

I try once more to shove him away but he covers my lips with his again, this time opening them with his tongue. As his tongue meets mine, he pushes inside me. I feel a stinging sensation, not overpoweringly painful, and he pushes harder, his breath coming in fast ragged gasps. I wrench my head away from his tongue, his lips.

'*Stop*, Hamid! Please! I beg you!'

But he keeps pushing harder and deeper. I put my hands on his chest in an attempt to get him off but he grabs my arms and holds them over my head while he pushes so hard I feel as if I'm being split in half. I'm at the heart of something so violent that I want to howl for my mother. I have time to realise that this is the dark side of those fantasies I enjoyed. In them I was in control; when I stopped, they stopped. Here, now, nothing stops. Tears stream down my face and then I hear Hamid moan loudly. His full weight falls on me and I am pinned beneath him for more than a minute as he whimpers and groans. I feel a hot liquid flow into me and I know in an instant what it is. He withdraws and raises himself on his hands. I shove him away. If only he'd waited! He has ruined everything, made the blackest misery out of my love for him.

I pull my underpants up and lift my chador over my head while he tucks his penis into his pants and zips himself up.

'Sorry,' he mutters.

I step past him on my way to the front door. I can't bear to look at him.

'Wait!' he calls.

I ignore him but hear his footsteps behind me. He puts a hand on my shoulder. 'Your book. Take your book.'

I snatch it from him and feel for the door handle, but can barely bring myself to open it. I'm certain people will be on the other side shouting at me that I am unclean, a harlot. With a deep breath, I yank it open, step outside and rush down the street, not making eye contact with anyone I pass. One glimpse into my eyes and even a total stranger will see my shame.

Thoughts seethe in my head. I don't need to look at my watch to know I'm late – very late. My mother will demand an explanation, and what will I tell her? That I am no longer a virgin? That I've been raped? Was it rape? I'd let things go so far before I said no. But he heard me tell him to stop and he didn't stop. He wanted what he wanted. Samira warned me. Why didn't I listen? I'm a vile, dirty slut and I'll never be able to marry. But it won't matter because Ali will kill me when he finds out.

I reach the front door of our house in such a state of distress that it takes me minutes of fumbling to fit the key into the lock. My enraged mother is waiting for me in the hall.

'Leila! Where have you been?'

'At the library.'

'Really? I was on my way to look for you, you fool of a girl!' She raises her hand to slap me but I step around her and rush to my room. Being treated like an eight-year-old is something I can't face at this moment. My mother storms after me and corners me in my bedroom.

'You're *forty* minutes late. It takes only twenty minutes to go to the library and come back.'

'I had to find a new book. I talked with Mrs Salimi.'

'Look at me!'

I lift my head and try to keep my gaze steady.

'Why are you so pale?' she demands. 'What's happened?'

'Nothing.'

'I'm not stupid. I know my daughter. I've never seen you so upset. Tell me what happened, Leila!'

'Nothing! You're scaring me. Nobody ever lets me make a mistake. I always have to be perfect. I feel like I'm a prisoner and I took too much freedom, and now I'll never get to leave the house again.'

'You're right about that,' my mother says. 'You're not going out to the library or to the orphanage or even to *rozeh*. You'll go nowhere. You'll stay with me every second. Since your sister has gone you've been out all the time, coming back late, and look at you now. Allah knows what happened, but I know there's more than you're telling me.' She leaves the room in disgust.

I burst into tears, stuffing a pillow over my face to drown my sobs. I weep until I have no tears left. I hang up my chador and hurry to the bathroom to clean myself. I have to wash away the day, Hamid, my disgrace.

Mother yells at me to come and help her in the kitchen.

'I won't be a minute.' I lock the door.

'Come here *now*,' she roars.

I climb into the shower, soaping myself furiously, as if what I endured were a coating on my skin that could be scrubbed off. I dry myself, pull my clothes on, stuff my soiled underpants beneath my mattress before running to the kitchen.

'Peel these onions, then chop them into the pot, and fry the eggplants. Why are your hands shaking? Why are your eyes red?'

'I think I'm getting sick.'

'I'm going to talk to your father.'

I look at my mother. 'What have I done that's so terrible? I was late and I promise I won't go out anymore. I'm just sick.'

My tasks done, I return to my room and pull my underpants out from under the mattress, take them to the bathroom and wash them. Torn to pieces though I am, I can still think in a practical way. But the part of me that is prepared to survive, prepared to wash underwear, scrub my body, fashion excuses for being late, is so weak. My greatest need is to die. That is what I crave – annihilation, non-existence. I take the razor from the cabinet and study the blade, touch it to the veins of my wrist. I know I won't use it, but I can take a few minutes' relief from heartache and humiliation by imagining my bright blood flowing from my body.

I can hear my mother completing preparations for dinner in the kitchen. She doesn't know that I am no longer the baby she takes me for. I have crossed a threshold into a dark place. My innocence is at an end. I thought I was approaching paradise but I was deluded. The sun has set on all my hopes, and my life from now on will be one of sadness and regret. Hamid, who I'd thought of as a beautiful man, is just like a million other men. He never shared my dream of marriage, a home together, children.

No, I will not cut my arms open with the razor. I will live and suffer. The prospect of paying penance with my suffering is the only hope I can hold onto. It's a bleak life that stretches before me. But just how great the suffering will be – no, I don't know that yet. If I did, then I *would* take the razor and rip my veins open, all along their length, and fall to the bathroom floor and die in a circle of my blood.

The Doctor

Early in December 1996 I move my family into a three-bedroom apartment in a safe section of Mashhad, near my in-laws. Azita wants to live closer to her family, and is pleased to be back in the city of her birth. I still have another eleven months of military service to complete in Quchan, and I plan to travel between the two towns every week, spending one or two days with my family and the rest working at the military base hospital.

This arrangement is far from ideal – I won't see enough of my wife and daughter – but I'm used to making do, having grown up in a destitute family where my father was often absent and my mother struggled constantly. My father drove a bus between Mashhad and Tehran and was regularly away for days at a time. I'd see him maybe once a week, but he was always emotionally remote. In spite of that, I would stay awake at night waiting for him to come home, and when he did, way after midnight, the smell of diesel on his clothes as he stepped into our single-room house was an aroma of delight and relief. The solitude I endured as a child prepared me for the sacrifices I made as a man.

But I want a proper family life for Newsha. She will never have to worry about where the next meal is coming from, and will never feel rats running across her bed in the middle of the night as I did, but food and material goods don't of themselves fashion a family. I want my daughter to be bathed in love, to know that her father adores her. I want to be someone she never has to doubt, as steady as a rock, utterly dependable. And I must admit that I want her to be exposed to my values as least as much as to those of her mother. I would like Newsha to be able to think more critically, employ more of her imagination, extend her sense of loyalty to take in the family of humanity. I want her to go to university and startle the professors with her intellect and wit. I want the world for her, quite literally. But for the next little while, I am going to be an absentee father, and it makes me sick at heart.

In Mashhad there's a herbalist by the name of Shafiq, who I've come to know over the past two years. He sells concoctions to women desperate to terminate pregnancies; he knows they are ineffective but he still sells them. Shafiq has contacted me two or three times to ask if I would be prepared to bring about the result that his 'medicines' cannot. He first approached me to intervene in the case of a truly wretched girl, and I did intervene, much against my better judgement. Now he wants me to perform a termination on a divorced woman, a certain Mrs Razavi.

'I'll be in Mashhad next weekend,' I tell him over the phone. 'I'll see her then.' If I put off the termination much longer, she will be beyond twelve weeks and it will be too late for me to do anything.

On the day, I park my car in front of a brick home in Abobarq, a new suburb of Mashhad. The doorbell rings musically at the high gates in the wall surrounding the house, and they swing open immediately.

A woman in her thirties is waiting at the door. She introduces herself as Nasrin, a friend of Mrs Razavi, and ushers me inside. Just before she closes the door, I notice a taxi parked in the yard.

'Is anyone else here?' I ask, pointing to the cab.

'Mrs Razavi lets her neighbour keep the car there. Pay no attention to it.' The woman leads me into a bright, tastefully decorated living room where Mrs Razavi comes forward. She is wearing a white chador and her face is plump, graced with a kind and welcoming smile. I immediately like her.

She leads me to a blue velvet sofa while Nasrin excuses herself to brew tea in the kitchen. My patient is evidently well provided for. The couch looks expensive, and above us hangs a crystal chandelier. The tea, when it comes, is served in beautiful china cups. Such a contrast to the poverty in which most of the women I attend to live.

I notice a little girl sitting under the dining table, scribbling colours onto paper and speaking animatedly to one of her dolls. She's wearing a plastic tiara and a pink tutu, like a fairy.

'Is that your daughter?' I ask, smiling towards the table.

Mrs Razavi replies fondly, 'Yes, her name is Jannat.'

'I have a daughter nearly the same age,' I say, surprising myself. I seldom speak about my private life to my patients. In the mood I'm in, the sight of any adorable child is likely to make me sob. I'm looking at this lovely little Jannat but I'm thinking of my beautiful daughter – the daughter I'm neglecting, the daughter whose welfare I'm jeopardising.

I put my cup down and adopt a more professional manner. 'I understand you're divorced,' I say.

Even though my tone is polite and unaccusing, Mrs Razavi's face reddens. 'Yes, Doctor. By the time I learnt I was with child I had already been separated.'

'How far along are you?' I ask.

'I think ten weeks.'

'I'll need to examine you. Where shall we go?'

Nasrin hurries back into the living room, as though summoned by a silent bell, and helps Mrs Razavi to her feet. I follow the two women down a long hall lined with artworks and family photographs. I feel a little body brush past me and I stand back as Jannat runs to her mother's side.

'I'm coming with you,' she insists, trying to take her mother's hand. She is wearing the stubborn pout that all girls her age use as a weapon to get what they want.

Nasrin intervenes. 'Your mother will be busy for a little bit, darling, so how about you and I have some ice-cream in the kitchen?'

I hope with all my heart that Mrs Razavi is strong enough to endure the pain without screaming and frightening her child.

The room we are to use is a good size, with a bed and dresser taking up one end and a desk and two chairs opposite them. A second door in the room stands ajar, and I am heartened to see that it is a clean white bathroom. Mrs Razavi's daughter won't have to see her hobbling along the hall with blood pouring down her legs.

'Doctor Karimi, you'll save my life by doing this,' says Mrs Razavi, using the same words all the women I help in this way feel moved to employ. She is sincere, and I am not so churlish as to shrug off such gratitude, but at the same time I'm thinking it would be a welcome change to hear a woman say, 'Doctor Karimi, I thank you for taking this insane risk on my behalf.'

'Shall I sit on the bed or the chair?' she asks. I notice the blinds have already been drawn tightly and extra blankets are folded neatly at the edge of the brass bed.

'The bed, please,' I tell her.

Folding her chador back, she allows me to examine her stomach, and once I am satisfied with the early stage of her pregnancy, I ask her to remove the chador completely. 'If you're quite certain this is what you want, I'll proceed.'

'Yes, Doctor. Go ahead, please.' Then she says, 'Will it hurt?'

I nod solemnly. 'Yes, it will hurt. You'd best be ready. And when I say it will hurt, I mean that it will hurt badly. I'm sorry.'

Her voice catches in her throat as she attempts to speak again. She brushes away tears, and it seems to me they have less to do with fear of the pain she faces than with the fact that the outcome of this ordeal will not be a living child, like her little Jannat.

She doesn't flinch as I inject her. 'How long is it going to take?' she asks, watching the Prostodin drain into her arm.

'Three, four, maybe five hours.'

I check her blood pressure and listen to her heart, satisfied that she is stable for the time being. I keep a close eye on her for the next fifteen minutes, relieved that she shows no dangerous reactions to the medicine.

Nasrin slips back into the room. 'I've put Jannat down for a nap. She's sleeping now,' she informs us. Mrs Razavi seems barely to hear her, her face turned away from the two of us as she stares blankly at the covered window.

I suggest to Nasrin that she stay and lend her support, and no sooner are the words out of my mouth than Mrs Razavi throws off the blanket and says, 'I'm going to be sick.' Nasrin rushes to her side, helping her to the bathroom.

I hear violent retching behind the door. Nasrin opens it, looking distressed. 'She can't stop vomiting, Doctor Karimi. Maybe you should come in.'

I go to Mrs Razavi's side as she heaves one more time. A small trickle of vomit runs down into the toilet bowl. 'It's okay,' I tell her. 'This is normal. Your stomach will settle down. Being sick is a good sign.'

An hour passes, and between bouts of nausea Mrs Razavi rests on the soft bed with her eyes closed, her face nearly drained of colour.

'The pain has settled down, Doctor,' she murmurs, breaking the long silence.

'I'm afraid that's a sign you need another shot.'

I open my kit to prepare the next needle. Nasrin shifts uncomfortably, clearly doubting that the older woman will be able to withstand another round of nausea and pain. And she has good reason for her concern. Two minutes of the medicine draining into her arm and Mrs Razavi is screaming her lungs out. She bites into the pillow in a vain attempt to stifle the pain, to suffocate the noise.

'What time is it?' she gasps when the pain lapses for a few seconds.

'It's half past one,' I tell her, puzzled that she asked. 'Why?'

'No reason,' she says, then lets out another heart-rending shriek.

Over the next hour, up until the third injection, and then the next hour after that, Mrs Razavi suffers such torments that I almost wish I could call the whole thing off. She is not a young woman. Her body can't cope with the rigour of an artificially contracted uterus; I know the pain can be almost as severe as childbirth. She is as pale as bone. I begin to doubt my own judgement in going ahead with the termination. I have to struggle to stay calm, to maintain a professional demeanour.

Nasrin turns her gaze to me again and again, as though she wants to say, 'This isn't right. No human being can survive what you're inflicting on her.' But she says nothing except with her eyes, which implore me to ease the suffering. And I can't do that.

Behind the creation of Prostodin lies a political agenda. The drug is designed for the desperate and the powerless. Those who depend on it do not feel they have the right to complain about the pain that attends its use. No medication that induced such agony would be prescribed for middle-class men. They wouldn't put up with it. But women with an unwanted pregnancy are not likely to say, No, this isn't good enough. Do more research. Produce a drug that doesn't cause such pain.

Mrs Razavi pleads for Nasrin to take her to the bathroom well after the third injection. She has violent diarrhoea, she is vomiting, and is so contorted she can't stand upright. The sounds I hear could be coming from a slaughterhouse.

Then comes an especially shrill scream, not from Mrs Razavi, but from Nasrin, who then throws open the bathroom door. 'Doctor, come quick! She's collapsed!'

And right at that moment, Jannat walks into the bedroom, her eyes still sleepy. 'Maman? Where's Maman?'

'Stay there, Jannat,' Nasrin calls from the bathroom, but in such a panicky way that it only heightens the little girl's alarm. She pushes her way into the bathroom to see her mother lying motionless on the floor. '*Maman!*' she screams.

I say, 'Please, Nasrin, take Jannat out of the room,' and she scoops the distraught child up and rushes her out. The screams echo down the hall.

I search for a pulse in my patient. It's weak, but it's there. I put my ear to her mouth and feel her breath against my cheek.

Nasrin hurries back in. 'What should I do?'

'Help me get her back to the bed.'

I swiftly hook her cannula to the saline solution, letting it flow in slowly. Nasrin is holding back tears as she follows my instructions to hold her friend's legs up to allow the blood to flow to her head. I'm watching the cannula. To my horror, the fluid stops running and the tube begins to fill with bright red blood. The vein has collapsed.

'Keep holding her legs up,' I urge Nasrin. 'I have to find another vein. Just keep her legs in the air. That's the most important thing you can do right now. Can I count on you?'

She nods rapidly, and hoists Mrs Razavi's legs up to rest on Nasrin's shoulders. I move quickly to the other side of the bed and check Mrs Razavi's left arm for a vein, stunned by how cold and pale her skin has turned in a matter of minutes. Dread settles in the pit of my stomach.

'Open your eyes for me!' I yell, yanking the tourniquet off her right arm and fastening it around her left. I feel along it until I find a vein and insert my last cannula. To my great relief the saline starts flowing through.

'Progress,' I tell Nasrin. 'Keep up the good work.'

Squeezing the bag of fluid between my two hands, I watch the saline move steadily. Mrs Razavi's heart beats fast and strong through my stethoscope. Her eyes flutter softly in her sleep. 'Mrs Razavi, open your eyes for me!'

They flicker open. She moves her lips but no sound comes out. Pale lips, frightened eyes, silent gasping. Kneeling next to her, taking her cold hand in mine, I try to coax her back to awareness of what's happening. 'Talk to me, Mrs Razavi, you have to speak. Try.'

A high-pitched shriek startles me and I whip around to find Jannat standing petrified at the door. She must be thinking her mother is dead. Nasrin tries to intercept her as she runs into the room but she ducks and weaves out of grasp and rushes to her mother's side.

'She just has a tummy ache,' Nasrin says quickly. 'She'll feel better in a minute. Why don't you go and make a pretty picture for her, Jannat?'

Three sorts of play-acting are being performed here in this small hell: Nasrin is creating a child-sized drama for the sake of Jannat; I'm enacting the role of the imperturbable doctor, when the truth is I'm scared out of my wits and feel like running away; and Mrs Razavi has for the past few hours been attempting to act as if she's involved in a standard medical procedure, when everything she experiences tells her that this is really massive trauma barely under the control of anyone at all.

I read Mrs Razavi's blood pressure as Nasrin once again escorts the poor child from the room: 90 over 65. Good enough for me. I click my fingers in front of my patient's face, startling her out of her daze. I check the fluid again. It is running well, so when Nasrin comes back I leave her with Mrs Razavi while I go to get some fresh air and regroup.

'Doctor, please don't go beyond the yard,' Nasrin urges as I leave the room.

'As you wish,' I say. But why should I not go beyond the yard? A feeling I've already experienced twice today returns – a sense of things going on that I haven't been told about.

I step into the yard and breathe in the cold wintry air, then light a cigarette and enjoy a long, slow drag. She has to start bleeding soon, I mutter to myself. My patient can't withstand any more injections. She's barely made it as it is, and she'll be under even more strain when the bleeding starts.

Walking back into the bedroom, I see Nasrin helping her friend out of the bed.

'I'm bleeding,' says Mrs Razavi, lifting a blanket to reveal the red-stained sheets beneath her. I leave her to the privacy of her bathroom, but within a minute she cries out, 'Doctor! Blood! A huge torrent of blood just gushed out of me! This can't be normal!'

'May I come in to examine you?'

'Please!'

I look down into the bloody toilet bowl, at the foetal matter bobbing on the surface. 'You'll be pleased to know it's almost over. You've miscarried. That gush you felt was exactly what we've been waiting for. Let's get you back to bed now.'

Lying down once more, she bleeds steadily for twenty minutes. Then it's over. Nasrin begins gathering up the blood-soaked sheets.

Kneeling at Mrs Razavi's bedside I inform her of the precautions she should take for the next week or so. While I'm talking, the phone rings. Nasrin darts a glance at Mrs Razavi.

'I'd better answer,' Mrs Razavi says, a note of alarm in her voice.

Nasrin fetches a cordless phone from the next room and Mrs Razavi gestures for Nasrin and myself to be silent.

'Hello?' she says, as calmly as she can manage. Her face grows tight with tension, but she continues to speak evenly. 'Oh, are you? Okay then . . . yes, I will . . . No, nothing. I'm just a bit sick. Okay, I'll see you soon, darling.' She hangs up and stares straight ahead, avoiding eye contact. She wordlessly passes the phone to Nasrin.

'Was that . . .?' Nasrin says, her voice trailing off.

Mrs Razavi nods grimly. 'He's coming home tonight.'

'No! Why?'

'I don't know. He didn't go to Bojnord after all. He's on the bus, coming home.' Mrs Razavi runs her hands nervously through her hair, tugging it hard.

'What's happening here?' I ask.

Nasrin looks at Mrs Razavi, who finally looks at me and crumbles. She begins to sob and heave. 'It was my husband,' she cries. 'He was supposed to go to Bojnord tonight but he's coming back home.'

'But you're divorced, aren't you?'

She lowers her head as if in shame. 'I'm sorry we didn't tell you.

We were afraid if you knew the truth you might not help me.'

I recall the cab I saw when I arrived. 'The taxi belongs to him, doesn't it?'

'Yes.'

'So if you're still with your husband, why are you terminating the pregnancy?'

Mrs Razavi refuses to meet my gaze, covering her face with her hands as she continues to sob. It is Nasrin who speaks up. 'She had an affair with my brother. Mr Razavi had a vasectomy two years ago.'

I'm at first flabbergasted, then furious. 'So if her husband comes home, he will kill her, you, me, and your brother. *And you knew this?*'

Nasrin shakes her head helplessly, tears springing to her eyes. 'What could we do?'

'Where is he now? How far from Mashhad?' I'm already rapidly collecting my supplies.

'Maybe an hour away. A little more, hopefully.'

Stifling my anger for now, I wrap up needles, bandages and tubes and pack them swiftly into my bag. When the last of the fluid drains into Mrs Razavi I remove the needles, unroll some bandage and lay her back on the bed. I put a bandage over the cannula spots on both arms.

'There will be bruising,' I warn. 'Make sure your husband doesn't see it or he'll ask questions you won't want to answer.'

Tearing out my script pad and pen, I quickly scribble a few necessary prescriptions, jotting beside them careful instructions and doses. I rest my hand on Mrs Razavi's shoulder, intending to deliver a brief lecture on the obligations of the patient to the doctor, but I can feel the tremor of fear running through her and realise how desperate and afraid she is. I spontaneously forgive her.

'Call me if there's severe bleeding, or if you run a temperature or have any unusual pain. You'll have some cramping and bleeding for a few days, which is fine. I need to know the results of your ultrasound. I've put an order for this on the script and I'll leave it with Nasrin so your husband doesn't find it.'

'Thank you so much, Doctor Karimi. Thank you with all my heart.'

I scan the room one last time; I mustn't leave a single trace behind. Satisfied, I say a final farewell to both women and leave the house.

As I pack my supplies into my car I see a tall man in his late forties walking towards me. I act natural, slamming the boot closed before climbing into the car. I watch through my mirror as he opens the tall white gates of the Razavi household and steps inside.

One minute, I missed him by one minute.

Should I take this as a warning to stop? Or is Adonai on my side for saving Mrs Razavi from stoning? Has He delayed Mr Razavi for a minute to let me make a clean getaway? I now know I'm on the radar not only of unmarried women with a baby in their womb, but also married women caught out in a love affair. Oh, wonderful! I might as well hang myself now and save the Islamic Republic the trouble.

For the next four days I live in a state of heightened anxiety. Under any other circumstances I would have stayed for a further three hours with a patient as weak as Mrs Razavi. Was she okay? Did her husband suspect anything? Had little Jannat said something?

Eventually I hear from Nasrin, who tells me that the ultrasound has shown nothing wrong. Mrs Razavi is fine.

I hang up the phone and drop my head into my hands. We have all survived.

Leila

I lie listlessly under tangled blankets. Crisp air sneaks through the cracks around the window frame, spreading a chill through the room. A patch of weak sunshine is thrown across the floor.

What have I done? What have *we* done? Doctor Karimi, this is not part of the love Gibran described so poetically. There is no link between the pleasure he portrayed and my own revolting coupling with Hamid. Betrayal licks at me with its hot tongue, covering me with a slime so repugnant I can't bear to wear my own skin. Red raised welts disfigure my arms from where I have scratched at myself.

Did he lie from the very start? The whispered vows of love, the touches and kisses that seemed brimming with sincerity, the nakedness of our very souls – were they all deception?

And what of my own betrayals? How minor his were in comparison with mine. Maybe I led him into this. Hadn't I accepted his gifts? Written to him about my feelings? Asked him to call? Gone to his house alone? Welcomed his touch? I have betrayed myself unforgivably, lied to my loved ones, involved my sister in sin, betrayed my mother's trust. Worst of all, I have betrayed the One I pray to.

What's left for me? In Allah's name, what is left for me?

I hurriedly dry my eyes at the sound of footsteps approaching my door. Moments later it is flung open and Majid crosses the floor in three giant strides. He kicks the side of my mattress and demands I prepare his breakfast. Had he found me with my wrists slashed, blood running freely onto the sheets, he'd have said, 'Bandage that and make my breakfast.'

I tidy myself up and dress for the day without looking into the mirror. I can't face my own eyes. What must others see when they look at me? Can they tell? Am I transparent? Is the anguish as clearly etched across my face as the scratches are on my arms? Once I wrap myself in my chador, covering my head in black fabric, will any living soul even notice my suffering? How many other girls like me are weeping behind this camouflage?

A few days ago I had considered calling Hamid, hoping he would apologise, offer to marry me, reassure me that he loved me. But I don't deserve his apology. I detest myself so intensely that I can't accept anything that would lessen my contempt. I have crossed a bridge that has collapsed behind me. Do you see, Doctor Karimi? On this side of the bridge live all the seduced, raped and ravished women of Iran, and we are like wraiths, no longer human. This is the land of the broken-hearted, of crippled virgins. We can never return to the land across the bridge, because the bridge has gone. We are like a colony of lepers. No one wishes to touch us, no one wishes to glimpse us. We are unclean.

I shuffle lifelessly into the kitchen and set about my chores. My brothers call out, 'Get a move on, you lazy slug! You're hopeless! What's the matter with you, moron?' No rage at their rudeness gathers inside me. I deserve their abuse.

Winter this year is cold and dark. For a month I drift through the motions of living. I've gradually learnt to behave, not only outwardly, but deep within. I am the perfect daughter, a model of obedient womanhood. Is this what all women go through? An experience so crushing and excruciating that it extinguishes the fire inside them? Did my mother suffer through something to make her submit so willingly? I succumb, I yield, I stay silent.

In late January I get physically ill. Is it possible to be sick from sorrow? The scent of saffron makes me queasy. I am plagued by constant nausea. I feel weak. I lie down wearily several times a day.

I keep these symptoms to myself. The less Mother notices me, the better. Already she watches me with narrowed eyes, knowing something serious happened the day I came home in such a state. Who knows what she imagines. Maybe she thinks I saw something hideous that shocked me badly – a man exposing himself in the street, something of that sort. If only that were it! And now my period is late. But when catastrophe looms ahead of us, we employ our imagination to search out every alternative. I tell myself I'm late because I am stressed. My period was two months late when I was studying for my final exams in high school. And I tell myself, You are sick because you wish to be dead. Because your heart is torn to pieces. Because you hate the sight of yourself. I never say, You are sick because you are pregnant.

Still, I must be sure. While Mother naps I find the general medical book that is kept beside the cookbooks. I scan the index, turning quickly to the pages on menstrual cycles. My eyes skim the page until I land on a sentence that reads: *The most common cause for a missed period in a woman of reproductive age is pregnancy.* And I can fool myself no longer. It's as if I needed to see it written before I let myself believe it.

I am not breathing. My lungs strain in panic, but there is no air. I clench my eyes shut, irrationally thinking that when I open them again I'll discover I've read the sentence wrongly, or that the words aren't there at all.

But there they are.

What do I do now? I have to talk to someone, but who? There's nobody. I no longer have anyone to talk to. I can't share this with Samira; she would die with worry if she knew.

Over the next week, I sneak quick peaks into the medical book. I learn to my semi-relief that I can test my pregnancy without involving a doctor. I think of the pharmacy closest to my house, devising a plan for how to get there and back without arousing any suspicions, or encountering anyone. Once again I wait day after day for my mother to leave the house, and eventually she announces that she is off to visit a friend. As she puts her chador over her head she looks at me, her eyes softening with sympathy.

'Why don't you come too? You haven't set foot out of the house in more than a month.'

'Maybe next time,' I say, my voice catching.

She comes to me, tipping my chin up so that my eyes meet hers. 'Something is wrong,' she says quietly.

As soon as I can no longer see her from the window I slip on my chador, for once welcoming its protection. I don't want anyone looking at me, I don't want a man to wonder what I might look like beneath its shapeless fabric. *I love my chador.* I cover as much of my face as I can without making it impossible to see.

The walls of the pharmacy are stark white, the lights hum overhead. A weary woman at the counter asks if she can help me.

'Pregnancy test, please.'

She hands over the packet, but when I reach for my wallet I realise that in my haste I've left it at home.

'I'll be back in a minute, just *one* minute!' I race back home, rush to my room, grab my wallet, run to the front door and fling it open in time to see my mother walking up the front steps.

'Leila? Where are you going?'

'To find you,' I tell her, a lie that comes to my tongue so fluently. 'I thought maybe it would be good to get out after all.'

'I was stuck with Mrs Sarabi. She carried on again about her son. But don't worry, I'd never arrange a marriage with him.' My mother steps into the house, pushing the door shut again.

A further two weeks pass without sign of menstrual blood. The nausea has gotten so intense that everything I eat causes me to retch. After lunch one day, my mother sets the wet dishes to dry on the counter and asks not to be disturbed while she takes a nap. I wait kneeling with my ear to her closed door until I hear the gentle rasp of her breathing. Hoping she will not wake soon, I sneak silently out the door and hurry to the pharmacy.

This time there's a man serving behind the counter. I keep my head down, feeling like a criminal, and say, 'I need a pregnancy test.'

'Yeah? When was your last period?' I glance up to see a mildly satiric grin on his face. 'Where's your husband?'

'It's for my sister.'

He gives a smirk as if to say, Oh really? He takes a packet from a drawer. 'Fifty toman.'

I hand him the money and tuck the white packet under my chador. Mother is still sleeping when I return. I've been gone less than twenty minutes. I judge that I still have time to take the test. Millions of women take it every day and pray for a positive result. Millions more pray for a negative one. I of course pray fervently with the second group. And like so many in that group, the desperate group, I am crushingly disappointed. The test is positive. One sexual experience in my life, and it has left me pregnant. I kneel on the bathroom floor staring unbelievingly at the blue lines on the test strip.

This is the cliff I've been walking towards. Now I'm plunging down through thin air and the only thing that will arrest my fall is death. I don't even attempt to think of a miracle that might save me. Miracles, love, desire, kisses, caresses, enchanting words – they all belong to a realm that I will never visit again. What I could not imagine has come to pass. My life is over.

The Doctor

The January air is so crisp and clear and bracing, I park a few blocks from my surgery to enjoy a brief walk in it. Winter has established itself, and the days are short and dark. We've had multiple snowfalls, and the pines lining the streets have been transformed into a vivid fantasy of green and white and rusty browns. It does me good to feast my eyes on this rich palette. I'm also feeling happy because Azita and Newsha are staying with me over the weekend, after which we'll all go to Mashhad. It's such joy to me, having my daughter kiss my cheeks and call me Daddy.

I greet Arash as I enter the waiting room, but when I answer my mobile phone and hear the dodgy herbalist Shafiq on the line, my mood withers in an instant. If I refuse to help him, he'll send an anonymous letter to the authorities. The fact that he charges women a ridiculous fee for directing them to my services appals me. Nietzsche's idea echoes in my ears: if one aspires to be a great person, one shall endure the tormenting leeches who latch on. Not that I aspire to greatness, but when I assented to save the first rape victim Shafiq preyed on, I also drew his poisonous fangs to my flesh.

I listen to his whining nasal voice with distaste. 'When can I see you in Mashhad?' he asks.

'Maybe next week. I'm coming for a medical conference.'

'I'll give you a call then. Could you please bring your gear?'

My conversation with Shafiq taints the entire day. I have nothing but problems with patients. Some with appointments don't show up, others show up demanding to be seen immediately, children howl nonstop, and one woman refuses to let me examine her even though she made the appointment herself.

The night is just as trying. Shortly after I arrive at the military hospital, Nemati phones for me to come to the emergency room. There's a soldier who's been shot. I go in to find a young man motionless on the bed, a hole in the middle of his chest. Blood covers his uniform and the sheets beneath him and is streaming onto the concrete floor. Nemati stands next to the bed with no idea what to do. A sergeant and two other soldiers who have brought in this wounded comrade stare at me for direction.

The bullet has pierced the chest and left a gaping exit wound in the soldier's back. I've seen horrific wounds like this before. I deduce that this one has been caused by an army-issue G3 automatic rifle fired at point-blank range. Only a G3 bullet could make such an enormous hole in a human body.

I ask the soldiers calmly, 'What's happened?'

'He put his G3 to his chest and shot himself,' the sergeant says.

'He'd had enough.'

Suicide is not rare in the military. The training is unnecessarily tough. For hours soldiers are forced to stand with fourteen kilos of ammunition strapped on their backs, around their waists, and over their shoulders. Their food is poor and most have no leave for months at a time. Many shoot themselves in the leg just to get a few weeks off. They remove a bullet from its shell and empty half the explosives to avoid shooting their entire leg off. The punishment for this is an extra two months of service after they heal, an acceptable price to a soldier desperate for a couple of weeks' respite.

This soldier's name is etched on a dog tag around his neck: Naser Kabiri. I go through the motions of checking his vital signs. There is no point in performing CPR.

'How long did he have left in the military?' I ask the other men.

One says, 'Only two months.'

Looking at Nemati, I say, 'Dead on arrival. Fill out the paperwork and I'll sign it. Call my mobile phone when you're ready or if you need me. I'm going outside for a few minutes.'

I need to calm myself down. The country isn't even at war but still soldiers are dying all around me. Why doesn't the government pay attention to these young men? The luckier ones might get a decent meal once in a while, but the majority have food slapped on their plates that is unappetising, cold and sometimes rancid. And there's rarely enough of it. Nobody cares about the soldiers' mental health. Tens of thousands suffer from depression or anxiety, but there are no counselling services. Commanders are hard on their men and at times ignore the certificates I write for medical leave.

Suicide is scorned in Iran, regarded as a sign of weakness or cowardice. Nobody sees it as the desperate act of a person who can no longer tolerate horrible conditions, loneliness, and pointless exercises. Islam considers suicide a sin, and this dead soldier's family will be fined for the cost of the bullet that ended his life.

A thick black cloud sits right over my head for the next three days. I can't stop thinking of that young man who put a high-calibre gun to his chest and blew a hole through himself. Everything in my training as a surgeon, and in my temperament as a human being, rebels against the infliction of wounds so grievous that my skills are rendered useless. Am I gloomy, grim, a sad sack by nature? I'm not. I love life, its colour and joy; the smile on the face of a child is for me the most wonderful thing in the universe. I want happiness for everyone. The truth is, I'm a type of Pollyanna, as the Americans say; an eternal optimist. I have known the bliss – yes, bliss – of saving a life that seemed to be over; I have saved men with wounds as appalling as that of the soldier who shot himself. For a surgeon, a pulse is like the breath of God moving through a human body. Give me a pulse and I'm happy. Suicide? I hate it, hate it. I want to say to anyone with a gun at his head, his finger on the trigger, 'Please, I promise you. Things will get better.' I have no right to say any such thing, but it's what I want to believe with all my heart. That things will get better.

The day before I'm scheduled to leave for Mashhad, Shafiq calls to make sure I'm coming. 'Don't forget the package,' he says. 'He's very sick. He could die without treatment.'

This is the code. A girl will commit suicide unless I terminate her pregnancy.

The next day, I pack a few ampoules of Prostodin in a flask of ice and set off with my family at four o'clock in the morning. Azita sits in the front next to me, Newsha sleeps in the back seat. By eight I've dropped them off at our apartment and am on my way to the conference at the Imam Reza hospital, a major university hospital where I did my training. The conference is on tuberculosis, which had been almost eradicated in Iran until the Soviet Union attacked Afghanistan in 1979 and hundreds of thousands of Afghan refugees, many of them infected, fled to Iran. Since then, hundreds of Iranians have died of the disease every year.

The session lasts five hours, and it's not until midafternoon that I reach Shafiq's shop in the Meydan Shohada district, in a distant part of Mashhad. Shafiq is a skinny, rat-like little guy. He stands at the counter in front of shelves stocked with bottles of herbal remedies, and also a number of expensive medications that even pharmacies don't normally carry. Many critical medications are not available in Iran, and patients have to pay high prices for them on the black market. Shafiq, with his links to drug smugglers, and corrupt Revolutionary Guards who are happy to take bribes, makes a fortune selling them to desperate people. The herbs are merely a cover for a much more lucrative business.

'Doctor Karimi!' Shafiq greets me with a big smile that reveals his ill-sorted mouthful of teeth.

'Listen, I don't have much time. Tell me about the case.'

He leans over the counter and lowers his voice. 'There's this poor girl who is fourteen weeks pregnant and has no partner. She is single, but thankfully she has a very good friend who is willing to pay.'

'Are you sure this isn't a trap?' Men who deal in illegal drugs are likely to draw the attention of the police.

'I know the man who's paying for it.' Shafiq opens his drawer and takes out a thick wad of notes. He pushes them towards me. 'Fifty thousand toman for you.'

Shafiq has no sympathy for the girl, and I have no doubt he's demanded at least a hundred thousand toman and already pocketed half for himself.

'Does she have any children?'

'No, but she's had two miscarriages.' Shafiq looks at me slyly and adds, 'She is a prostitute.'

In Iran prostitution is punishable by whipping and execution, and every year hundreds of women, some under the age of eighteen, are hanged or stoned to death for it. But still women turn to prostitution. Some have been kicked out by their families. Some are poor and uneducated and have no other way to feed themselves. Some are orphans. Most are addicted to opium or heroin. A pregnant prostitute will be beaten by her pimp then thrown out, leaving her without income or means of survival. There are no charities in Iran that pick up homeless people and house them, no charities that extend pity and help to a starving prostitute. These people simply die of hunger and neglect, are found dead in alleyways and gutters and deserted lots.

I've been hoping in my heart of hearts for a way out. I wanted to hear that the prospective patient was a woman with three kids who didn't want a fourth. I would have been free to say, 'Tell her no. She'll have to cope with another child.' And I wouldn't care even if Shafiq blackmails me. I would satisfy his unquenchable greed with a false promise of the next job, the next top-dollar customer. But once again I have no choice.

I will do the termination with injections, not by curette. I can't afford the risk of catching hepatitis C by using curette and suction on a patient whose medical history I do not know.

Shafiq gives me an address and a phone number and I leave his shop quickly. As soon as I reach the privacy of my car I ring the number from my mobile phone. A young man answers. I arrange to meet him and my patient after the conference that evening at an address in Alteimor, a dangerous slum on the outskirts of Mashhad.

And all through the conference, I strive to find an excuse I can give Azita. She will be deeply suspicious of what I've been up to when I return late. Other women would perhaps think their husband was having an affair, but Azita will think only one thing: that I have been performing a termination. She will say, 'And that was more important than spending time with your daughter? A dirty, disgusting whore means more to you than Newsha?' I decide, finally, to enlist my mother in my scheme of deceit. She knows I perform terminations, and is forever warning that I will destroy the peace and security of her old age by getting myself hanged. But she will help me nevertheless. She will call Azita and tell her I am visiting her friend Haji Heydar in hospital. Haji, she will say, has had a heart attack and she wants me to look in on him. Haji hasn't had a heart attack, and he is of course no friend to my mother; he is a vile human being if ever there was one. But the excuse will suffice.

Alteimor is a disgusting place. It's the part of town where criminals gather, a sort of bad-guy ghetto. I would normally avoid the place like the plague, which is stupid in a way because I grew up in one of the most notorious slums of Tehran, and later in another slum in Mashhad, where families of six or eight people lived crowded together in rat-infested buildings. I ran barefoot in the dirty streets and ate on the bare floor with my hands – when there was something to eat, that is. I was one of the children who cried from constant hunger, and I would eat out of the garbage cans at school after the other kids had left. My brother and my mother and I slept huddled on a bare mattress wearing everything we owned to stay warm. I'd never heard of something called a birthday. Alteimor could have been my home.

It's dark when I reach there. People lie curled up under trees, craving shelter. A storm has roared in from the north and rain is coming down hard. As I step out into it a thug on the sidewalk tosses away his cigarette butt and comes towards me.

'Doctor Karimi?' The man's left eye is noticeably bigger than his right one, and a scar runs from the centre of his bottom lip to beneath his jawline.

'Yes. I'm Doctor Karimi.'

'Kamal. We spoke earlier. Follow me.'

We walk along the verge of a muddy road. I can make out a wasteland at the end of it. There are no more houses beyond. Kamal stops at a wooden door and I follow him into a small, dim, cold room. The building is not a house at all, but a shed. In the middle of the room a portable oil heater hisses. Sitting beside it is a woman dressed in jeans and a blouse, no chador. She staggers to her feet and manages a weak, 'Hello.' She's a drug addict: dark circles beneath sunken eyes, her face as grey as ash, her lips cracked.

I glance about for a place clean enough to do the procedure. A worn, cheap rug covers the floor; a thin blanket is tossed at the end of a thin foam mattress in a corner. I notice on the blanket a metal opium pipe. I know opium well. I've treated a number of addicts. The drug is expensive in other parts of the world but it's cheap in Iran. Most is produced in Afghanistan, then transported to the West through Iran and Turkey. Along the way, dope for the Iranian market is siphoned off.

The woman is too weak to stand for long and soon sits back on the floor. I squat beside her. 'Are you the patient?'

She nods. The room has no furniture, no kitchen area. I wonder when she's last eaten. How will she possibly survive the vomiting and diarrhoea to come?

'Before we begin I need to examine you,' I tell her.

She seems baffled by this.

Kamal barks, 'Lie down so the doctor can examine you.' Like a zombie, the woman shuffles to the mattress and flops on her back.

I check her abdomen. She's so thin I can feel her kidneys. I can also feel the dome of her uterus above her pelvis; she's around twelve weeks into the pregnancy. 'How old are you?' I ask.

'Twenty-two.'

I would have placed her closer to forty. 'You're not allergic to anything, are you?'

She shakes her head and I tell her I'm going to give her injections every hour until she miscarries. 'It's not going to be easy,' I warn. 'There will be a lot of pain. You'll have diarrhoea and you'll vomit until you feel like you're dying.'

Kamal says in a matter-of-fact way, 'It's fine, Doc. She's a strong girl.'

I open my bag and am grieved to see that the ice in my flask has already begun to melt. 'Do you have a fridge here?' I ask.

'No, Doc,' Kamal says. 'Nothing like that.'

Prostodin lasts at room temperature no longer than three hours. I take out the first ampoule, cut its top off and drain the liquid into a syringe. The woman has little flesh on her arm, but she doesn't flinch or whimper as the needle pierces her skin. I have adrenaline and dexamethasone handy in case she has an anaphylactic reaction, but when I check her blood pressure it's stable.

She lies back on the mattress as if she intends to sleep. I sit beside her and ask her name.

'Shahin,' she says, opening her sunken eyes.

'You're not on the pill?'

Kamal answers for her. 'No. She's a stupid girl. I pay for the pills but she forgets to take them.'

Shahin whispers, 'My life is a misery.' She closes her eyes and murmurs, 'I'm better off leaving this world.'

I go outside for a smoke while I'm waiting for the Prostodin to kick in. The rows of abandoned houses look haunted; they remind me of where I spent my childhood. A stray dog shuffles along the road, so skinny I can count his ribs when he stops to sniff me. He's the canine equivalent of the woman inside: starving, wretched, better off dead.

Shahin's retching breaks the deathly silence. I grind my cigarette out and head back inside. I find her vomiting into a rusted metal basin. Kamal sits in a corner, smoking.

I hold Shahin's shoulders. 'Don't worry. The medicine's supposed to make this happen.'

She returns to the mattress and attempts to lie down, but the cramps are too severe. She presses her knees against her chest in pain. There's nothing I can give her to ease her suffering. A few minutes later, she drags herself to the toilet, where she stays for a long time.

'Please make sure she's all right,' I tell Kamal. 'If her blood pressure drops too low she could pass out.'

Kamal yanks the toilet door open without knocking and says, 'What the fuck's going on in there? Get out.'

Shahin picks herself up off the floor and walks unsteadily to the mattress.

'Are you all right?' I ask her, and she nods. Unlike most of my termination patients, she doesn't cry out from the pain. Hers is the stoicism of the unloved, the degraded. So little of her is noticed, so little sparks any concern from others that she has surrendered the right to complain about anything, even agony. I could never kiss her cheek, partly because that would violate a surgeon's ethics, and partly because she is so withered, but I wish I could.

A few minutes later, I give her another injection, this time in her right arm. She becomes sick immediately and pushes past me to get to the basin.

Kamal lights another cigarette with the butt of the one he's just finished. 'How long before it's done, Doc?' he asks me.

'Anywhere from one to three hours.'

'This is disgusting. Stupid cunt.'

At that moment, Shahin collapses to the floor with a thud. I hurry to her side, trying to wake her. Her eyelids flicker. Kamal hauls her to her feet and drops her onto the mattress. 'Damn it,' he grunts.

I grab my stethoscope and listen to her heart. Far too fast. I check her blood pressure. Far too low. I prepare to hook her up to intravenous fluids, but her arms are so thin I can't find a vein.

'She's used them all,' says Kamal. She's no more than a commodity to him, like a beaten-up old car that he hopes to get a few more kilometres out of before abandoning.

I check the tops of her feet, but she's used all those veins as well. I rotate her feet and ankles, holding them up to the light; all the veins are gone. I have only one option – the jugular vein. It's an extremely dangerous process but there's no other choice. Very carefully I slide a cannula into her jugular, aiming it towards the heart, avoiding the delicate valves. Success. I start the fluids, but I have to keep the drip slow. Soon she needs to go to the bathroom.

Kamal says, 'Stay there, idiot. Can't you see your neck is all hooked up?'

'I'll take her,' I say, and help her to stand. I hold the saline beside her as she first stumbles to the basin. She tries to vomit, but there's nothing left in her stomach.

I take her to the bathroom and am horrified to discover the toilet is nothing more than a feculent hole in the floor. There's a jug of water in the corner for her to wash herself. She squats over the hole for a few minutes, clutching her stomach in pain, but there's no blood.

Another two hours drag by, marked by bouts of vomiting and severe cramping. The only encouraging sign is that her blood pressure has come up slightly.

'How much longer?' Kamal asks again.

'Maybe another hour or two. I can't tell.'

'I can't wait around anymore.' He stubs out his cigarette. 'Behave yourself,' he tells Shahin over his shoulder as he leaves. 'I'll see you tomorrow.'

I stare after him in disbelief. How can he possibly leave this sickly woman here on her own? He hasn't even bothered to ask me if she'll need someone with her when it's time for me to go.

After the third injection, Shahin can no longer bear the pain. She's on the edge of the mattress, moaning and rubbing her stomach, whispering over and over, 'Allah, please help me. Please help me, Allah.'

About half an hour after Kamal leaves, I tell Shahin I need to check her blood pressure again.

'Can it wait for a minute? I have to go to the bathroom.' A minute later she calls out, 'I see blood!'

I go to check on her, and despite her extreme pain she thanks me. 'I'm sorry I'm not doing better with the pain.'

'Don't be sorry. You're going to be all right.'

But the bleeding doesn't progress and I have no choice but to give her the last injection. While she drags herself into the bathroom one more time, I check my watch. Almost ten-thirty. I step outside, call Azita and tell her I'm still at the hospital with Haji Heydar.

Azita says, 'With Haji Heydar? Do you think I'm simple-minded? I didn't believe your mother when she called me, and I don't believe you.' She hangs up.

I sigh and shake my head. She'll be angry with me for days, turning her back when I talk, refusing any peace offerings.

Inside, I find Shahin on the mattress, rocking herself to ease the pain. I squat in front of her and rub her shoulders. 'Do you have any relatives who could look after you? A mother or father or sister? A friend?'

'I grew up in an orphanage. I have no one. Kamal is the only one I have. My angel.'

Kamal is her angel? Dear God.

Finally, at eleven-thirty, her bleeding becomes more severe, and the pain so intense she faints in the bathroom again. I have to drag her back to the mattress. Once I settle her, I check her blood pressure once more: 97 over 65. Not too bad. She's as skinny as a pencil, but she's got a lot of fight in her.

A few minutes later, we return to the bathroom, and this time she passes tissue.

I examine her abdomen and I'm encouraged to find it soft. Her bleeding has slowed down considerably and her blood pressure has risen to 98 over 80. Her heart sounds fine. I check her tongue to make sure she isn't dehydrated.

'I'm writing some prescriptions for antibiotics and iron tablets,' I tell her, futile advice no doubt. 'I want you to drink lots of fluids and eat some meat. You have to build up your body, Shahin. Are you listening to me?'

She nods, eyes closed. She has miscarried and the pain is gone, but her skin is still pale and cold to the touch.

'How are you feeling?'

'Much better,' she says and unexpectedly opens her eyes and gazes up at me. 'Thank you so much,' she whispers. 'You can leave now. I'll be fine. Thank you for not shouting at me or leaving me here to die. Blessings on you.'

I scribble my phone number on a piece of paper. 'If the pain comes back or there's too much bleeding or if you get a temperature, you call me, okay?' I have to say this, but I know she'll be back at work in a day, or at the most two. She may still be bleeding but her clients won't take much notice.

'Okay.'

'Do you know how much Kamal paid Shafiq for this?'

'One hundred and ten thousand toman.'

One hundred and ten thousand toman, and Kamal can't find a place where this wretched girl can suffer in just a fraction more comfort. He must figure he can make ten times that sum out of her before she dies. And she will die. She'll close her eyes one day, maybe a year down the track, fall asleep, her heartbeat and respiration will dwindle to nothing, and it will be all over.

'You take care of yourself,' I say, and then I walk to my car and drive as fast as I can out of Alteimor.

Leila

Picture me, Doctor Karimi, whispering prayers to ghosts. I mean the ghosts of women who loved the wrong man, as I had; loved so deeply that they accepted kisses and caresses before marriage. The ghosts, too, of women betrayed and violated, like me. These women in their sorrow gather about me at night. They say, 'Leila, there is only death.' I whisper back, 'Help me to die. Show me the way.'

My sisters in sorrow murmur tenderly, 'A knife. A sharp knife. Plunge it into your heart. Or Leila, the poison your mother keeps to kill the insects that attack her roses.'

I ask, 'Are there other ways? Please tell me.' And Doctor Karimi, they answer me so softly, so sweetly, with such understanding. 'Leila, Leila, find a high place and leap. Take a rope, coil it around your neck.

Go to the highway where the cars and trucks speed past and kneel before them. Leila, you will feel nothing.'

I remain in communion with these sister-ghosts for hours. It is like a ceremony of welcome for death. I feel their breath on my cheeks. I feel their fingers stroking my forehead. I whisper to them, 'Oh, is there really only death?' And they whisper back, 'Yes, sister, yes, beloved, there is only death now for you.'

Then, in the early hours of the morning when the house is still and silent, I think of Hamid. Maybe he would help me? Maybe if I reach for him, he will reach back. He must. He surely must.

I get the chance to call him when my mother leaves to shop for groceries one afternoon. She doesn't offer to take me, knowing that I now prefer the solitude of home. I watch from the living-room window as she makes her way through the carpet of snow, then I pick up the phone and dial Hamid's number. My heart doesn't quicken with anticipation, my pulse doesn't race with excitement. The thought of marrying him now, after he has abandoned me, makes me sick, but it is the only hope I have to survive.

The phone rings three times before a woman answers. 'Hello?'

I hang up quickly. It is the voice of the woman who has answered the phone before. Who is she? Has Hamid mentioned a sister or auntie? Minutes pass, then I pick up the phone and dial again.

And again she answers. 'Hello?' she says, impatiently this time.

I say, 'May I speak to Hamid, please?'

'He's not here right now. Can I ask who's calling?'

I hesitate. 'This is Mrs Sabeti, I'm a . . . business partner. When will he return? It's urgent.'

'Mrs Sabeti? I'm sorry, I don't know who that is. What do you need to talk to Hamid about?'

'It's private.'

'Well, excuse me, but I am his wife. What business would he have that I'm unaware of?'

The phone slips from my hand. It swings back and forth by its twisted cord and I can hear a faint 'Hello? Hello?' as I sink to the floor.

I thought my grief had already taken me as low as it could. I thought I'd reached the depths of my sorrow. Oh, but I was very, very wrong. I writhe on the cold tiles of the living-room floor, wrenched by pain. And then I stop and lie quite still.

'He is married,' I say aloud. 'Of course! *Of course!*'

I begin to laugh hysterically, but the laughter stops and I rise to my feet and become a monster. I pick up pots and pans and crash them on the kitchen bench, I run to the wall and claw at it, I run to another wall and bash my skull against it, I shriek like a goblin, I race to the bathroom and face the mirror and spit at my reflection. I cannot breathe. I throw back my head and strive to find air. I am burning, I am a torch. I howl and howl, not giving a thought to the possibility of my mother returning and finding me transformed into a demon. I don't care. I don't care. Nobody on earth can ask me to bear this pain. I phoned Hamid believing all my love for him had faded to nothing, but it is still there, still alive, and now it is dying its true death; that's what is burning inside me, the love I thought was already dead.

I find the strength to go back to the living room and return the phone to its cradle. And I calm down enough to realise that Mother can't find me like this. A few minutes ago, I didn't care. Now I do. I straighten the pots and pans in the kitchen. I must survive long enough to kill myself. I must stay sane until I can cut open my veins, or find a rope, stuff poison down my throat. It is the vision of my death to come that keeps me alive.

After twenty-two years of being frightened of my mother, of her temper and stern looks, her remonstrations, she is now frightened of me. I am sullen. I barely speak, and when she tells me to do something I glare back at her. She fears that I have lost my wits, that I am the victim of a disease that has eaten my brain. My expression reveals nothing, but my eyes, I know, glitter with hatred and anger. Mother tells me one morning that she has called Samira and asked her to visit me. I slam the pot I am holding down so hard that the entire bench trembles.

'I don't want her here!' I shout.

'Leila, your sister! You love Samira!'

'I don't need her pity. She's a married woman now with a perfect life. Our ties were broken when she took a husband.'

I can see my mother's confusion and heartbreak. I see her own loneliness each time I shove her away from me.

My sister comes to visit me despite my protests and I reluctantly follow her into our room. I am ice. My arms remain at my sides when she hugs me tightly.

'Leila, please,' Samira whispers, 'I'm so worried about you. Please tell me what has happened. Is it that man? From the boutique? Did he hurt you?'

I wrap my arms around myself tightly so that Samira cannot take my hand.

'Leila,' she says tentatively, eyes seeking mine. 'Please let me help you.'

'There's nothing to help. Go back to Saeed. That's where you belong now.'

I know I'm hurting her. I don't care. I know, too, that my mother is waiting outside the door, hoping Samira will be able to coax some answers from me.

Samira shakes her head, leaves the room and says a quick goodbye and an apology to Mother before leaving for home.

When my mother goes to a *rozeh* the next afternoon, I cloak myself in my dark chador and black boots before rushing out the door and down the snowy street to the ancient herbal-medicine shop. It is cramped between two stone buildings deep within the winding alley of a side street by the bazaar. I shuffle inside, into the reek of burning incense and dried herbs. Big burlap bags full of seeds and grains are stacked against the walls. Dried vegetables hang from rafters. Herbs of all colours fill glass jars that reach to the ceiling.

Haji Hosein Attar, the shop's mysterious owner, is measuring out fine powder on his brass scales. His glasses slip down his long nose as he sprinkles the last few grains onto the plate. An old woman with sagging skin and tufts of snow-white hair that have slipped free of her chador stands impatiently by his side, her quivering hands impatient for her package. I approach the counter quietly. Haji Hosein is known to be temperamental.

'Forty-five toman,' he says to the old woman.

She drops coins into his waiting hand and glances at me with suspicion on her way out of the shop.

Haji Hosein turns to me, offering perhaps a quarter of a genuine smile. His face is wrinkled with age, his lips are thin, his hands lined and creased from the plucking, cutting, cooking and packaging that he has carried out for decades.

'Salam, Haji,' I say.

'Salam, my daughter, what is troubling you?'

'Is there something for miscarriage?' My voice is strong and it surprises me. It occurs to me how different I am now. A month ago, I would never have had the courage to stand where I do now, speaking with such confidence.

Haji raises an eyebrow at me. 'To prevent miscarriage or to induce it?'

'To force it.'

Haji holds my gaze. He is issuing a challenge that I accept. He rubs the white stubble of his chin.

'All right,' he says, pushing his chair back as he stands. 'Wait here.'

He disappears behind gold silk curtains for a minute, then returns with his hands full of roots of some sort. 'This is a strong plant. Boil these roots and drink the tea every morning for five days.'

Haji finishes his careful measuring, tucking each root into brown packaging and tying a tight string over the wrapping. He keeps his eyes downcast, respectful of the delicate nature of the situation. 'That will be sixty toman,' he says when he's finished.

'Will this work?'

Haji sighs and lifts his shoulders. 'My child,' he says, still not looking up into my eyes, 'our fate is always in the hands of Allah.'

The tea that I hope will save my life is prepared by boiling a root until evaporation has left a yellowy-green residue in the pot. This residue is mixed with hot water in a cup. The taste of this baby-killing tea is vile, but so it should be if I am to believe in its potency. If it were pleasant I would be disappointed. I prepare the tea each morning while my mother is occupied elsewhere, take the steaming cup back to my room and sip it slowly until nothing is left.

On the fifth day, I find three bright drops of blood on my underwear. They are like jewels. I fall to my knees and utter rapid prayers of gratitude.

My gratitude is premature. I check twenty times over the remaining hours of the day without finding another droplet of blood.

It's the same the next day. And the next. I have to accept that the herbal remedy has failed.

The following day I rise from bed early, well before my mother is up and about, trudge down the hallway, past the kitchen, out the side door and across the snow in my bare feet to the rusted shed in the corner of the backyard. This is a storage shed where we keep big sacks of onions and potatoes for the winter. Within, the shed is draped with cobwebs that catch in my hair, which I've left uncovered. Mice scurry across the floor as I make my way to the sacks.

I have already made preparations. A rope hangs over a rafter, dangling down low enough for me to tie a hefty sack of potatoes to one end. I laboriously hoist the sack to a height of about two metres, then awkwardly lower myself, still supporting the weight of the sack by holding firmly to the rope, until I am lying face up on the dirty floor. The sack is poised above my abdomen. I close my eyes, put my lower lip between my teeth to forestall any screaming, then release my grip on the rope. It lands with a thud exactly where it is meant to.

The pain is shocking. My abdomen feels as if it has absorbed the kick of a horse. I gasp without taking in any air. I lie there on the floor writhing about with my mouth opening and closing like some huge fish thrown onto a riverbank. I regain my breath at last but keep lying there, panting, waiting. I'm hoping for a massive gush of blood from between my legs. Nothing comes, and I tell myself to raise the sack and let it fall again. But my body rebels, it will not allow me to inflict such pain a second time; besides, there's no strength left in my arms. I can taste blood in my mouth and slowly raise my hand to investigate. I have bitten my lip. I turn my head sideways and spit blood into the dust.

This is what I have come to: lying on the filthy floor among years of mouse droppings, hoping to force my body to abort my growing child by pounding it with a hefty bag of potatoes. Such squalor, such depravity. Doctor Karimi, even now, looking back, I weep for my wretchedness.

I limp silently back inside before anyone notices my absence, and in the bathroom I find not even one drop of blood on my nightgown.

That night I dream I'm in a huge, dim room. I can hear a little girl sobbing and I turn around and around to determine where it is coming from. Every time I think I've located the cry and head towards it, it changes direction. I stumble about, hands groping, bumping into things as sharp as needles, as hard as rocks. Then I realise the weeping girl isn't in the room at all. I stagger outside and find myself in a desert. In the dark I can make out the shadows of snakes crawling around and scorpions stalking me. I open my mouth to call for help but no sound comes out, and I know that nobody will come to help me.

Then the dream shifts and I am in a landscape of light. I hear the crying again, and see the figure of a child in the distance. I run towards her, a little girl with long black hair sitting on the ground and holding her head on her knees as she sobs. When she looks up I see that her face is covered in blood. She has big, dark eyes with a circle of gold around her pupils, just like mine. She says, 'What are you doing to me, Maman?'

I scream in my sleep, waking myself up. Gasping, I try to orientate myself. The house is absolutely silent but the little girl's voice echoes in my ears. As I become fully awake, I put my hand on my stomach and feel the distinct, solid bump right above my pelvis.

The next morning, I stand in the booth of the payphone at the street corner. Snow is falling. The phone rings once, twice, three times. I glance about, praying not to be recognised. It is five o'clock, not yet dawn. I finally hear a sleepy response on the other end of the line.

'Aunt Sediqa,' I say with a trembling voice. 'It's me, Leila.'

The Doctor

Azita and Newsha are with me in Quchan for three days this time, and I've taken those days off from the military hospital. If I want to have a marriage – and I do – I have to spend time with my wife and my daughter. Another benefit of this short holiday will be that I'll be able to work on my book, *Battle of the Gods*, a project dearer to my heart than medicine. I'd learnt at an early age the similarities and differences between the gods people pray to. I've written about these themes before, and have also translated books about them, but my work has been banned from publication because the fanatics in power despise anything but total adherence to strict Muslim beliefs. I have no doubt the government watches me closely, which makes seeing patients for free and paying for their medicines dangerous.

Not to mention the terminations. I've lost count of the number I've performed in the last three years. I've stopped thinking about the toll they take on my nerves. But now this.

We arrive home after a day out to find the apartment trashed. Drawers have been ripped out, their contents flung everywhere, and anything of value gone – the television, stereo, furniture. Even things of no value to anyone else have been taken, including my videotapes of Newsha as a baby. Heartbreaking.

I stand amidst the debris in a state of shock. Nobody expects their home to be robbed. It's like a violation, property rape. The police have come and gone, promising further investigation. Azita is on the verge of hysteria, terrified the burglars will return while we're asleep and cut our throats. As my initial shock eases, a fear takes hold that this could be to do with my illegal procedures. Has somebody in power learnt of them?

The fingerprint men come early the next morning. Both are young, with well-trimmed beards, and eyes that dart across the carnage. They both wear black trousers, but one has a white shirt with blue stripes and the other a blue shirt with white stripes. On any other day I'd find that amusing, but nothing can shake my sombre mood.

'If there are prints here, we'll find them,' one of them promises, and after about an hour he comes up with two good prints. 'These will help,' he says.

'At least two people did this,' the other one says, brushing a door-knob for prints.

As I'm due to start work again I send Azita and Newsha back to Mashhad on the bus. When I arrive at the hospital to begin my shift, my immediate boss, Colonel Sadiqi, is waiting for me. He has heard of the break-in somehow.

Taking me aside he says, 'Here's some advice for you, Doctor

Karimi. Don't try too hard to find out who did this. I've lived in Quchan for forty years and I know a lot of people. Never point to anyone unless you're one hundred percent sure.'

I wonder why he has offered this advice. Does he think I'm about to accuse somebody?

Dealing with the aftermath of the robbery takes up most of the week, and I call Shafiq to tell him I have to postpone a termination he's conned me into performing.

'You promised,' he whines.

'I have to take care of things here. Tell the gentleman it may be three weeks.' In our conversations, we always refer to the patient as 'the gentleman'.

Shafiq says, 'That's impossible.'

'Then find someone else.'

'All right, all right. But please come as fast as you can.'

Sergeant Adidi, one of the police officers investigating the burglary, phones with a report while Arash is in my office going over the schedule for the day. Arash moves towards the door so I can take the call privately, but I gesture for him to stay.

The sergeant says, 'We know all the thieves in the area. We know their styles and where they work, and this doesn't match any of them. It looks like your house was targeted by someone who doesn't like you. Do you have any enemies?'

Do I have any enemies? I might have a hundred. Some father, some brother, who found out that I administered Prostodin to his daughter, his sister. A husband who has beaten a confession out of his wife. A government agent told to devote himself to watching my movements, and who might have been searching for Prostodin, not knowing I keep it in the refrigerator. Maybe he covered it up by making it look like a burglary.

'I don't have any enemies at all,' I tell Sergeant Adidi. 'What about the fingerprints? The men thought they got some good ones.'

'We have a file with more than two thousand fingerprints. We can't go through every file looking for a match.'

'So what was the point of fingerprinting?'

'They'll help if we get a good lead. Right now we're going to check out people who deal in stolen goods. We already have the word out.'

I hang up and put my head in my hands. 'He thinks I was targeted,' I moan. 'Have I brought this on my family, Arash?'

Arash puts his hand on my shoulder. 'Listen, I have an idea.' He sits down across from me. 'I know an old thief here in town who went to school with my father. They've stayed friends through everything. He's a drug addict and will do pretty much anything to earn drug money. If you're willing to pay, he'll ask around and see what he can find out from the other criminals he knows.'

The next night, Arash and I drive to an old brick house on the outskirts of Quchan. 'Wait here,' Arash says, getting out of the car before I can protest.

A few minutes later, he returns with a tall, slim man about fifty years old. His grey moustache almost reaches his chin. Every feature of his face brands him as an addict. His eyes are sunken in dark circles of flesh, his skin elsewhere has a yellowish tinge, his hair is dry and lifeless.

He introduces himself as Hassan. In the two or three minutes of our chat, he finishes one cigarette and lights another. He says, 'Let's go to your house so I can have a look.'

In my apartment he glances here and there, making mental calculations. He asks for details of the stolen items. What brand? What colour? How many?

'They watched you,' he says. 'They made sure you'd be in Mashhad. Then they cut your phone and power, jumped in, stole everything that would fit in their van, and trashed your house. I can't tell you their names, but I can find your things. It'll cost you ten thousand toman, and no police involvement in any way.'

'For that kind of money I'll want some guarantee.'

'No guarantees. That's my price. I have to travel to find your items. They won't be in Quchan, and when I find them I'll have to buy them back. That's the rule. You'll need to pay them something like twenty thousand toman to get your things back.'

I was outraged. 'Why the hell should I pay them?'

'I'm not going to mess with these people. Even the police won't. Quchan isn't a safe place. Maybe you don't see it because of how you live, but there are gangs all over this city. Drug gangs. Thieves. You mess with them and they'll cut off your head. You have a wife and daughter. You need to be very, very careful.'

'The only things I want back are the videos of my daughter. I don't care about the rest.'

Hassan says, 'Is that right? Well, don't tell anyone or the price will go sky-high.'

He calls me at my office two days later. 'Meet me at my house,' he says.

'When?'

'When do you think? Now.'

I jump in my car and drive to Hassan's house. He's waiting for me outside, leaning against the fence and dragging on a cigarette. He has such a disreputable look that I have to ask myself once more if I was right in the head when I agreed to get involved with him.

Hassan slides into the passenger seat beside me. 'I found the guy who fucked your place over,' he says. 'You can forget about getting your stuff back. He won't deal with us.'

'He won't accept money? That's absurd!'

'Yeah, whatever you say. Doc, you have enemies in Quchan. Did you know that?'

'What do you mean?'

'I mean enemies, Doc. Guys who hate your guts. Your stuff's gone for good.'

'What do we do next?'

He gives a brief laugh. 'What do we do next? We do nothing, Doc. You go home, I go home, and that's it. Better pray these guys don't come back. Next time they might take your head away with them.'

He gets out, slams the door shut, and shuffles off to his house without a backward glance. I'm left thinking about these enemies I'm supposed to have. I drive away with a sick feeling in the pit of my stomach.

Once again, Colonel Sadiqi is waiting for me when I arrive at work. He calls me into his office and tells me to shut the door behind me.

'Doctor Karimi, do you remember I warned you not to accuse anyone about what happened at your house?'

'Yes, sir, and I haven't.'

'No, but you've been chasing the matter in other ways. Listen carefully. There are more than forty doctors in Quchan, and many of them, including me, have been practising here for more than twenty years. You came here only last year and opened a surgery and you're so busy you had to extend your hours. Do you know why that is?'

I say, humbly, 'No, I don't know why that is, sir.'

'Then I'll tell you. Because you provide free services, and sometimes you pay for the medications too. Did you know that's against the law?'

'Yes, sir, I know that.'

'Many doctors aren't happy. You've stolen their patients. The robbery at your apartment is related to that.'

'Sir?'

The colonel leans forward and rests his arms on his desk. He beckons with his finger for me to lean closer too. 'The worst thing you can do is look for the people involved,' he says quietly. 'You understand? It could cost you your life. The best thing you can do is charge a normal fee like the other doctors, or close down your practice in Quchan. You'll leave next year anyway, when your military service is finished, right?'

I nod.

'I'm telling you this because I respect you as a doctor and a writer, and I don't want anything tragic to happen to you or your family. You're an intelligent man, Doctor Karimi. I don't have to spell it out, do I?'

So that's it. Not the terminations, but the charity cases. Does the colonel imagine I'm making my fortune out of these wretched people? Does he think I'm stuffing a bank account in Switzerland with the tomans of the poorest in Iran? I don't have the courage to look him in the eye and say, You know what? Fuck you. But nor can I say to the suffering people who come to me, No, I'm afraid I've been warned off, I can't help you anymore.'

I don't have a solution. I imagine I'll continue accepting patients without payment. I'll have to make sure that Azita and Newsha never come to Quchan. These people who want to frighten me off, maybe they'll accept that I'll be leaving Quchan before long and back off. I have the courage to keep going, but it's just ordinary courage, not superhero stuff. If some guy puts a blade to my throat and says, 'Next time you provide free service, I'll open your throat,' I'll probably say, 'You win.'

Leila

Aunt Sediqa hears my story, told over the telephone in the early morning with snow falling and my whole body trembling. She listens to all of it and she embraces me in her love. Not a murmur of censure, not a single harsh word. She says, 'Leila, you will come to Mashhad. You will stay with me. We will make a plan.'

There are monsters in the world. And there are angels. Listening to my aunt, warmth comes into my heart for the first time in months. Tears stream down my face. *We will make a plan* – Doctor Karimi, I can't tell you what comfort those words brought me. It was not simply about believing in a way out of my agonising situation; it was hearing kindness, human kindness, in the voice of someone who would go to any lengths to rescue me.

Aunt Sediqa calls my mother. She says, 'I have suffered a misfortune, sister. I have fallen over on the ice and broken my leg. Can Leila come to Mashhad and care for me for a few weeks?'

My mother commiserates. 'I will talk to Leila's father, but he will surely see the need for Leila to come to you.'

My father, with some reluctance, says that I can go. Majid will accompany me. My father is worried that my mother will be left burdened with all the work of the household – which is to say, he is worried that his own needs, and those of my brothers, might be compromised. But he will not stand in the way. He says, 'Wife, Sediqa is your sister. What help Leila can be I don't know. But I suppose she must go.'

Aunt Sediqa's three-storey building is in an old middle-class area of Mashhad. She lives on the second floor, and Majid complains angrily about lugging my heavy suitcase up the steep flight of stairs.

I knock on the door and Aunt Sediqa calls, 'Push the door, it's open.' I follow behind Majid, keeping a safe distance in case he discovers the truth and turns on me.

Lovely handmade Persian rugs cover the tidy front room. Several indoor plants rise from intricately painted pots set near the window, and inexpensive but tasteful art adorns the walls. A small hallway off to the right opens into an immaculate kitchen and a corridor to the left leads to two small but comfortable bedrooms.

'I'm in my room,' Aunt Sediqa calls out. 'Please, come in.'

We enter and I see my aunt in bed with a blanket covering her leg – relief washes over me. She smiles at the two of us as we lean down to kiss her cheeks.

'Hello, darlings, sorry I can't get up.' She gestures to her covered leg.

'How are you feeling, Aunt Sediqa?' Majid asks, his discomfort at being in his aunt's bedroom apparent. My brother is entirely a product of his culture. If he lives to be a hundred years old, no original thought will ever enter his head.

Aunt Sediqa shakes her head sadly. 'Silly, clumsy me. I was going downstairs when I tripped and fell down ten steps. The ambulance took me to the hospital. They X-rayed me and said I had broken my left leg in two places, but luck was with me and it will heal without surgery.'

'Oh, it must be painful,' Majid says sympathetically, then frowns and tips his head to one side. 'But I thought you told my mother you slipped on the ice?'

Aunt Sediqa is up to the task of explaining this contradiction. 'Who knows what I said yesterday? They gave me so much medicine I'm not sure I could have told you my daughters' names. But no, there was no ice involved. I simply set my foot on the steps wrongly and went tumbling down until I hit the landing. Now I can't move without help.'

'Don't worry. Leila's here to help,' says Majid.

It strikes me how our deception of my brother has left him believing I am a virgin when I am not, and that my aunt has a broken leg when she doesn't. He is standing here with two women and knows nothing of the most important facts about either of us.

After a cup of tea, Majid says his goodbyes to Aunt Sediqa, telling her to take care of herself. To me he says, 'See me out.'

At the door, he says, 'You're not here on a little holiday. Take care of Auntie. I'll be calling to check that you're doing what you're supposed to for once.' Then at last he is gone.

I run back to my aunt's bedroom and throw myself down beside her on the bed. I hug her tightly and she returns the embrace, allowing me to sob my heart out.

When my tears are spent, we talk well into the night. I tell her the circumstances of my infatuation with Hamid, of my folly. I confess that I have already tried to kill the baby.

She pats my hand. 'Oh my poor darling,' she says. 'Poor foolish girl! Men are not like us, Leila. Love for them is so often a pathway to your body. Poor, poor darling.'

We come to no conclusion about the way ahead. Tearfully I admit what I have yet to fully accept myself: that I love my unborn child with the entirety of my being. 'But I know I can't keep her.'

Aunt Sediqa doubts she can keep me with her long enough for me to give birth in her house. 'And even if I could, what would we do with the child? Where could I say it came from? If anyone found out you were the mother, you'd be arrested and tried for adultery.'

'And my baby? What will become of my baby?' I grasp my aunt's hands in mine, hoping for an answer, but she simply shakes her head and tells me there is no way of knowing.

The next morning, Aunt Sediqa takes me to the Imam Reza shrine to ask for Allah's guidance. I have made pilgrimages here with my family in the past, but never before have I entered the sacred grounds with such reverence. As we wind our way through courtyards and corridors, I barely notice the crowds of tourists gawking at the magnificent arched arcades, marvelling at the elaborate tile work, mirrors, calligraphy and designs that cover every available surface in so many colours.

When we reach the shrine and enter the part of the mosque reserved for women, we step out of our shoes and wait with other women dressed in plain black chadors to participate in the midday prayer. A hush settles on us, and I kneel with the other pilgrims, bowing to the ground and touching my forehead to the small stone that lies there.

Over the next few weeks, my aunt and I go from herb shop to herb shop in search of a better potion to induce a miscarriage. Most of them do nothing, but some make me so violently ill I am certain I will die along with my child. One gives me a headache so intense that light nearly blinds me with pain. Another pushes me into a deep sleep for more than eighteen hours.

I jump rope a dozen times a day, hoping the strain will cause me to miscarry. I do sit-ups and run around and take hot baths with infusions of herbs that are said to end pregnancy, but all that changes is the size of my stomach. My trousers and skirts are too tight to fasten, and even my aunt worries that someone will notice the bulge if the wind blows my chador too tightly against my body.

After one long day of strenuous exercise I drift off to sleep with my muscles aching. I feel something flutter in my stomach and wonder if I'm going to miscarry after all. I wait, tense, for blood to start running down my legs, or for cramping in my abdominals. Instead I feel the fluttering again.

I put my hand on my abdomen. 'Is that you, my daughter?'

The word for 'spring' in Farsi is related to the word for 'pregnant'. How apt, and for me, how bitter. Together with the passing of spring has come the acceptance that my pregnancy is so far advanced that miscarriage is now most unlikely. My stomach is round and firm. The baby delights me by moving frequently, especially when I try to sleep at night, and I smile every time she kicks – I am sure it is a girl. The delight is always short-lived.

Aunt Sediqa continues to come home from shopping trips with new herbal solutions. There are probably more herbal concoctions for inducing miscarriage in Iran than any other country on earth. When my aunt isn't looking I flush them down the toilet. The baby is no longer just a mass of tissues, she is almost fully developed, with a heart and brain and even a soul, I believe, just like mine.

My parents are anxious for me to come home. There is too much work for my mother to do alone, and even though Samira comes by several days a week to help, both my parents think I should return. Aunt Sediqa conjures up stories to buy more time, but we both know it is running out. My mother has already suggested that Aunt Sediqa move into our house, but Aunt Sediqa says, in a voice convincingly full of regret, that the doctor has told her she can't travel. If we can only hold on here in Mashhad for ten more weeks, I can have my baby. I don't care what happens after that.

Then the one thing I've never allowed myself to think about comes to pass. One morning, as my aunt and I clean up after breakfast, with the windows wide open so we can hear the birds singing from the rooftops, my mother phones and says, 'Leila, I've got some exciting news for you.'

My stomach tightens, and the baby, feeling the tension, kicks in protest. 'What is it, Mother?'

'Someone's coming to ask for your hand!'

'Who?'

'Your cousin Kazem.'

Oh dear Allah! Kazem! Have I not made it clear enough that I detest the man?

'Mother, please, no.'

'He's bought a house in Quchan, his business is booming, and he wants to settle down. He was here last night with his parents, and his mother wants to come and talk formally about it. Your father has already said yes to his brother. You can't let him down. You're twenty-two now. You should be married.'

'I'm not ready. This is too sudden. I need time.'

'Time for what? Do you want to stay home with me forever? I'm going to arrange for us all to meet next week.'

'Not next week. Aunt Sediqa still can't walk. The doctor says if he doesn't see improvement soon he's going to operate.'

'We can send Samira to look after her for a week or two. Under these circumstances, her husband will agree.'

'Can't it wait for just a few more weeks? If we rush this, Aunt Sediqa won't be able to come to the wedding, and I couldn't bear that. *Please*, give it another few weeks?'

Mother considers the request, and deciding it is reasonable enough, says, 'Okay, I will arrange it for three weeks from Friday. Then no matter what, Majid will come to bring you home. Now give the phone to Aunt Sediqa so I can give her the news. She'll be so happy for you.'

That night, when we sit down for dinner, Aunt Sediqa tells me she has made up her mind. She will call Hamid.

'Please, no! That will only make things worse.'

'I'd love nothing more than to do as you ask, Leila, but this time I have to go against your wishes. This is his fault, and he has to do something about it. At least I have to tell him what he has done to my niece.'

'But what can he do? He's married!'

'We'll see.'

The next morning, I sit listening while Aunt Sediqa phones Hamid's shop. I feel like a sheep waiting to be slaughtered. She holds the phone close to my ear so I can hear both sides of the conversation.

'Hello, Mr Hamid?'

'Yes, speaking.'

'My name is Mrs Moradi. I'm Leila's aunt. You remember her, I'm sure?'

A pause. 'Which Leila are you talking about?'

It is utterly pathetic, but a wave of longing sweeps over me at the sound of Hamid's voice.

'The girl you took to your house. Do you remember now or should I say more?'

'Yes, yes, I remember Leila. Is she all right?'

'Actually, I have some news for you. She's pregnant with your child.'

For minutes there is only the sound of Hamid's breathing. Then: 'I have a customer. Let me get rid of him, then I'll lock the door so we can talk.'

Two minutes pass. Aunt Sediqa puts her arm around me and pulls me in as close as she can.

'Did you say she's pregnant?' Hamid asks when he returns.

'Yes, six months.'

'No, it can't be.'

'Mr Hamid, the child is yours. My niece has been hiding in my house in Mashhad for months, and now she has to go back to Quchan. Now, listen to me carefully, young man. I know you're married, and I'm sure you're aware of the consequences of this. Leila has three brothers who will kill you if they find out.'

Hamid listens in silence.

'The reason I called is to get help. You have to do something. Maybe you can find a doctor to fix this. Maybe you can marry her. You figure it out.'

I can't believe what my aunt is saying. If Hamid marries me, everyone will find out my secret and my aunt's life will be in danger for hiding me.

'Okay, let me think about it,' Hamid pleads.

'Take down my number and call me in no more than a week. I don't have to tell you how serious this is.'

I run to my room and bury my face in the pillow, sobs shaking my body. I had dared to let myself imagine that somehow things would work out, had even allowed myself to enjoy feeling my daughter moving inside me. In a rush I see the impossibility of my situation all over again. But it's worse now. I'm robbed of the small speck of dignity I had left. Aunt Sediqa has told him he must do something, even marry me.

She comes to my bedside and sits down. 'Leila my darling, this had to be done. I'm sorry. Do you see?'

'Oh Aunt, I see nothing, nothing.'

Aunt Sediqa pats my arm. 'We are fighting a battle for your life, my darling. We can't afford to be squeamish. That man, that Hamid, he must help. It is his seed that did this. He must be made to help.'

The Doctor

I have just started my day at the surgery when Arash enters my office and asks if he can have a word with me before I see my first patient.

'Of course,' I say, and gesture for him to take a seat.

He drops into the chair. He opens his mouth to speak but blows out air instead. Then, running his hands through his hair, he says, 'Doctor Karimi, I have a friend. I'm not particularly close to him, but our families have known each other for many years. He's a married man with a child, but unfortunately he saw a girl a couple of times. He feels so embarrassed about it.'

'He "saw" a girl?'

Arash averts his eyes in discomfort. Iranian men are never comfortable talking about sex. It's bred into them, this uneasiness.

'He saw her in . . . in an intimate way.'

'I understand.' I know where this is going, even though I have never told Arash about the terminations. He's at risk enough through his involvement in the free treatment of school children.

'Nothing more than a casual relationship – an accident, he calls it. The girl called him a couple of days ago and told him she's pregnant with his baby. He doubts it, but she's putting pressure on him to do something about it.'

'Why are you telling me this?'

Arash lowers his voice. 'He's come to see me to ask if there's a doctor who can terminate her pregnancy. It's a matter of life and death. The girl's brothers will kill her, and his family will be torn apart, if it comes out.'

'But your friend doubts the child is his, isn't that what you said?'

'Well, I suppose he would say that.'

I'm beginning to dislike this friend of Arash's already. He appears to be admitting that he had sex with this girl, but that the pregnancy is some other man's work. 'So he wore a condom and that's why he doubts the child is his. Is that it?'

'No, no. I think he just wants to deny responsibility. I don't know him that well, like I said.'

'Arash, I feel sorry for the girl but I can't help. Termination of pregnancy is illegal, as you know. The punishment can be death.'

'Doctor Karimi, the girl's life is on the line, I've heard —'

'What have you heard?'

'Sorry, I didn't mean to offend you.'

'I'm not offended. Yet. What did you hear?'

'A woman living in Mashhad told my sister something about a girl you helped. She was tremendously grateful.'

I push my chair back and walk to the window. If word has got back to Arash from Mashhad, I could be in deep trouble soon.

Arash stands and comes to my side. 'Doctor Karimi, you haven't done anything wrong.'

'Arash, you know I have enemies in this town. You know what happened to my apartment. I can't take any more risks.'

'I know that. I truly do. I'm your friend. You've done a lot for me. You gave me a job and have been wonderful to the children at my sister's school. But this is an emergency. The girl's been hiding in her aunt's house in Mashhad because her family will kill her. They won't just be angry, they'll take her life for disgracing them. You know what this country is like. I promised Hamid to beg you for help.'

My exasperation mounts. Every single time, the unexpressed code is that I'd be a monster to decline.

'How far along is she?'

'I'm not sure, ten weeks, maybe more.'

'What do you mean, maybe more? Is it ten weeks or not?'

'It could be fourteen. Possibly.'

'Arash, termination isn't technically possible after fourteen weeks. Sixteen at the most, and that's too far gone for me.'

'Please, you have to make an exception. It's a matter of life and death.'

A matter of life and death – how many times have I heard that now? How many more times will I hear it? And for some reason I suddenly recall my mother's voice, telling me the story of the day I went missing at the age of three. I was always running in the streets of our slum, according to her, and that day she searched for me everywhere.

'And so did almost all the people in the slum,' she told me. 'I looked in the deep gutters, and the evil well in one of the back streets – that well had swallowed a number of children over the years. I checked every lane and every corner. Nobody could find you. It was getting dark and I was losing hope. I went back to the well and sat there looking into its dark mouth, crying out your name again and again. Children got kidnapped all the time in the slums, I knew that, but I was sure you had fallen into the well, and that I would never see your big brown eyes again. Suddenly Haji Javad ran to me, yelling excitedly, "I found him! I found him!" He grabbed my hand and together we ran for six blocks, until we came to you. You were asleep on the ground in front of a pastry shop.'

My mother would wipe away her tears at this point in the story. 'You'd sat there staring at the cakes and cream puffs until you passed out.' Then she would sigh. 'After my mother left me with Uncle Abraham at the age of four so she could live with her new husband, she never visited me again and my heart broke. When I fell in love and eloped with your father to Tehran, then found out two weeks later that he was already married to two other women, my heart broke still more. And it broke all over again when I went into premature labour alone in the middle of the coldest night in winter, and I dragged myself to the snow-covered streets and gave birth to you in the back of a stranger's car. I didn't think there was anything left to break until that evening I found you asleep and hungry on the ground, and then my poor heart shattered completely. That night, I vowed to do anything to protect you and provide for you.'

I have always known very well what my mother did for me. I was twelve when I found out that she had surrendered her body to the evil Haji Heydar, the devout Muslim who was already married, who abused her for cheap sex. Seeing my mother under his obese, grunting body was the point at which my own heart shattered. I left school to work full-time in the bike repair shop where I already had a part-time job, so I could buy my mother's pride back. When she realised this a few weeks later, she stormed into the shop with tears rolling down her cheeks and yelled, 'You promised me! You promised me you would become a doctor! To help people, the people of the slums, the poor people, and me. You promised!' She was shaking a finger at me. I was speechless.

I went back to school. I studied hard. I excelled in my exams in the final year. I went to university. I became a doctor. And I helped women. All because I remembered my mother's words to me.

Had I promised her to be rich? No. Did I promise to buy cakes daily for every kid in the slums? No. Did I promise to be kind? Yes. I am not allowed to live a normal life. I am not allowed to sleep comfortably at night. I have not survived the slums in order to get rich or famous or comfortable. I am here to say yes, I can help you.

A matter of life and death: I know all too well what that means. One of us must die, the patient or the doctor. It is the patient who must be saved; it is already too late for me. I know the black car will come.

'Doctor Karimi?' Arash prompts. 'What are you thinking?'

'Where is she?' I murmur.

'In Mashhad. I can get the address or ask her to come here.'

'I'd rather do it in Mashhad. Maybe at my place there.'

'Thank you so much, Doctor Karimi. Hamid will be . . . well, he'll be relieved.'

'Arash, your friend can go to hell. I'm thinking of the young woman.'

Hamid arrives at the office in the early afternoon and Arash sends him in. He's tall, good-looking, well groomed. It's easy to imagine a young woman succumbing to his charms. We exchange polite greetings, then he says, 'I know you're a busy man so I won't waste your time. This girl —'

I interrupt him. 'Does this girl have a name?'

Hamid seems baffled by my question for a moment. Then he sees what I'm getting at, which is to say, good manners. 'Leila. Her name is Leila.'

'Please go on.'

'Doctor, her life is in great danger. If we can't fix this situation the whole story will come out, and I'll lose my family. Her family is very religious. Backward, even. They don't understand the world has changed. Her brothers are known to be quick to fight. They'll kill me.'

I close my eyes briefly in distaste. I dislike this man. His plea centres on what could happen to him. This alone makes me want to protect the young woman, Leila. I have little doubt that this slick individual seduced her, not caring that it would ruin her life.

'I'll pay you anything you ask,' Hamid goes on. He takes out his wallet, thick with bills. 'Say the price. One hundred thousand toman? One hundred and ten? Twenty? I can give it to you now. I came prepared to pay any price you name.'

'Put that away. I'll see her first. Then I'll make my decision. I'm not making any false promises. I'll see her in my house a week from Thursday.'

'That's ten days away. Is there any way to see her sooner?'

'No, that's the best I can do.' I scribble down the address and hand it to Hamid.

'The fee?' he asks.

My distaste grows. I think to myself, Did this Leila love this man? What was she thinking? He's a narcissist.

'One hundred and fifty thousand.' That's the figure I give him. The money will go towards buying medicine for my impoverished patients.

'Done,' he says. 'I'll have it for you any time you want it.'

I think, My, my, you are frightened, aren't you?

'This conversation,' I tell him, 'regardless of what I decide, never goes further than this room. Do you understand?'

'Yes,' Hamid says, standing. 'Thank you, Doctor Karimi. You've saved my life.'

'Have I indeed? If I do this, it will be to save the girl's life. You're incidental.'

Hamid nods, as if in humble agreement. 'Yes, yes. Of course.'

Having been in Mashhad visiting my family for two days, I am getting ready to go back to Quchan when my mother-in-law suddenly becomes very sick. Azita wants to stay at her parents' house to look after her, which means that Newsha, despite my decision following the burglary, must come with me. She will spend a few days mostly being cared for by Arash's sister, and Azita and I agree that we'll all return to the Mashhad apartment on Friday. But in fact I will be driving to Mashhad on Thursday to see Leila, so Newsha will have to stay with me while I carry out the termination. How I will keep her out of the way, I don't know. I'll think of that when we get there.

Thursday is a day of rain and mud. My medical bag is packed with everything I'll need, and I set off with Newsha in the back seat singing to herself. Hamid had told me to expect a call from the young woman's aunt, Mrs Moradi, early in the afternoon. Once in Mashhad, I park two blocks away from my apartment in case Azita drives by for some reason and notices my car. I carry my daughter in my arms.

Newsha says, 'Why don't you drive your car, Daddy?' and I answer, 'Well, I need some exercise, that's why.'

Inside, I sit Newsha in front of the television to watch cartoons and fix myself a cup of tea. My hope is that she will fall asleep, and stay asleep for the entire period of the termination, not even waking when the patient screams. This is hopelessly optimistic, I concede. My life is full of hopelessly optimistic plans.

Within thirty minutes Mrs Moradi calls. I tell her I'm ready and waiting. 'You have my address,' I say. 'Please be very, very quiet when you arrive. I don't want to disturb the neighbours.'

'I understand.'

Less than an hour later my doorbell rings. I press the button to let Leila and her aunt through the first set of doors, and then walk into the hall as the two women in black chadors glide up the steps. Opening my door wide, I step aside to let them enter. I ask them to take a seat, and awkwardly they sit down beside each other on a sofa.

'Doctor Karimi, thank you for seeing us,' says Mrs Moradi respectfully.

'That's all right.' My glance has taken in an alarming detail regarding Leila. She is a long way gone in her pregnancy, more than the ten or twelve or fourteen weeks I was told.

Mrs Moradi is about to speak when she picks up the sound of the cartoon down the hall. She gives me a questioning look.

'My daughter is watching television,' I explain. 'I'm looking after her today.'

Mrs Moradi nods. Then she takes Leila's hand and says, 'As you know, my niece Leila is pregnant. She's been hiding at my place. Her family live in Quchan, and she has to go back to them in three days. If they find out about her pregnancy —'

I interrupt her. 'The man who came to see me told me all the details, but I'll have to see how far along your niece is before I can proceed. We need to move quickly. My wife is at her father's house; she's not aware I'm doing this and would never agree. She isn't expecting me back till tomorrow, but her father lives only a short distance away. I also need to tell you that it's going to be very painful, but your niece cannot yell or the neighbour will hear. She has to be absolutely quiet.'

'We understand.'

I turn to Leila, who has held her head low since her arrival. 'Leila, I'm going to need to examine you. Is that okay?'

'Of course,' says her aunt for her. Taking Leila by the hand, the older woman follows me into the room I use as a surgery when I'm in Mashhad. I ask Leila to lie down on the bed and lift her chador above her waist. She complies, but her embarrassment is painful to witness. She is an extraordinarily beautiful young woman, her eyes the most tender and appealing I've ever seen. There is something like poetry in her sorrowful expression.

A sixty-second examination is all I require to conclude that Leila is far more than fourteen weeks pregnant. 'You must be kidding,' I say under my breath. I take a tape measure out of my bag and establish Leila's fundal height.

'This is ridiculous. You're over seven months along.'

Leila has her head turned away from me. The moment I speak, she lifts her hand to her mouth, as if to stifle a cry.

'Termination is impossible after sixteen weeks. You have a complete baby here. I'm sorry, there's nothing I can do for you.'

Leila's hand shoots out and catches mine. She holds it tight. Her beautiful black eyes are turned towards me now. 'Doctor Karimi, I have to go back home in three days. I can't go like this.'

'I understand, but it's too late.'

'Doctor, look at me, please,' Leila whispers, her hand still clasping mine. 'Can you save my child?'

No other words would have made me give further consideration to her case, but of all the women who've come to me with an unwanted pregnancy, Leila is the first who has ever asked me to save her child.

I stand looking down at her. The expression in her eyes is imploring, of course, but I see more than that. It is as if I were looking at the archetypal image of the woman who surrenders to the craft of the seducer, who opens her heart and releases the bounty of her love in a most ill-advised way. Seduced and abandoned – it's an old, old story, and Leila, in her tenderness and beauty, summarises millennia of suffering, millennia of heartbreak and despair.

I ask her softly, 'How much time do we have?'

'The whole three days.'

I don't have nearly that much, of course. I scoop up my black bag from the floor and leave the room, stopping only briefly to talk to Mrs Moradi. 'I'm afraid you're going to have to act as babysitter for a short time. I have to get some things from the hospital. I'll be back soon. If anyone calls or knocks on the door, don't answer. You both need to be absolutely quiet. Newsha will probably just keep watching cartoons. If she comes out, give her a drink of milk and humour her.'

I drive to Imam Reza hospital, where almost everyone knows me from when I worked there as an intern, rush into the treatment room and fill my bag with supplies – larger gauze cannulas, syringes, a microdrip, five ampoules of Syntocinon. I am received with impressive respect by the staff, and somehow this gives me more courage.

'Is there anything I can help you with, Doctor Karimi?' asks a curious nurse.

'I've got it,' I answer. 'An emergency. No time to explain.' I rush back through the ward and sprint to my car.

When I get home I take the stairs two at a time. Mrs Moradi is in the living room looking perplexed.

'Newsha was okay?' I ask.

'Not a peep from her,' says Mrs Moradi.

'Good. No time to waste.' I stride past her to Leila in the adjoining room. She is as I left her, except that she has pulled her chador down over her stomach and legs.

'Remember I said time was short?'

Leila nods.

'I meant it. I don't have time to explain. Roll up your sleeve.' I insert a cannula into the cubital fossa of her left arm and set up a bag of normal saline next to the bed. I drain the Syntocinon into a syringe, inject it into the bag of fluid, and adjust the microdrip until the drug is flowing at the correct rate into Leila's vein. The whole thing takes less than ten minutes. I lift her chador and examine her abdomen carefully. I push and poke in critical spots with both hands. The baby's head is down. That's good. To Leila, I say, 'You're going to have strong cramps in a few hours. I'm inducing labour. This is the only option. I'm not sure if your baby can make it, but if what matters most to you is that I try to save it, there's no other way.'

Tears spring into her eyes. 'Thank you, Doctor. Oh, thank you, thank you.'

I check her blood pressure: 112 over 78, very good. I listen to the baby's heart, which is beating strongly. This is a child who wants to live. 'I'll be right back. Just lie there and let the medicine work.'

In the living room I find Mrs Moradi pacing in small, nervous steps. She says, 'She'll be all right, then?'

'She's going to give birth, Mrs Moradi.'

Mrs Moradi sinks onto the sofa.

'This can take hours, and I have to stay close to Leila to check her and the baby regularly. Listen carefully for any sound coming from the stairway and come and get me if you so much as hear a door open.'

Half an hour later Leila experiences weak cramps and I adjust the microdrip to a faster rate. I listen to the baby's heart with my obstetric stethoscope. 'You're both doing fine.'

She attempts a smile. Her lips shape the words, 'Thank you, Doctor,' without any sound issuing.

I return to the living room to explain the situation to Leila's aunt, but before I can utter a word, she says, 'I want to tell you about my niece. She's not a wild girl. She's the most innocent girl in our family. She didn't deserve this. That bastard used her and threw her away like garbage. I hope he suffers the rest of his life. My poor niece's life is ruined.'

'Maybe it's not ruined,' I say. 'Maybe not. Have a little faith, Mrs Moradi.'

Some hours later, I hook Leila up to the second bag. I tell her not to drink any water; I'm worried that her sodium levels will drop. Her blood pressure is stable and her pains are getting stronger every hour – a good sign, certainly – but it could still be hours before the baby is born.

I take a break then and call my wife from the living room. She, of course, believes I'm still in Quchan with Newsha. 'I'll be home in the morning,' I tell her. 'I'll sleep better tonight if I know you're at your parents' house. Think of something relaxing we can do this weekend, all right?' Then I add, 'Newsha is sound asleep.'

I hang up, confident that my wife won't return. I take a deep breath and think for a minute. I check on Newsha, who has indeed fallen sound asleep, just as I'd hoped. I cover her with a blanket, realising with a feeling of misery that I've neglected to give her a proper meal. Why the hell can't I get my priorities right? Before anything else, I should be seeing to Newsha's welfare. What's wrong with me?

I need Mrs Moradi to be present for the next task. 'I must check your niece's cervix. It might be easier for her if you're with her.'

'Of course.'

When we enter the makeshift surgery, Mrs Moradi goes to her

niece and pushes back her hair. 'How are you doing, darling?'

'I'm fine, Aunt Sediqa.'

I put on my gloves. 'I'm going to examine you to see how much your cervix is dilated,' I explain to Leila.

She closes her eyes, so embarrassed she can't even look at her aunt. I try to be as gentle as I can be, but birth is not a delicate process. 'Relax,' I say. 'It'll be over in a minute.' Then: 'You're four centimetres dilated. You're doing very well.'

Leila smiles fully for the first time, then closes her eyes and puts her hands over her stomach and whispers a song – or a prayer – for her baby.

A little after midnight I listen to the baby's heart again, as I've been doing regularly for hours. Leila's contractions are much closer together, but the baby's heartbeat is weakening.

'Leila, I know you don't like this, but I have to check your cervix again.'

She nods and shifts her position for me. Her aunt has gone back to the living room, after I insisted that she try to sleep a little. 'Leila will need you later,' I tell her.

The cervix is seven centimetres dilated. 'That's good,' I say, 'but your baby's in distress. Its heart rate is dropping and I need to deliver it quickly and put it in an incubator. I'm going to adjust the microdrip to the fastest rate, so the contractions are going to come faster and harder. Remember what I said before about not screaming?'

Leila nods.

'Good. You're doing great. I'm going to have to break your waters.' At this moment Leila panics and her heart races. I check her blood pressure and it's critically low. She must be getting water intoxication from the Syntocinon, a complication that can be extremely dangerous. I might lose her and the child. I insert another cannula in her other arm and attach a bag of normal saline to bring her blood pressure up. This is risky too, because too much fluid can jeopardise her electrolyte balance. But I have no choice.

I listen to the baby's heart and it's still slowing down. Her baby is suffocating. I have to deliver it soon or it won't make it. I leave the room to splash some water on my face and give Leila a few minutes to revive. One glance at me from the living room and Mrs Moradi realises that things are not good. I step into the bathroom and look into the mirror. Big, deep, dark circles are showing under my eyes. I try to stay calm and positive, but I simply don't know what more I can do now to save Leila and her baby.

Walking back to the birth room I notice that Mrs Moradi isn't in the living room anymore. I find Leila moaning in pain. She looks so pale. She is definitely poisoned by Syntocinon, and that's life-threating. I try to talk to her. I shake her hard but she can hardly open her eyes. She mustn't go into a coma; that would be fatal.

'Leila jan!'

The door to the room is flung open and a middle-aged woman hurries in with Mrs Moradi. She pays no attention to me but rushes to Leila and holds her arm. 'Leila jan, stay strong, I am here!'

Who the hell is this? Where did she come from? She rubs Leila's forehead and keeps saying, 'Leila jan, I am here.'

I stand there in silence until finally I say, 'Excuse me, who exactly are you?'

The woman says, 'I am Fatima. I am this child's mother.'

Leila opens her eyes, sees her mother and bursts into tears. 'Madar jan, I am sorry . . . I am so sorry.'

'There is nothing to be sorry about, Leila jan. You will be fine.

You will get through this. I know you will.'

Mrs Moradi is standing silently in the corner of the room. Fatima sits next to Leila, comforting her with tender words and stroking her forehead. I hear her whisper, 'I understand, my darling. I knew you were in love, and I know your heart is broken.'

She weeps, still caressing her daughter's forehead. 'I was in love too, but I had no chance, I was given to your father by my family. Don't be ashamed.'

Then she explains to me that her sister had told her the truth a few days ago, and Fatima has been lying to her husband and sons so that Leila could stay safe with her aunt. It amazes me to see how this mother's love has been able to overcome what must have been a lifetime of training in prejudice.

Inserting a speculum to gain a better view, I turn on a spotlight and see the head of the baby bulging through the cervix. I put a couple of gauzes under Leila, then with the utmost caution, so as not to lacerate the baby's head, I draw my blade across the amniotic sac. A strong flow of water gushes out and Leila moans with pain. I feel her abdomen. Her uterus is in complete contraction. The baby is about to be born.

'Come on, we're going to hospital,' I say, snapping my gloves off.

'Hospital?' says Mrs Moradi. 'Doctor, she can't go to the hospital.'

'The baby is premature. Leila's going to give birth any minute now. I need you to help me.'

I take the drips out of Leila's arms, and together Mrs Moradi and Fatima and I carry her down the steps and into the back seat of my car. Leila does not say a word, does not so much as moan. Anyone else would have been screaming, writhing in pain. Instead Leila bites her chador. I tell Mrs Moradi to stay in the apartment with Newsha until I return.

I make it to the hospital in less than fifteen minutes. 'Open the gate, I have a pregnant woman here!' I yell at the guard. I drive through the grounds at about five times the speed limit and pull up outside the entrance to the maternity ward.

'Listen to me,' I tell Leila, holding her chin up so she will look into my eyes. 'Can you hear me?'

She nods.

'Go inside and say you're over seven months pregnant and you've fallen downstairs and your waters have broken. They'll take care of everything. Make up a name for yourself. They'll be too busy to check. Fatima, you can help your daughter?'

'I can,' says Fatima, and gently she helps her out of the car.

As they reach the top of the steps and Fatima opens the door, Leila turns back to look at me. I'm watching from the car, while trying not to be seen. Nobody should know I'm here.

Supported by her mother, Leila lifts her hand and attempts to wave. It requires an extraordinary effort. She's in diabolical pain. Looking at her dark eyes, the beauty and suffering in her face, I feel an almost sublime sense of justification, of gladness for being here, and for having been with Leila so much of the day. I think, Hang me if you like, I could not leave that young woman to the despair that was strangling her. I could not.

'My Adonai bless you,' I whisper.

I wonder if I will ever see her again.

Two weeks pass. I am at my surgery in Quchan, waiting to see my next patient, when my mobile phone rings.

'Hello, Doctor Karimi?'

I immediately recognise her voice. 'Leila, is that you? Are you okay?'

'Yes, Doctor, thank you.' A silence follows. And then: 'I am back home, Doctor Karimi. I am getting married next week.'

'Oh . . . Okay, that sounds good.'

That silence again.

'I saw her,' she says, and she is sobbing now. 'I held my daughter in my arms . . . on my chest . . . for two minutes. I called her Zahra, and that is her name. Zahra.' I can hear the pain and grief in her voice. She is shattered.

All I can manage to say is, 'A lovely name, Leila.'

'I gave them a false name and I escaped from the hospital.'

'Good, so they can't find you. That's good, Leila.'

'I don't think I can do this, Doctor. I love my daughter.' And she cries, 'I want my Zahra!'

I have absolutely no idea what to say. 'But you can't do this, Leila. You will lose your life, and your baby.'

She weeps; I listen. Perhaps she thought there was some miracle I could conjure up, some magic that would restore her daughter to her. But all I can offer are more ineffectual words. 'Please be safe, Leila. Please. It must be this way.'

I can hear her struggling to control her tears. Finally she masters her voice. 'I am sorry to call you, Doctor. I won't bother you again.'

Two days later, I find Hamid in my waiting room when I arrive for work. I gesture for Arash to follow me into my office.

'Send that man away. I want to forget I ever met him.'

'You're sure?'

'I have nothing to say to him.'

Arash leaves, only to return a minute later. 'Doctor Karimi, Hamid's horribly distressed. I think you'd better see him.'

I don't like the sound of this. Has something terrible happened to Leila? I'd assumed Hamid had come to pay me, and the last thing I want is his money, but he wouldn't be upset if he'd simply come to settle his debt.

'Show him in then.' I lean back in my chair and wait impatiently for Arash to usher Hamid in. His eyes are red, his hair is uncombed, he's unshaven.

'Have a seat, please.'

He slumps into a chair and holds his head in his hands.

'What's happened?' I ask him. 'You look awful.'

He bursts into tears, his chest heaving.

'Is it Leila?'

Reaching into his pocket he takes out a crumpled white envelope and places it on the desk. 'I received this two days ago.'

I pick up the envelope and pluck out the letter inside.

Dearest Hamid

The reasons for me living have vanished. But I know that suicide is an unforgivable sin and I am not to commit more sins. I have accepted that I must continue my unhappy life. This is my punishment for what I have done and I accept it.

This is the last time I will contact you. I feel I have accomplished the one task Allah had for me in this life. When I learnt I was carrying your child, I decided to end my life, but when I saw my child in my dreams, I knew I had to bring her to life. She is perfect and beautiful. I named her Zahra. I held her in my arms for two minutes. I felt her heart beat. I heard her breathing quietly on my chest, then I let her go forever.

The nurse told me we would have our whole life to spend together, and I think those were the harshest words I've ever heard, because I knew those two minutes were all either of us would ever spend with each other.

My parents have arranged for me to marry my cousin next week, but I am still in love with you.

I ask only one thing of you, Hamid. I beg of you, save our daughter. Give her the life I cannot. Please, Hamid, tell Zahra I will always love her.

I feel tears welling in my eyes. I cross the floor to open the window. A cool breeze drifts in. I take a pack of cigarettes out of my pocket, fumble for a lighter, and with unsteady hands light up.

'Doctor Karimi,' says Hamid, 'I know you think I am a horrible man, but I never had any evil intentions. I love Leila. I am so sorry. I had a dreadful problem with my wife and she left with my son. In that time I met Leila, but things went back to normal in a couple of weeks and my wife came home. I am living in a loveless marriage but I can't divorce her because I have a child with her.'

'I'm sorry,' I say, and I do feel sorry for him, but nothing like the sorrow I feel for Leila. I return to my chair and spread my hands out across my desk. 'What will you do, Hamid? Will you adopt the child, as Leila asks? You *are* her father.'

He shakes his head, unable to meet my eyes. 'I can't. I have a family.'

Disgust rises in me. What is the point of this wretched man coming to see me if he can't grasp the opportunity he has for redemption? Leila's love and generosity seem utterly wasted on him.

'I want you to leave,' I tell him. 'In all honesty, I can't bear the sight of you for another minute.'

He stands slowly and pulls a wad of bills out of his pocket. 'Here's the money I owe you. I appreciate what you've done.'

I shove his hand away. 'Go now,' I say. 'We will not need to see each other again.'

Hamid seems about to say something more, but changes his mind. He stands and leaves the room with his head bowed. I watch from the window as he gets into his car and drives away.

The crumpled envelope and letter remain on my desk. I put the letter in my pocket, pick up my jacket, and walk out to the waiting room. Ignoring the patients who are there to see me, I tell Arash, 'I am sick. Cancel all appointments this afternoon.'

'Is everything all right?'

'No,' I say. 'Everything is not all right.'

I didn't know it then, but things would get a lot worse – for me, at least – before they got better.

The black car finally came for me in February 1998, in the year following the birth of Leila's daughter. I was walking home in Mashhad from a publisher's office when a black Peugeot suddenly pulled over alongside me. Four strongly built, bearded men emerged from it and forced me into the back. I was informed that I was under arrest by the intelligence service and I was taken to an unknown prison. The reason for my arrest was never clarified, but there were multiple options: I wrote about subjects that grated with the fundamentalist government; I performed illegal medical procedures; and I was a Jew by virtue of my mother's ancestry.

I was born in Iran, as was my father, and his father – my bloodline goes back 2700 years, to the country that was called Persia. For three millennia my ancestors lived in Iran and called it home; they fought for its territory, and for its pride and independence. But the first words the interrogator said to me when I was arrested were, 'You are not an Iranian, you are a Jew!'

In prison I was brutally tortured for sixty-two days. My principal interrogator, a man who went by the name of Samadi, told me he could hang me any moment he chose. And having done so, he could, indeed would, destroy my family. He was a man without any scruples whatsoever when it came to his job. There was no torture he would not contemplate, no limit to the lengths he would go in the prosecution of his brief – that brief being the destruction of all enemies of the regime. He was not exactly a zealot, more a man who took great professional pride in getting results. There were times when I looked into his eyes and saw the angel of death.

But while Samadi made me wish for death, he had a better plan for me. I was released and forced to become a spy for the intelligence service. I was put to work gathering information, mainly on Jews, to be used to accuse them of spying for Israel. In March 1999 the government finally fulfilled its evil plot and arrested thirteen innocent Jews for espionage, the sole purpose of which was to put pressure on Israel to release Hezbollah terrorists from its jails.

By then my mission for Samadi was accomplished and I saw it in his eyes: an intention to kill me. I had to escape. And on 14 July 1999 I managed to flee Iran. If a miracle is something that holy men perform, or a phenomenon that goes against the laws of physics, then my escape was not a miracle, it was simply luck. But to me it felt like a miracle, even though it had its roots in my own actions.

On the day of my eleventh birthday, 31 December 1978, the Islamic revolution was at its peak. The Shah of Iran had declared a military curfew, and anyone found in the streets after four in the afternoon was to be arrested or shot. My family were sitting at home listening nervously to BBC news about the demonstrations. It was one of those rare occasions when my father was home. There had been a massacre earlier that day in which many people were killed by the military. We heard constant gunfire, and tanks were patrolling the streets like monsters walking in hell. Suddenly there was a bang on our door, and my father opened it to find a trembling young man begging for a place to hide. He was one of the demonstrators, and my father, a fierce monarchist, refused to help him. But I pleaded with my father, and eventually he allowed me to hide the man in his bus.

Later that night, when it was finally safe to come out of hiding, the man, Ali Mazaheri, climbed out of the bus and shook my little hand. 'I owe you my life, Kooshyar,' he said.

Years later, when I was running for my own life in July 1999, I had only one hope, and that was to get a fake passport. Ali Mazaheri was the head of the passport office.

'You have only forty-eight hours,' he told me when he handed me the passport. 'If you are arrested, I will be hanged too.'

I crossed the border to Turkey. I had sent my wife and daughters (I now had a second, Niloofar) ahead of me. I left behind all my wealth and assets. I left my books and my medical profession. I believed then that I would be unable to practise as a doctor, or be an author, in a foreign land. Most preciously I left my memories and my dear friends.

I became a fugitive in Turkey for thirteen months. Azita, Newsha, Niloofar and I survived on next to nothing in Ankara. I had returned to the poverty of my childhood. Asylum seekers such as us were a despised class in Turkey. We were called *yabanji*, savages, because of the way we lived, eating discarded scraps of food, begging for a few coins. I was stealing electricity and food on a daily basis. At times the rats of Ankara made a better living than I did. Our only shelter was a hovel three floors below ground, given to us by a Turk who found some pity in his heart. I couldn't legally take employment, and what jobs I found paid next to nothing. I begged for food from a charity that provided one small meal a day to impoverished Muslims. Had I revealed that I was Jewish I wouldn't have been given anything. We shivered in our basement room, the temperature in winter plunging to minus-fifteen. Azita looked at me with scorn and disgust. What she and the girls were living through was because of me, and Azita never let me forget it.

A long, exhausting interview with an officer of the United Nations High Commissioner for Refugees in Ankara finally yielded results when I was recognised as a legitimate political refugee. Nevertheless it took another ten months for my family and me to be flown to Australia, where we would be permitted to live under a resettlement scheme for people who had fled political persecution.

I wept with relief, then wept again when I said goodbye to the friends I had made in the refugee community, people dear to my heart. The powers that rule the universe – gods, spirits, disembodied forces of some sort – seemed to have fashioned a program of task and trial for me, withholding reward until I'd been taken to the brink of madness and physical exhaustion. After emerging from a childhood of privation into an early adulthood full of promise and the prospect of a good career, I lived with the fear of being hanged as an enemy of the Islamic state, and then knew poverty again. In Sydney, following a further period of struggle and working as a poorly paid labourer for almost three years, I found safety and a measure of prosperity when my medical credentials were finally validated. However, Azita had decided to separate from me. I did not blame her. Living with a man like me is not an easy task. I hope and pray that she forgives me.

I am now working full-time as a doctor once more. I have a respectable job and a comfortable life, and when I walk in the streets of Sydney with my brand-new shirt and shining suit, nobody sees the numerous scars beneath. Those on my stomach have been there since my father's second wife tried to kill me in the house fire. Those on my chest are from when Samadi burnt me with cigarettes to force me to cooperate. But the deepest scar is in my heart, from when I hung up the phone the last time I spoke with Leila.

In 2014 I met a lovely Australian woman. A selfless human being who humbles me in every aspect of living. If I am allowed to use the word miracle, I would use it to describe my fate crossing hers. Misha is the hope, the love, and the beauty that keeps my heart alive. She has made Australia my home.

I cannot return to Iran while the current regime holds power. This is a great sorrow. I am a Jew and yet Iran will forever seem my homeland. A time comes every few days when I find myself staring at nothing, a rapt expression on my face, and the voice of whoever is talking to me dies away to nothing. I am listening to the racket of the bazaar in Mashhad, the shouts and curses of merchants striving for the attention of the throngs of people passing by, the musical babble of a thousand voices chattering in Farsi. I can see myself as a kid of nine or ten, ducking and weaving through the crowded streets, searching for some dodge that will earn me a few toman. Then the scene fades and I am gazing at the face of Leila. Such beauty, such bravery. *Doctor, can you save my child?* Iran is the Ayatollah and his lofty arrogance, the Revolutionary Guard and its brutality, the Basij militias and their malice, the mullahs and their hidebound ideology – but it is also that beauty and bravery in Leila's face.

I have been trying to find out, through my contacts in Iran and through the Red Cross and the UN, what happened to Zahra. But it is a difficult quest to find an orphaned girl in a land of a thousand orphanages. I don't even know her surname. I am told the Iranian government ensures that female orphans are married before the age of eighteen. Every night I pray that Zahra has not been forced to wed a forty-year-old man who is already married. A voice in me insists that one day I will find her. I know there is nothing I can do for her, but when I eventually see her I want to carry out Leila's request.

You are as innocent as your mother, I will tell her. She loved you with all her heart.

ACKNOWLEDGEMENTS

I am enormously indebted to my daughter, Newsha, and to Robert Hillman and Nancy Hill for assisting me with the writing of the original manuscript.

Thanks to two remarkably talented and extraordinarily precise editors from Penguin, Meredith Rose and Rebecca Bauert. To Pippa Masson and Fiona Inglis, my superb literary agents at Curtis Brown, who made this dream come true, I owe thanks for advice and support.

I would like to express special gratitude to Ben Ball, Publishing Director of Penguin Books. I also owe boundless thanks to the men and women who are the characters of this nonfiction. Some carry their real names, but the identities of most have been veiled by pseudonyms.